6139454c

WINE
APPRECIATION

WINE APPRECIATION

500 *Wines for* 100 *Occasions*

DAVID WILLIAMS

Foreword by Elin McCoy

UNIVERSE

First published in the United States of America in 2013 by
UNIVERSE PUBLISHING
A Division of Rizzoli International Publications, Inc.
300 Park Avenue South
New York, NY 10010
www.rizzoliusa.com

2013 2014 2015 2016 / 10 9 8 7 6 5 4 3 2 1

Printed in China

ISBN: 978-0-7893-2702-4

Library of Congress Control Number: 2013933402

CONTENTS

The 100 Occasions

Foreword *by Elin McCoy*

ONE HOT SUMMER AFTERNOON, I was reading in a hammock and sipping from a glass of cool, crisp, thirst-quenching German Riesling. A bee buzzing nearby also clearly appreciated the wine's flowers-and-honey aroma: It dove right into the pale chilled liquid kamikaze-style, as though seduced, just as I was, by the perfect harmony between the warm sun, the sound of the nearby surf, and the refreshing, aromatic white.

A basic wine truth, too rarely acknowledged today, is that most of us think about wine in relation to specific occasions, whether a beach picnic, a grand formal dinner, an anniversary party, a romantic weekend, or a casual barbecue. And no wonder. Wine has been an important companion to life's rituals, events, and meals from the very beginning of its 8,000-year history. Like other Egyptian pharaohs, Tutankhamun was buried with pitchers filled with red wine. At Greek symposia, wine was a vital accompaniment to philosophical conversations and poetry contests. Wedding toasts evolved, we think, from raising a chalice of wine as an offering to the gods in ancient Greece; the first recorded toast was supposedly given at a Saxon wedding feast more than 1,500 years ago. By the late 19th century, the savvy Champenois, recognizing the wine/occasion connection, exploited opportunities for their bubbly to become synonymous with the very idea of celebration. We all know how a particular wine continues to carry powerful memories of when and where it was served. For me, a sip of Pol Roger Champagne still evokes the day my son was born, when he was toasted with warm fizz in paper cups in a sterile hospital room.

Yet surprisingly, the wine mentality of the past couple of decades has bypassed this long history in the hunt for the "best" wines, often defined as those achieving a perfect 100-point rating. Those points ignore the most obvious wine question: perfect for what? A rich, plush Pétrus from a great vintage wouldn't have been nearly as enjoyable to sip on my warm afternoon as the light, chilled, low-alcohol white that seemed like a metaphor for summer. The wine slid seamlessly into the day's story.

In contemporary culture, hundreds of diverse times and places call for wine to be part of the story. Season, mood, whom we're with, and where all influence the types of foods we choose to eat, so why not the wines we pick, too? "If I could find a wine that went well with my Cheerios in the morning, I would even have it for breakfast," quipped an interviewee in a 2011 study of wine occasions. Unlike 20 years ago, drinkers today have thousands of wines to choose from, and therein lies much confusion.

Plenty of books rate the world's best wines, but this one is perhaps the first to go much further and guide us to the wines that fit the stories of our lives, reflecting and enriching the way we actually drink.

Introduction *by David Williams*

A FEW YEARS AGO, I signed up for one of those postal DVD clubs that, for a monthly fee, sends you a movie from your wish list every time you return one. It seemed like a fine idea to begin with: a seemingly limitless choice from the whole history of cinema—and unlike at the local rental chain store, no fines for late returns. After a while, however, I noticed that it was taking me longer to get around to watching the movie each time, until it got to the point where I wouldn't even open the envelope before sending it back, let alone watch the thing.

The problem, common to everyone else I've ever spoken to who's used one of these clubs, was easily diagnosed: There was a gap between the optimistic, self-improving person who filled the wish list with intellectually nourishing works of great artistic import (subtitles, generally black-and-white, challenging approach to character and form) and the exhausted, unthinking post-work couch potato who actually received the envelopes but wanted nothing more than some mildly diverting, mildly amusing entertainment to soothe his tired mind in the brief hour or two between work and bed.

I realized, in other words, that although the films that have lingered longest in my memory and affected me the most—the films I would think of as the best I'd seen—could all be described as challenging in some way, I didn't always want to be challenged. Sometimes you're more in the mood for *Borat* than Bergman; sometimes (actually, most times) *Annie Hall* seems more appealing than *The Sorrow and the Pity*.

It's a simple point—one that might be condensed to that weary old phrase "horses for courses"—but it is equally valid, and frequently overlooked, when it comes to wine. Too often when we choose wine, we get caught up, even a little anxious, in a hunt for the "best" or what we feel we *should* like, rather than looking for something that fits our mood or the occasion. It's a way of looking at wine that is reflected in most books on the subject, which generally tend to fall into the "greatest and the best" genre. Up to a point, I don't have a problem with that. In the right hands, this critical approach makes for entertaining reading and provides a useful service in promoting worthy producers and putting the underperformers in their place. All the same, in their rush to rank wines and create a pantheon of great bottles, collectively these books (and their burgeoning online equivalents) present a rather distorted picture of how most of us actually approach wine in our day-to-day lives. Perhaps they even get in the way of our enjoying it to the full.

The fact is that for most of us, for most of the time, the finest wines, the acknowledged classics and greats, *aren't* the right wines. Budget has its miserable say in that, of course: Critical acclaim can push up the price of a wine in a way that just doesn't apply to books or films; but there's more to it than that. Even if I had the money to open a bottle of—to pick a particularly pricey example from this book—Giuseppe Mascarello's Barolo Monprivato every night, I wouldn't. There's no doubt that the couple of times I drank this undeniably great Italian wine were among the most memorable wine experiences in my life. But this powerful red just wouldn't cut it if I happened to be eating a plate of spicy Thai noodles or some delicate fish by a beach on a hot summer's evening. Its attention-demanding, ethereal complexity would get lost, too, at a loud and busy party. And its bristly tannins would grate if I were having some white-wine–loving friends around for dinner. In all of these cases, in fact, something much more simple, more humble, would be a better choice.

Context, in other words, is everything with wine. Who you are with, what you're eating, where you are; your mood, the time of year, the weather; your evolving tastes, the money you have in your pocket, the scale and kind of occasion, the many trivial things that happen on a given day… All have an influence on your choice. And it's that sense of wine as a part of life, rather than as a free-floating aesthetic object, that I have tried to get back to with this book.

A number of the wines included here would make it on to many wine writers' selections of desert-island choices—the kinds of wines that may well have a profound effect on you if you're in the right place at the right time and feeling open to the experience. And every wine featured here is an excellent example (or at least one of my favorites) of its type in its price bracket. But this isn't another rundown of the World's 500 Best Wines. It's not another vinous *Billboard* chart.

What I hope to do instead is provide a little fun, a little inspiration, and to fit wine a little more closely to life, in all its messy glory. You may be marking a major life event, like getting married or divorced. You may be pondering what to have with your takeout Chinese or perusing the list at a Michelin-starred French restaurant. Or you may simply be watching *The Hangover Part II* or a seven-hour slice of avant-garde from a fêted Hungarian auteur on your post-work sofa. But whatever you're up to, I hope that somewhere in these pages there will be a wine that feels right for you.

As its subtitle suggests, this book is divided into 100 "occasions," covering events both major and minor in an individual's life. It's arranged roughly chronologically, though many of the events are applicable whatever stage you are at in life. You can also navigate the book by referring to the thematic index of occasions (see p. 242). Each event is color-coded, matching one of seven types of occasion:

Personal Highlights (milestones such as birthdays)	**Love Life** (from a first date, to a diamond wedding anniversary)	**The World of Work** (from college graduation, to retirement)	**Festive Times** (celebrations such as Christmas, New Year, or Thanksgiving)	**On the Town** (from an Italian restaurant, to a neighborhood bar)	**Let Me Entertain You** (when you have guests, such as a vegetarian or a wine snob)	**Daily Life** (from the best wines for springtime, to a weeknight at home)

Each occasion features five wine choices (and an index of all 500 wines is on pp. 244–55):

A **top choice** that best fits the occasion and **four alternatives** based on style, budget, or both.

L'ECOLE NO. 41 COLUMBIA VALLEY MERLOT

FROM Washington State, USA
STYLE Rich Red
GRAPE VARIETY Merlot
PRICE $$$
ABV 14%

WINE PRODUCTION IN WASHINGTON STATE only really began to take off in the late 20th century, but it already has a deserved reputation for producing some of the world's best reds from Merlot, a grape variety that originally hails from Bordeaux, France. From one of the state's top, pioneering producers, this is the perfect introduction to Washington's charms: layers of black and red fruit, smoothly presented with fine tannins, and a quality of brightness that is the hallmark of all Washington's best wines.

Drink it with: Your comfort food of choice—and as a Brit, that would be the mashed potato-topped lamb mince of shepherd's pie; for Americans, it would more likely be meatloaf. But there is power and depth enough in this wine to handle most red-meat dishes, such as steak, burgers, and roasts.

BUDGET BALM

Chilean Merlot is a ubiquitous budget choice in supermarkets around the world, much of it defiantly ordinary and unexciting. But this, from one of the country's leading producers, is a cut above, with its depth of juicy plum and blackberry fruit.

Santa Rita 120 Merlot, Central Valley, Chile
14% ABV $ R

THE EXTRAVAGANT CHOICE

Along with St-Emilion, Pomerol in Bordeaux is where Merlot reaches its greatest heights—nowhere higher than at this magnificent estate, where, with a little help from the Cabernet Franc variety, it achieves a scintillating, perfumed, silky elegance. This wine can turn a bad day into a great one.

Vieux Château Certan, Pomerol, Bordeaux, France
13.5% ABV $$$$$ R

IF YOU DON'T DO MERLOT

If you've been put off by the many inferior Merlots out there, then Pinot Noir made at the plumper, riper end of the spectrum can offer a similarly luxuriant brand of escapism. Saintsbury's sun-filled example will certainly soothe stressed out nerves.

Saintsbury Carneros Pinot Noir, Carneros, California, USA
14% ABV $$$ R

THE WHITE-WINE DRINKER'S BALM

This is a richer style of Chardonnay from a Burgundy producer working in the Ardèche region, farther south in France. It has a mellow, luscious feel, with no rough edges—the kind of wine you can sink into but without the sawdust and butterscotch sweetness of many oak-aged Chardonnays.

Louis Latour Ardèche Chardonnay, PDO Ardèche, France
13% ABV $ W

For each wine, there is a brief description of the **color/style** (*see abbreviations below*) and **origin**, plus an indication of the likely **alcohol level and price** (*again, see the key below*). The latter are offered as an indication only, since alcohol levels may vary from vintage to vintage, and prices vary greatly depending on several factors.

ABBREVIATIONS AND PRICE GUIDE

ABV – *Alcohol by Volume*	SpR – *Sparkling Red*	$ – *Under $10*
R – *Red*	SpRo – *Sparkling Rosé*	$$ – *$10–20*
W – *White*	SW – *Sweet White*	$$$ – *$20–30*
Ro – *Rosé*	SR – *Sweet Red*	$$$$ – *$30–50*
SpW – *Sparkling White*	F – *Fortified Wine*	$$$$$ – *Over $50*

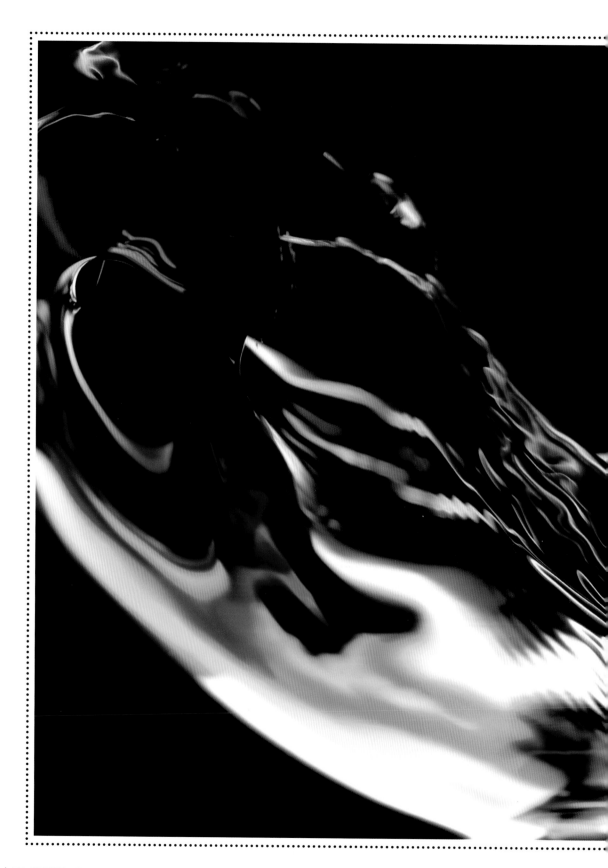

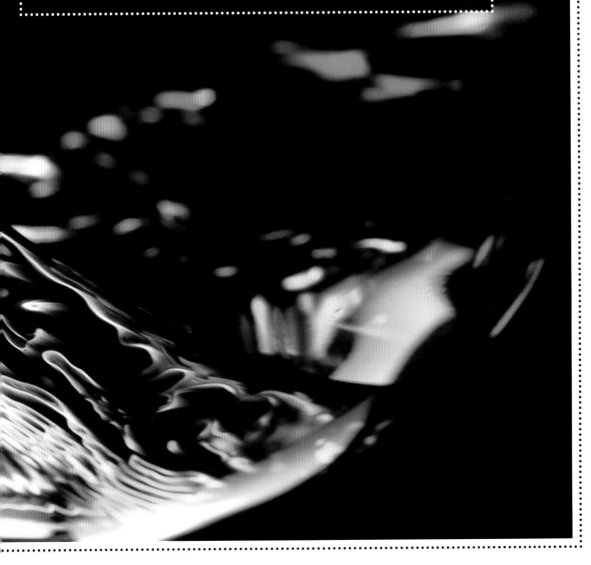

Section 1
100 Occasions

Spring

HERE IT COMES AT LAST. CAN YOU FEEL IT? The warm, ticklish air sweet with blossom and the first cut grass of the year, alive with birdsong and the laughter of children playing in the street; the music of radios drifting through open windows and your whistle as you work. The first real day of spring gets into your veins, an electric quickening as your spirit thaws and soars—an indestructible mood that was given you free: frisky like the violin of Stéphane Grappelli, weightless like Vivaldi. Do we ever feel more connected to nature, more subject to its rhythms and moods than now, when all of life is waking up anew? On days like these, we want only to be outside; we've fallen in love with the world again, and it's given us butterflies. If only we could capture this mood, if only we could bottle it and keep it for those darker, more difficult days. Impossible? Well, there are people who sometimes get close. Some vintners make wines that really do seem to express the joys of spring. It's there in their scents and flavors: blossom, grass, young fruit. And it's there in the way they feel and make you feel, their energy, their joie de vivre, the way they seem to dance and skip across the tongue.

"She turned to the sunlight
And shook her yellow head,
And whispered to her neighbor:
'Winter is dead.'"

FROM *"DAFFODOWNDILLY"*
BY *A. A. MILNE*

FRANÇOIS COTAT SANCERRE CAILLOTTES

FROM
Sancerre, Loire, France
STYLE
Crisp, Dry White
GRAPE VARIETY
Sauvignon Blanc
PRICE $$
ABV 13%

IN THE GENTEEL SURROUNDS and on the chalk, flint, and, in this case, limestone soils of Sancerre in France's Loire Valley, the Sauvignon Blanc variety is at its most spring-like. Generally speaking, you'll find less of the explosive tropical fruit and gooseberry that you find in New Zealand's Marlborough versions—the flavors are quieter, greener, flintier, and crisper than those. François Cotat's wines are particularly graceful, but they pulse with energy, too; there's a stony mineral quality, with citrus, nettles, grass, and flowers. And if flowery descriptions don't do it for you, suffice to say that the wines are also invigoratingly dry, crisp, and refreshing.

Drink it with: *You could take a bottle outside with a baguette and a creamy goat's cheese like the local Crottin de Chavignol—one of the classic and hard-to-beat wine-and-food matches—or else serve it with smoked salmon or a simply prepared delicate white fish, like lemon or Dover sole.*

SPRING MELT

With aromas and flavors as delicate and subtle as its delightful name suggests, this is a light, dry white from the Alpine French region of Savoie. Made from Jacquère, a grape variety unique to the region, it charms with its nose of blossom and subtle citrus, and it's as pure and pristine as an Alpine stream.

Domaine de l'Idylle Cuvée Orangerie, Savoie, France
12% ABV $$ W

OUI, C'EST LE PRINTEMPS

A lighter red wine—made from Syrah in France's Northern Rhône Valley from biodynamic vines and in a way that is designed to be quaffed rather than contemplated —this has the region's classic black-pepper twist and a floral dimension to the crunchily succulent black fruit.

Dard & Ribo C'Est le Printemps, Crozes-Hermitage, France
13% ABV $$ R

A RICHER SPRING WHITE

Rather more forthright in its fruit, aromas, and texture, with ripe, juicy orchard fruits such as pear, quince, and apricot, this wine from the Austrian-influenced far northeast of Italy also has a flowing mineral coolness that refreshes and chimes with the mood on warmer spring days.

Cantina Terlano Pinot Bianco Vorberg Riserva, Alto Adige, Italy
13.5% ABV $$$ W

A SPRING QUARTET

The delicate, low-alcohol Kabinett style of off-dry Riesling produced in Germany's Mosel Valley is wine's equivalent of Mozart's jaunty "Spring" string quartet. Fritz Haag's version is a benchmark of its racy, lacy charms that could well see you humming along to Beethoven's "Ode to Joy."

Fritz Haag Brauneberger Riesling Kabinett, Mosel, Germany
7.5% ABV $$ W

First Date

THE DILEMMA ON A FIRST DATE is how much to reveal of yourself. Not (only) in the high-school sense of first base, second base, and so on, but in how much to show of your tastes, your personality, your foibles. There is an art to this artificial situation that calls for specialist skills. You want to show you have interests—passions, even—but you don't want those passions to look like obsessions: Best to conceal that 30,000-strong (and climbing) collection of baseball cards for the time being, with a simple "I like baseball"; best to restrict your thing for 1980s hair metal to a casual, "I still play my old Bon Jovi LPs from time to time." It's the same with your drink order. Nothing extreme: no high acid, tannin, or off-the-wall flavor; neither too expensive nor too cheap; just an easy-drinking wine with enough character to suggest you like and know about wine but you're not obsessed with it. New Zealand is the country that answers this need most consistently: The overall standard is very high, and the wines tend to appeal to the novice and connoisseur alike. They are, in fact, safe but delicious, which, when you think about it, is more or less the message you want to get across about yourself.

"Wine gives courage and makes men more apt for passion."

OVID

SERESIN ESTATE PINOT GRIS

FROM
Marlborough,
New Zealand
STYLE
Rich White
GRAPE VARIETY
Pinot Gris
PRICE $$$
ABV 14%

SAUVIGNON BLANC BROUGHT New Zealand its international reputation, and it still dominates the country's production, with Pinot Noir assuming a similar position for reds. On a first date, however, you don't want to be too obvious, and the country's many other varieties are every bit as interesting. Pinot Gris is better known as Pinot Grigio, under which name it makes crisp, light, occasionally neutral whites in northern Italy. Inspired by producers in Alsace, France, the Kiwis use the variety to make rich and powerful wines, with a distinctive spicy quality and often with a touch of sugar. This one is just off-dry, with the opulent richness of quince, red apples, and pears: mouth-filling but not overbearing.

Drink it with: *This will work well accompanying buttery roast chicken, pork with apples, or—with that note of spice and sweetness—curries with a gentle heat.*

A BIGGER-BUDGET CHOICE

You don't get all that much Cabernet Franc—a red variety that is most associated with the Loire Valley in France—in New Zealand, but this wonderful, perfumed middleweight red, with its subtle violet notes, red fruit, and leafy freshness, suggests there should be much more.

**Pyramid Valley
Howell Family Vineyard
Cabernet Franc, Hawkes
Bay, New Zealand**
12% ABV $$$ R

SOME ICEBREAKING BUBBLES

Is a first date too soon for sparkling wine? Not necessarily, since a jaunty "Why don't we have a bit of fizz" could help break the ice. And this one is very good. Made by the winery behind the original Kiwi cult wine, Cloudy Bay Sauvignon Blanc, it's a toasty, refined, Champagne look-alike.

**Cloudy Bay Pelorus NV,
Marlborough,
New Zealand**
12.5% ABV $$ SpW

THE ONE TO HAVE WITH RED MEAT

There may be no better match for a peppered steak than Syrah, with its complementary notes of cracked pepper, earth, and meat, to which this example, from New Zealand's best area for the grape variety, Hawkes Bay, adds raspberry and blackberry fruit.

**Mission Estate Syrah,
Hawkes Bay,
New Zealand**
13% ABV $$ R

THE LOW-ALCOHOL CHOICE

Slightly sweet—though you wouldn't know it because of the balancing dose of freshening acidity—this German-inspired Riesling from a winery run by a pair of medical doctors is agile and light on its feet, with floral and stone-fruit flavors.

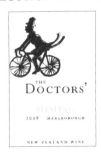

**Forrest
The Doctors' Riesling,
Marlborough,
New Zealand**
8.5% ABV $ W

Chinese New Year

BRINGING IN THE NEW YEAR is the most important celebration in the Chinese calendar and a fine excuse for a party in the rest of the world. Traditionally, festivities begin with a banquet on the eve of the first new moon of the new year, finishing with a lantern festival, complete with parades, to mark the full moon 15 days later. Like Christmas in the West, both New Year's Eve and New Year's Day are very much family occasions for the Chinese, a time for gathering around the table for a feast and to cherish and remember both the living and the dead. What actually goes on the table varies greatly from region to region, but there is a number of common ingredients and dishes, many of them playing a symbolic role as much as a gastronomic one. All New Year's Eve banquets will feature fish, for example, since in Mandarin Chinese the word for fish sounds like "save more." Similarly, *nian gao* (cakes made of sticky rice, sugar, chestnuts, Chinese dates, and lotus leaves) sounds like "getting higher year by year"; the Chinese believe that the higher you are, the more prosperous your business will be.

"A thousand cups of wine do not suffice when true friends meet, but half a sentence is too much when there is no meeting of minds."

TRADITIONAL
CHINESE PROVERB

DOMAINE ZIND HUMBRECHT HENGST GEWURZTRAMINER

FROM
Alsace, France
STYLE
Off-Dry White
GRAPE VARIETY
Gewurztraminer
PRICE $$$
ABV 12%

A CHINESE NEW YEAR'S EVE FEAST features such a range of sensations, spices, textures, and levels of sweetness, all served—in the traditional Chinese way—as a single spread, that it presents a stern challenge to find a sufficiently versatile wine.

Drink it with: *This bottle from one of Alsace's finest producers, Zind Humbrecht, has the degree of sugar required to match both the sweetness and the occasional hot, gingery spice. It also has sufficient acidity to cut through the fatty meat and fried dumplings, as well as a spectrum of opulent spicy aromas and flavors—ginger, litchis, musk, roses—that is harmoniously and suitably oriental in range.*

BUDGET CHOICE

Many tannic red wines don't really work all that well with the complex interplay of spice and sweetness in Chinese food. But if you're a red-wine drinker by preference, then this punchy, full-bodied rosé, which has a touch of sweetness and some very expressive strawberry fruit, is the next best thing.

Finca Las Moras Shiraz Rosé, San Juan, Argentina
14% ABV $ Ro

UNCONVENTIONAL CHOICE

Most people regard Sherry as a fortified wine to be sipped as an apéritif, but it can also work tremendously well with food. This very powerful dry example is, like Chinese food, rich in savory/umami flavors, with heady, intense notes of walnuts and figs.

Lustau Almacenista Obregon Amontillado del Puerto, Sherry, Spain
18.5% ABV $$$$ F

CELEBRATE WITH BUBBLES

A fine fizz, inspired by Champagne, which once played a major part in Sino-American relations: President Richard Nixon served this very wine at the historic "Toast to Peace" in Beijing in 1972. A 100 percent Chardonnay, it is full, rich, and toasty, with a very refined mousse and cleansing, refreshing acidity.

Schramsberg Blanc de Blancs, California, USA
12.9% ABV $$$ SpW

AUTHENTICALLY CHINESE

China has really caught the wine bug over the past decade or so and is making some increasingly interesting wines. This crisp but fruity white, made from the German grape variety Riesling, has just the right level of limey acidity and tropical flavors to match a New Year's fish dish.

Domaine Helan Mountain Premium Collection Riesling, Xinjiang Uygur, China
11% ABV $ W

4 St. Valentine's Day

IT DOESN'T MATTER if the object of your affection is your husband of 60 years or if you're on a first date. You've set aside any distaste for greeting-card schmaltz—all that shop-bought sentimentality and artificial pink that hang around St. Valentine's Day. No, this is not the time for cynicism and snarky remarks; this, make no mistake, is a time for good, old-fashioned, unironic romance. And so, as you splash on an extra dash of aftershave or perfume for luck, as you pull on your most revealing dress or your most flatteringly cut shirt while humming along to the tune of "That's Amore," you decide that tonight you will call on wine choices that are unashamedly romantic. From the name on the label to the colors and flavors inside, these wines are seductive and sensual, just like you (at least tonight, anyway).

"Drink to me only with thine eyes, and I will pledge with mine; or leave a kiss but in the cup, and I'll not look for wine."

FROM *"SONG TO CELIA"*
BY *BEN JONSON*

LOUIS JADOT CELLIER DES CROS SAINT-AMOUR

FROM
Beaujolais, France
STYLE
Fragrant Red
GRAPE VARIETY
Gamay
PRICE $$$
ABV 12.5%

ST-AMOUR IS ONE OF THE SMALLEST of the ten villages, or crus, that are permitted to put their name on the label in the region of Beaujolais. Its name is, in fact, derived from the Roman soldier who converted to Christianity and founded a monastery in the area, Saint Amateur, but that hasn't stopped local growers capitalizing on its associations, and it is a fixture of Valentine's menus in restaurants across France on February 14. Something in this wine, made by the very reputable Louis Jadot, really is conducive to romance, however: Think silk sheets, cherries, and roses.

Drink it with: *A true gentleman, this wine is a culinary diplomat, matching foods from meatier fish (tuna), to white and red meat, or even a rustic local dish such as tripe topped with Gruyère cheese. Like all dry wines, it has its limits, however: It won't work with the sweet course or the Valentine's box of chocolates.*

THE DOWNTOWN ROMANTIC'S CHOICE

From the B-movie-inspired label, to the full-bodied, full-flavored red wine within, this is a wine for those who prefer bold statements of passion to a witty, eyebrows-raised, slow seduction. If it were a romantic movie, it would be *True Romance* rather than *An Affair to Remember*.

Some Young Punks, Passion Has Red Lips Cabernet/Shiraz, McLaren Vale, Australia
14% ABV $$ R

THE UPTOWN ROMANTIC'S CHOICE

Les Amoureuses—which translates as "The Lovers"—is a special vineyard in the special wine village of Chambolle-Musigny. J-F Mugnier's version is both powerfully deep and gracefully light-hearted—the vinous equivalent of one of Shakespeare's sonnets.

Jacques-Frédéric Mugnier Chambolle-Musigny Premier Cru Les Amoureuses, Burgundy, France
13% ABV $$$$$ R

TO GO WITH THE VIOLINS AND ROSES

The bottle would not be out of place in a boudoir in a 1970s romantic mini-series. And the wine, made from Moscato grapes, has a similarly sweet, perfumed character that won't appeal to everyone—but it is just about the perfect accompaniment for strawberry desserts.

Bottega Petalo Il Vino dell'Amore Moscato, Veneto, Italy
6.5% ABV $$ SpW

THE MANDATORY PINK FIZZ

There probably isn't a restaurant or wine retailer in the world that doesn't promote pink Champagne on Valentine's Day. If the wine is as good as Billecart-Salmon's elegant, red-currant-scented example, however, then it's hard to resist.

Billecart-Salmon Brut Rosé NV, Champagne, France
12% ABV $$$ SpRo

Start of the Evening

THE BEE GEES ARE DOING THEIR funky choirboy-at-the-disco thing on the stereo. You're looking good in your new clothes in the mirror. It's Friday night, the bright lights and beats and glamor of the weekend arrayed before you like an all-kicking can-can line at the Moulin Rouge. You feel like John Travolta in *Saturday Night Fever*, like Bianca Jagger on her way to Studio 54. It's a feeling that says tonight is going to be one of those epic occasions that will feel, in retrospect, like it had its own pre-scripted narrative. There will be adventures, flirtations, and world-righting conversations, confessions, surreal encounters, and full-throated, belly-deep laughter —a world so far from the weekday grind you'll find it all too hard to come back there on Monday morning. Those thoughts can wait, though, because right now you're completely in the moment, like a ballplayer at the plate; you are entirely in the party zone. You hear your friends arriving outside the window, and something in the hectic, syncopated hum of their chatter tells you they are in much the same skittish mood. Time to get out the glasses, open the fridge, and uncork the white wine—energetic and exhilarating—with which to start the weekend with a bang.

"No one looks back on their life and remembers the nights they got plenty of sleep."

ANONYMOUS

LIVIO FELLUGA PINOT GRIGIO

FROM
Friuli, Italy
STYLE
Aromatic Dry White
GRAPE VARIETY
Pinot Grigio
PRICE $$$
ABV 12%

AS YOU READ THIS, someone somewhere in the world is starting to ease into their evening with a glass of Pinot Grigio. The crisp and dry north Italian white has become, over the past few years, many people's default by-the-glass or supermarket wine choice. It can verge on the bland, anonymous, and industrial, and most of it, alas, is exactly that. However, Livio Felluga, working in the northeastern region of Friuli near Slovenia, uses the variety to produce something arrestingly aromatic, with ripe tropical fruit, a martini-like twist of herb and spice, and acidity that makes it dance across the tongue. So it's well worth going the extra mile or two to discover the real McCoy.

Drink it with: *This wine's incisive freshness would cut through the comforting richness of a seafood risotto, a dish that will provide the slow release of energy you'll need for the evening to come.*

DISCO JUICE

Pulsating with the classic aromas and flavors of Marlborough Sauvignon Blanc—passion fruit, elderflower, a touch of guava—but with an extra level of citrusy vibrancy and verve, Dog Point's Kiwi classic is as crowd-pleasingly uplifting and energetic as Donna Summer in full flight singing "I Feel Love."

Dog Point Sauvignon Blanc, Marlborough, New Zealand
13.5% ABV $$ W

WALTZING INTO THE WEEKEND

Native to Austria and rarely found elsewhere, Grüner Veltliner makes wines with a distinctive white-pepper spice seasoning, which in this case lifts the pear and apple fruit in an effortlessly graceful, lively Strauss waltz of a dry white.

Domäne Wachau Terrassen Grüner Veltliner Federspiel, Wachau, Austria
12.5% ABV $ W

A LATIN FIZZ TO GET THINGS MOVING

Light pink in hue, delicately aromatic on the nose, and punchily red-fruited on the palate, with a zip and a zing of quickening acidity and finely caressing bubbles, this Spanish sparkling rosé is comparable to Champagne in both quality and its capacity to lift the mood.

Raventós i Blanc de Nit Cava, Spain
12.5% ABV $$ SpRo

EARLY-EVENING PARTY RED

As the sun sets and the neon lights call, here's a lighter red wine with a quicksilver quality to match a restless, excitable mood. From the increasingly fashionable Ribeira Sacra appellation in Galicia, northwest Spain, it uses the Mencía grape variety to delightfully silky, perfumed effect.

Guímaro Tinto Ribeira Sacra, Galicia, Spain
13% ABV $$ R

Easter Day

For the committed Christian and steadfast atheist alike, Easter is a family time, where the centerpiece of the celebration is a sit-down meal. In much of the world, that traditionally means roast lamb, which in itself is a reflection of both the Christian and the secular sides of Easter. The lamb is a particularly potent symbol for Central and Eastern European Christians, representing the Lamb of God; while for the secular, the first new-season lamb has a more atavistic connection to pagan celebrations of the end of winter. Much the same can be said of Easter eggs: a symbol of rebirth for the Christian and of spring's fertility for the pagan. And then there is the wine: Central to the Christian story and to Dionysian rites of spring, it, too, is an important part of Easter, whatever your belief system. For the roast lamb (and for that alternative US favorite, boiled ham) look for medium-bodied red wines such as those produced in Bordeaux and Rioja, ideally with a bit of age (five to ten years or more), by which time they will have softened and become more savory, mimicking the tender flavor and texture of the meat.

"Well pleaseth me the sweet time of Easter That maketh the leaf and the flower come out."

Bertran de Born

FEUDI DI SAN GREGORIO LACRYMA CHRISTI BIANCO

FROM Campania, Italy
STYLE Rich Dry White
GRAPE VARIETY
Blend
PRICE $$
ABV 13.5%

THE NAME, OF COURSE, is the draw here: Could there be a more appropriate Easter bottle than one named "Tears of Christ"? In fact, the origins of the name, which relates to vines grown on the lava-scarred slopes of Mount Vesuvius in Campania, southern Italy, are disputed. One account has the tears of Jesus Christ, weeping at the beauty of the Bay of Naples as he ascended to heaven, causing the scars; another version has Jesus crying as Lucifer fell from heaven. Another local myth dates back still further. In this account, it was Bacchus, god of wine, whose tears of joy brought vines to the slopes of Vesuvius. Whichever myth you prefer, the white blend made by Feudi di San Gregorio on those slopes today would be worth talking about even without the compelling backstory. This is a rounded, mouth-filling dry white, with expressive honeyed exotic fruit, rippling orange-citrus acidity, and a mouthwatering mineral quality.

Drink it with: *Have this with the Easter dinner if you're roasting a bird or with Easter fish on Good Friday.*

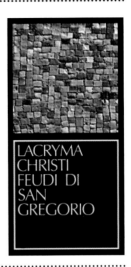

BUDGET CHOICE FOR LAMB

The mellow flavors and textures of traditional Rioja—the dusky red and black fruit, coconut, and savory leather, and the soft, melting tannins—have a lot in common, somehow, with a tender, pink roast lamb. For sheer value, few can match the quality of Bodegas Montecillo's classic Reserva.

Montecillo Rioja Reserva, Spain
13.5% ABV $ R

TREAT FOR LAMB

The red wines of Bordeaux, with their firm tannins and bright acidity, are a classic match for the fat and flavor of lamb. In a region where price still closely follows official classification, the low-ranked but high-performing (and delicious) Château Chasse-Spleen is one of the best-value red wines around.

Château Chasse-Spleen, Moulis en Médoc, Bordeaux, France
13.5% ABV $$$ R

FOR CHOCOLATE EGGS

Whether in the form of eggs, bunnies, or a dessert, Easter is a time for chocolate. Few wines have the combination of power and sweetness to make a good partner, but this sweet fortified red wine—a southern French alternative to Port (also a good match)—has what it takes: a rich but still sprightly melange of fig, date, and dried cherry.

Domaine la Tour Vieille Banyuls, Roussillon, France
18% ABV $$ F

A HOLY WINE

One meaning of Vin Santo is holy wine, though strictly speaking here it refers to a sweet wine made on the Greek island of Santorini. White grapes are dried on straw mats in the sun for two weeks after harvest to concentrate the sugar before being aged in barrels for six years. The result is a luscious, slightly chewy, sweet wine for Holy Week.

Hatzidakis Vinsanto, Santorini, Greece
12.5% ABV $$$ SW

7 Blind Date

NOT EVERYONE GOES on a blind date looking for The One. There's fun to be had in just meeting someone new, fun in the flirtation, in trying to piece together their background and quirks. And in this, the process is very much like the wine-tasting equivalent of the blind date—blind tasting—where wines are presented with their identity, origin, and price concealed. For professional wine buyers, this can serve a serious purpose: Some feel they can get a truer picture of the wine's quality without being biased by its reputation. But it can also be fun, a guessing game that engages the brain and the senses and could work as an icebreaker on a blind date in a restaurant. Just ask the sommelier to pour you, say, five small glasses of wine on a theme to compare and contrast; it could be five whites or reds from different grapes, five wines from the same grape in different places, or five wines from the same place and grape but from different producers. It's up to you—though remember that, like the date itself, a blind tasting tends to work best if you don't take it too seriously and you're prepared to make a fool of yourself.

"What is research but a blind date with knowledge?"

WILLIAM HENRY

WARWICK ESTATE THE FIRST LADY UNOAKED CHARDONNAY

FROM Stellenbosch,
South Africa
STYLE Fruity Dry White
GRAPE VARIETY
Chardonnay
PRICE $
ABV 14%

CHARDONNAY MAKES a great theme for a blind tasting because it is a grape variety that is made in so many different styles around the world, its flavor and texture dependent to a great extent on both the climate and soil where it is grown and the ways in which it is treated in the winery. In this case, the grapes have ripened in plentiful sun in the historic South African region of Stellenbosch, which helps bring the wine its ample ripe orchard-fruit flavors, but it has been fermented and aged in neutral stainless-steel tanks, so has none of the toasty, buttery character associated with oak-barrel aging. That makes it an ideal starting point for an exploration of what's known in wine-speak as the varietal flavors of Chardonnay—the taste of the fruit rather than the vessel.

Drink it with: *This has sufficient body to go with chicken but is also perky enough to suit white fish.*

LEAN AND STEELY

The next Chardonnay in the lineup is, like the Warwick Estate, unoaked, but it tastes very different. There's a salty, steely quality, bracing almost, under the tender green apple— the product of the chalky soil and cooler climate of the Chablis region to the north of Burgundy, France.

Domaine Brocard Chablis, Burgundy, France
12% ABV $$ W

A LITTLE BARREL AGING

Here is a slight change in geography, a little farther south in Burgundy, but the influence of oak is the most significant difference in this great-value (for Burgundy) Chardonnay. It has a creamier texture, more savory tones, and a nuttiness to go with the incisive acidity.

Domaine Jean-Marc Pillot Bourgogne Blanc, Burgundy, France
13% ABV $$ W

A WARMER CLIMATE

Although nothing like as big and rich as many examples from the state, this Chardonnay still feels much more ample and ripe in its fruit character than the previous pair of wines— the product of the warm California sun, as well as the oak-aging—but it's nicely freshened by a kick of lemon citrus.

Waterstone Carneros Chardonnay, California, USA
13.5% ABV $$ W

CHARDONNAY WITH BUBBLES

Finally, a chance to see what Chardonnay tastes like in sparkling form— a style known as blanc de blancs in Champagne. It is adapted here, in the same region as Warwick Estate, to fine effect to create a wine that has layers of patisserie and toast resulting from contact with the yeast cells in the bottle as it ages.

Villiera Brut Natural Chardonnay, Stellenbosch, South Africa
11% ABV $ SpW

Mother's Day

8

On Mother's Day, many of us will choose wine as a gift. But, since every mother has her own personality and tastes, recommending a single wine for this occasion is no simple matter. One solution might be to pick out something that will match that other popular Mother's Day gift, a box of chocolates. But even this is not as easy as it sounds, since chocolate is one of those foodstuffs that regularly appears in lists of impossible food pairings in magazines and wine guides. What makes it difficult? Well, the sweetness of chocolate rules out dry wines completely: Generally speaking, if the food is sweeter than the wine, the wine's bitterness will be emphasized or, in the case of lighter styles, its flavors will be lost entirely. The sheer force of flavor in chocolate, particularly as you climb up the ladder through the different cocoa percentages, also has the capacity to overwhelm most wines. And there are different types of bitterness in both chocolate and wine that taste fine independently, but clash when put together. A difficult match, then, but not an impossible one: Many styles of Port have the necessary mix of robust fruit and sweetness to cope, as do similar styles produced in France's Maury and Banyuls regions. And if those styles seem too strong, you could switch to flowers rather than chocolate, or simply choose a dry red, white, or fizz with a floral bouquet.

"The heart of a mother is a deep abyss at the bottom of which you will always find forgiveness."

Honoré de Balzac

WARRE'S OTIMA 10 YEAR OLD TAWNY PORT

FROM Douro, Portugal
STYLE Sweet Fortified
GRAPE VARIETY Blend
PRICE $$
ABV 20%

IN GENERAL, IT'S SOUND ADVICE never to judge a wine by its label. But when you've gone to the trouble of making everything else you've bought look so appealing, it would be a shame if the wine were to let the aesthetic side down. In a region not known for taking risks with its packaging (though a lot of those traditional Vintage Port bottles are almost more appealing for not trying too hard), the modern minimalism and clear glass of Warre's Otima is a stylish exception. More importantly, the wine inside, as is generally the case with this fine old producer, is just as impressive if not more so: a blend of casks with an average age of ten years, though lighter in feel than many Ports, it's still rich with dried red and black fruit and lingering notes of fruit-cake spice.

Drink it with: *Powerful and sweet, Port is one of the few wines that generally works well as a complement to chocolate, the style depending on the cocoa content and sweetness, as well as any added flavorings.*

A CHOCOLATE PARTNER

The sweet fortified wines made from Muscat (Moscatel) in Setúbal near Lisbon are not as well known as those Portuguese classics Port and Madeira, but they have a similar chocolate-friendly depth and richness—and, in this instance, an aromatic fruitiness as well.

Bacalhôa Moscatel de Setúbal, Portugal
17.5% ABV $$ F

SPLASHING OUT

Now owned by the more famous house of Bollinger, Ayala is a fine producer in its own right, and this rosé, a blend of Chardonnay with the red Pinots Noir and Meunier, is gracious and delicate with its fine mousse and strawberry and red currant flavors— a maternal treat.

Ayala Rosé Majeur Brut NV Champagne, France
12% ABV $$$ SpRo

A DRY RED THAT SAYS IT WITH FLOWERS

Argentina isn't known for the quality of its Pinot Noir, but this Patagonian estate, run by the grandson of the creator of the legendary Tuscan wine Sassicaia, has shown how good it can be in the country's cooler climes: so pretty, floral, and elegant.

Bodega Chacra Barda Pinot Noir, Río Negro, Patagonia, Argentina
12% ABV $$$ R

A DRY WHITE GIFT

From a top vineyard and made by a small family-run firm in Alsace, this is a strikingly pure and fragrant dry white that goes easy on the floral grapey aromas associated with Muscat, adding a fennel and dill-like herbal nose and brisk citrusy freshness. Ready to drink, but your mother can stash it away for a few years if she likes.

Dirler-Cadé Saering Grand Cru Muscat, Alsace, France
13% ABV $$$ W

The Proposal

9

YOU'VE BEEN THINKING ABOUT how you're going to do this for weeks. Now you're starting to wonder if you shouldn't have been a little more spontaneous. You've done that thing they do in the movies, turning to the mirror time and again with your prepared line, and immediately wished you hadn't: Whatever you say doesn't sound quite right, you just don't look quite as dashing as you'd hoped, and you're starting to feel the nerves. Maybe that's the point, that the proposal is in itself a kind of test; if your intended laughs you out of the room, well, it was never meant to be. Problem is, you do so much want it to be—if only you could be more commanding, more suave, more Cary Grant or Katharine Hepburn about it. Still, even if you haven't quite got the script and delivery perfect yet, at least you know you've got the mise-en-scène right. You've booked a weekend away in the finest hotel you can afford; you've scouted the most romantic location. All that remains is the wine: a bottle full of romance and glamour, but a little out of the ordinary—dazzling, exotic, sensual, Viognier, which at its best is as irresistible as you hope to be.

"It is always incomprehensible to a man that a woman should ever refuse an offer of marriage."

EMMA TO MR. KNIGHTLEY
IN EMMA
BY JANE AUSTEN

DOMAINE DE TRIENNES VIOGNIER

FROM Vin de Pays du Var, France
STYLE Aromatic Dry White
GRAPE VARIETY Viognier
PRICE $$
ABV 13%

VIOGNIER IS A TRICKY GRAPE to get right. It needs a bit of sun and warmth to achieve proper ripeness, but if the vintner isn't careful, the variety has a tendency to become unappealingly fat and listless in the mouth, a kind of ungainly, overperfumed splat of tinned peaches in syrup. This Provençal partnership between two of Burgundy's most respected producers avoids the pitfalls. It has Viognier's trademark aromatic intensity, all honeysuckle, white peaches, and apricots, but while it's weighty and rich on the palate, it has a certain raciness, a cut and thrust, that makes it an irresistible pleasure to drink.

Drink it with: *Gorgeously ripe and round, this Viognier needs no partner, but if you're making your proposal over dinner, maybe steer your partner toward full-flavored dishes involving pork, chicken, or meaty fish such as turbot or sea bass.*

BUDGET CHOICE

Viognier has become a popular grape in France's largest and most experimental wine region, the Languedoc-Roussillon, in the past couple of decades. Laurent Miquel makes several examples with a remarkable consistency, balancing sumptuous honeyed apricot and crisp mandarin-like citrus.

Laurent Miquel Nord-Sud Viognier, IGP Pays d'Oc, France
13% ABV $ W

MONEY'S-NO-OBJECT CHOICE

The tiny Château Grillet appellation in Viognier's spiritual home, France's Northern Rhône Valley, has just one eponymous producer, now owned by the billionaire proprietor of Bordeaux's no-less-legendary Château Latour and producing only Viognier with a remarkable complexity of fruit, flowers, and verve.

Château Grillet, Rhône, France
13.5% ABV $$$$$ W

A RED WITH VIOGNIER

Producers in the Northern Rhône appellation of Côte-Rôtie have traditionally blended a little Viognier into their red wines made from Syrah, giving them a little aromatic lift and helping fix the color. Many top Aussie producers have been inspired to do the same, and this sumptuous, powerful red, with its explosive, violet-edged black fruit, is a delightful expression of the style.

Yering Station Village Shiraz/Viognier, Yarra Valley, Australia
14.5% ABV $$ R

AN ITALIAN ALTERNATIVE

Greco di Tufo, a white grape variety from the hills of Campania in the south of Italy, shares some of the qualities of well-made Viognier—in this case offering both the blossom and the fruit of the orchard (quince, peach), as well as a certain nuttiness, in a full but dry and elegant white, with a crystallized citrusy bite.

Terredora Loggia della Serra Greco di Tufo, Campania, Italy
13% ABV $$ W

At a Steak House

THERE ARE FEW GREATER OR MORE atavistic pleasures than the elemental combination of fire, iron, and earth found in a well-cooked steak: a steak that is charred black and crisp by the fearsome heat of a smoking grill on the outside but is melting, almost tofu-like in texture, on the inside, the blood streaking into the crisp French fries without which it just would not be the same. Many places can lay claim to offering the ultimate steak—from Texas, with its T-bones, to Lyon and its *steak frites*; from the barbecues of South Africa and Australia, to the great steak houses of New York and Chicago. But the country where steak has permeated the culture most definitively is Argentina. On impromptu street-side grills, in fancy restaurants, at family *asados* (barbecues) . . . steak is everywhere here, the meat sourced from the vast plains, the pampas, that fan out from the capital Buenos Aires, and always accompanied by a glass or two of the local *tinto*. No wonder the Argentinians have historically been among the world's largest consumers of red wine. The intense, full-bodied Malbecs in which the country specializes are the ideal wines for the national dish—and the perfect choice the next time you take your seat amid the checked tablecloths and dark wooden panels of a classic US steakhouse.

> *"White wine is like electricity. Red wine looks and tastes like a liquified beefsteak."*
>
> JAMES JOYCE

PULENTA LA FLOR MALBEC

FROM Mendoza, Argentina
STYLE Dry Red
GRAPE VARIETY Malbec
PRICE $$
ABV 15%

IF IT WERE A PERSON, Pulenta's delightful Malbec would be a "metrosexual" man of the world: Physically imposing but in touch with his softer side, he's well groomed and not afraid to dab on a little cologne. Translated into wine-speak, that means the juice has plenty of alcohol and tannin (or structure), but it feels sleek and juicy in the mouth, while the nose is floral, mingling violets with red and black fruit. This is a benchmark Malbec from high-altitude vines (980–1,200 ft.).

Drink it with: *Steak, of course, but also the other elements of a classic Argentinian* asado—*the corpulent blood sausage (*morcilla*), chicken, kidneys, liver, and so on. There's also enough acidity to cope with a spicy tomato salsa.*

ARGENTINA WITH AN ITALIAN ACCENT

Itinerant winemaker Alberto Antonini helped found this winery in Mendoza, the latest in a long line of Italians to bring their expertise to bear on Argentinian wine and society. Here he's fashioned a wine of intense perfume and power, with a twist of Italianate bitterness.

Altos Las Hormigas Malbec Reserva, Valle de Uco, Mendoza, Argentina
14% ABV $$ R

MONEY'S-NO-OBJECT CHOICE

A Franco-Argentine collaboration, Achaval Ferrer makes a range of Malbecs of unmatched finesse. It may be inky dark to look at, but the summer-pudding fruit flavors in this graceful, aromatic, and supple red from a single vineyard are entirely transparent.

Achaval Ferrer Malbec Finca Mirador, Mendoza, Argentina
13.5% ABV $$$$ R

IN THE PARISIAN BISTRO

The classic bistro lunchtime *steak frites* is lighter, the meat cut thinner, than in a US steak house. So, too, the wine in your *pichet*—a leafy Cabernet Franc from the cool of the Loire, with a texture that is crunchy and refreshing rather than velvety and lush.

Domaine Filliatreau Saumur-Champigny, Loire, France
13% ABV $$ R

IN THE ALL-AMERICAN STEAK HOUSE

A vinous modern classic, Napa Valley Cabernet, goes with a culinary modern classic, the steak house. The softly swarthy tannins and ripe, almost sweet fruit combine with the fat of the tannin for a scientifically proven combination.

Frog's Leap Cabernet Sauvignon, Napa Valley, California, USA
14.5% ABV $$$ R

THE STEAK-HOUSE WINE LIST

The steak house is perhaps the USA's greatest culinary gift to the world. The formula is deceptively simple: high-quality aged beef and a searingly hot grill. One of the most highly regarded in New York is Sparks Steak House in Manhattan, and its wine list reveals exactly the kinds of wines that fit well here: It's a veritable *Who's Who* of Napa Cabs, Argentinian Malbecs, and brawny southern European reds.

11 On a Camping Trip

As with most things in life, our attitude to camping rather depends on that first, formative experience. If, at some point in your childhood, you've been through the trauma of waking up in what seems like a muddy interior lake, your favorite books and toys destroyed, the canvas providing no more of a barrier between the angry sky and your sodden sleeping bag than a single sheet of tissue paper would, then it's fair to assume that you'll grow up to be one of those people who, at best, sees camping as budget vacation accommodation of the very last resort. But if your early camping experiences relate to warmer climes, to vast night skies filled with stars, birdsong, and the scent of pines and wood smoke in the warm evening breeze, or dew-soaked morning grass (such a delicious feeling in your flip-flops) and the distant lowing of cows, then you may think it's touched with a kind of magic. The wine to take on a camping trip should appeal to both extremes. For the naysayer, it will provide comfort, warmth, and a fast track to sleep; for the wide-eyed enthusiast, it's all about echoing the wild scents and flavors of the great outdoors.

> *"In all things of nature there is something of the marvelous."*
>
> *Aristotle*

PÉREZ CRUZ CABERNET SAUVIGNON RESERVA

FROM Maipo, Chile
STYLE Powerful Red
GRAPE VARIETY
Cabernet Sauvignon
PRICE $$
ABV 14%

THE MAIPO VALLEY, which begins as the suburbs of the capital Santiago start their ascent into the Andes, is Chile's most established wine region and is synonymous with Cabernet Sauvignon. Typically, the style here is intense and deep-colored, with a black-currant-pastille fruit character. These are wines that would provide succor to any reluctant campers shivering in their fleece on camp chairs they can only think of as a "not-sofa." For the outdoors types tuning up their guitars beside the campfire, it's the characteristic Maipo waft of mint, eucalypt, and bay leaf that brings out the Walt Whitman.

Drink it with: *Sausages and baked beans, a can of meat stew, or a hunk of meat that has come straight from a wood-fired barbecue.*

FOR THE CAMPFIRE

South Africa's Pinotage variety is not always to everyone's taste. The wines often have a mix of cherry bubble gum and ashtray that is hard to love. In the right hands, however, it makes robust but supple red wines with black fruit, where that ashy quality is transformed into an attractive note of wood smoke.

**Bellingham
The Bernard Series
Bush Vine Pinotage,
Stellenbosch,
South Africa**
14% ABV $$ R

THE SMELL OF GARRIGUE

Pitch up a tent in the south of France, and the air is thick with the smell of *garrigue*, the aromatic scrubland that covers the hills. Along with olive and blackberries, this sleek red blend, made by a Dutchwoman in vineyards in those same hills, evokes those scents beautifully.

**Mas des Dames
La Dame, Languedoc,
France**
13.5% ABV $$ R

BY A STREAM

A wine to have with the fish you've caught yourself that very morning, this is a Catalan blend of Sauvignon Blanc and the local Macabeo. It is weighty and aromatic, bright-fruited and fresh, and touched with the scent of wild herbs such as tarragon and fennel.

**Castell del Remei
Blanc Planell,
Costers del Segre, Spain**
13% ABV $ W

IN THE BUSH

Like Chile's Maipo, Coonawarra is strongly associated with Cabernet Sauvignon with a very pure, ripe black-currant character and a distinct note of the eucalyptus trees that are such a feature of the Australian landscape. Wynns Black Label is a benchmark of the style.

**Wynns Black Label
Coonawarra Cabernet
Sauvignon, Australia**
14.5% ABV $$ R

12 Bachelor Party

LIKE MUCH TO DO WITH MARRIAGE, the bachelor party has fallen prey to competitiveness. Where once the groom was content with a single, albeit boisterous, night out with the guys, now there is a feeling that nothing less than a debauched weekend, possibly even a week, preferably some place exotic, will do. There is inflation, too, in what constitutes an acceptable level of misbehavior: If a bachelor party hasn't included a brush with death or the law, if some apocryphal story of excess has not been bettered, then what was the point of having one? In its essence, however, the bachelor party hasn't really changed. It remains an almost ritualistic expression of maleness: a boozy, innuendo-laden opportunity to indulge in the kind of practical jokes, risqué banter, and tomfoolery that were tacitly encouraged by coaches at high school but would quickly earn you a disciplinary hearing in the world of work. In this environment, only the toughest wines survive—powerful reds from robust varieties like Shiraz or Tempranillo that would never attract effete descriptions like "pretty" or "elegant" as you sip them in some godforsaken bar at 4:00 a.m. and wonder if the true purpose of the bachelor party might be to make the groom yearn for married life to begin.

> *"Take the tone of the company that you are in."*
>
> LORD CHESTERFIELD
> IN A LETTER TO HIS SON

TWO HANDS GNARLY DUDES BAROSSA SHIRAZ

FROM Barossa, Australia
STYLE Powerful Red
GRAPE VARIETY Shiraz
PRICE $$
ABV 15%

THE IDEA THAT Australia only produces enormous wines with bold fruit flavors and high alcohol is more than a little outdated: Modern Australian wine is far more diverse than that. But those blockbuster wines are still out there, and the Barossa Valley in South Australia is where the best of them are made. Two Hands, a relative newcomer in a region with a long winemaking history, has a knack of combining intense, deep, dark fruit with a svelte texture. This wine, named for the very old "gnarly" Shiraz vines that produce the grapes, is robust but fragrant—there is even a touch of floral perfume, but don't let on that you've spotted it tonight.

Drink it with: *Hearty wine, hearty food. This is one for the grill, bloody steaks, high-quality burgers—meat!*

BUDGET CHOICE

Grant Burge makes some of the Barossa's top reds; here the net is cast a little wider, with grapes taken from across the wider region of South Australia, for a sweetly fruited (but dry) wine, with juiciness as well as power.

Grant Burge Benchmark Shiraz, South Australia
14% ABV $ R

THE ONE TO STOP A FIGHT

Mollydooker is an Aussie term for a southpaw, and this wine certainly has an offbeat pugilistic power: concentrated, almost thick and viscous in texture, with lots of alcohol, but also a very appealing purity of blackberry fruit—a big wine, with a soft side.

Mollydooker The Boxer Shiraz, South Australia
16.5% ABV $$$ R

THE MACHO CHOICE

Australia doesn't have the monopoly on powerful red wines. Toro in Spain's northwest is another, here using very old Tempranillo (known around here as Tinta de Toro) rather than Shiraz vines for a chewy dark black coffee and black-fruited wine that lives up to its name (El Recio translates as "Tough Guy").

Matsu El Recio Toro, Spain
14.5% ABV $$ R

BIG, RED—AND FIZZY

An Australian specialty (it's an Aussie Christmas dinner tradition), sparkling Shiraz is a bit of an acquired taste but one worth getting used to, pitting the toasty flavors and fizz of Champagne and the grunt and guts of a straight Shiraz—as in this hardy example, one of the few that is readily available outside Australia.

Wyndham Estate Bin 555 Sparkling Shiraz, South Australia
13.5% ABV $$ SpR

Father's Day

WE MAY LOVE OUR FATHERS DEARLY, but it takes a special kind of person to be able to spend their life working with their dad. For those born into a family business, as a great many wine producers still are, it is not always an easy task. They may feel the pressure of continuing a business that has been in the family for centuries. The two generations may have opposing views of what to do with the business. But tradition and innovation do not need to clash—many an inspired idea has come from the creative tension between age-old, deeply held values and new, cutting-edge techniques. Of course, no doubt even the most outwardly harmonious intergenerational partnerships have their moments of strife. But on this day dedicated to fathers, it makes sense to honor the businesses that work out of their shared family values and whose wines express the powerful bonds of love, responsibility, and loyalty that hold them together.

"By the time a man realizes that maybe his father was right, he usually has a son who thinks he's wrong."

CHARLES WADSWORTH

FILIPA PATO NOSSA BRANCO

FROM Bairrada, Portugal
STYLE Off-Dry White
GRAPE VARIETY Bical
PRICE $$$
ABV 12.5%

ONE OF THE GREATEST Father's Day gifts is to see your child succeed, and it is certainly one that Filipa Pato, daughter of the celebrated Luis, has managed to give. The wines she makes under her own label are the equal in quality of her father's (high praise indeed) but with a stylish flair that's all her own. This oak-aged white, made from the local Bical variety, has pithy grapefruit-and-lemon zestiness and an oatmeal-like savoriness.
Drink it with: *Its weight and textural depth make this a wine to serve to your father with roast chicken or pork.*

VATERTAG

Armin Diel is the head honcho at this fine German estate, but his daughter Caroline now has responsibility for the vines and, with the support of winemaker Christoph Friedrich, the wines. This off-dry white has a racy energy, lacy delicacy, charm, and steel.

Schlossgut Diel Riesling Kabinett, Nahe, Germany
10.5% ABV $$ W

AN AMERICAN FAMILY

Father-and-son team John and Doug Shafer have between them created a modern American classic in Shafer Hillside Select, a quintessential Napa Cab from the Stags Leap District. Full of black fruit, it's glossy and dense, but harmonious.

Shafer Hillside Select, Stags Leap District, Napa Valley, California
15.5% ABV $$$$$ R

FESTA DEL PAPÀ

The Antinori family are Tuscan wine royalty, having been in the business since the late 14th century. Current paterfamilias Marchese Piero Antinori runs the business with his three daughters, Albiera, Allegra, and Alessia. They produce a broad range of wines, of which this deep, slick, cherry-driven Tuscan red blend is a reliable fixture.

Villa Antinori Rosso, Toscana IGT, Tuscany, Italy
13% ABV $$ R

A FATHER'S DAY GIFT

One of a number of British families that helped shape the history of the Port trade, the Symingtons are still going strong, with three generations working in a business that owns names such as Cockburn's, Dow's, Graham's, and Warre's. This typically sumptuous but fragrant Port is made entirely from grapes grown in a single vintage on the family's beautiful Quinta do Vesuvio estate.

Quinta do Vesuvio Single Quinta Vintage Port, Portugal
20% ABV $$$ F

Summer

An important facet of wine that is too often overlooked, by vintners as much as by consumers, is refreshment. We can become so caught up in all the other things wine can do—its startling range of flavors and textures, its ability to capture the essence of a specific place and year, or the way its alcohol makes us feel—that we forget that this ability is perhaps its primary role. It's a drink, in other words, and as such it should be able to quench our thirst. All the best bottles—even the richest, headiest red wines and Ports, even the wines that are designed to age for decades—have this quality. It's a pulse of energy or brightness that means we do not simply admire them for a sip or two; they call us back for another glass. But while every wine worth drinking is refreshing to a degree, there are wines for which refreshment is the sole raison d'être. If wines were pieces of music— with the refreshment factor the rhythm keeping us listening/drinking, and the flavors the melody appealing to our emotions and intellect—then these wines would be almost all rhythm, their fruit flavor stripped back, their acidity pronounced, insistent, but not shrill; the dance track, the samba band, rather than the symphony. Red, white, or rosé, these are the wines of summer, beaded in an ice bucket, waiting to slake our thirst, waiting to dance.

"Wine is sunlight,
held together by water."

Galileo

QUINTA DE AZEVEDO VINHO VERDE

FROM Portugal
STYLE Dry White
GRAPE VARIETY Blend
PRICE $
ABV 11%

IN PORTUGUESE, VINHO VERDE literally translates as "green wine," as in young (it's a style that is intended to be drunk within a year) rather than relating to the color (though as it happens, the landscape in this corner of northern Portugal is verdant). With its slight spritz and nervy acidity—in this instance, just the right side of tart—it has the refreshing quality of a *citron presse* made with a lightly sparkling soda water, but there is subtle peach and flowers here, too, and a low alcohol content that makes drinking it on a summer afternoon an effortless pleasure with no painful or sleepy consequences later in the day.

Drink it with: *Seafood, perhaps served in the Portuguese style with a peri-peri sauce.*

A BASQUE FOR A BISQUE

The grape variety here, Hondarrabi Zuri, is almost as hard to pronounce for non-Basque speakers as the wine's name, but it's a quintessential summer wine, similar to Vinho Verde in its spritzy, lemony tang, while the stony mineral characters add to the cooling, thirst-quenching effect.

Txomin Etxaniz Chacoli, Spain
11% ABV $$ W

A CRUNCHY SUMMER RED

Almost all the Vinho Verde that we see outside of Portugal is white, but the region makes rosés and reds, too, in an equally eye-watering, tangy style. The acidity can be too much for those used to more ample, lush reds, but chilled down it has the tart clarity and crunch of cranberries.

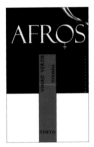

Afros Vinhão Tinto, Vinho Verde, Portugal
13% ABV $$ R

A VOLCANIC WHITE

Greece's Assyrtiko grape variety produces wines with a distinct note of preserved lemon and lemon zest that invite you to imagine Mediterranean citrus groves. From the volcanic island of Santorini, this pristine white also has notes of minerals and exotic spice.

Hatzidakis Santorini Assyrtiko, Greece
13% ABV $$ W

FOR THE CÔTE D'AZUR

A plate of salade niçoise, a bowl of bouillabaisse, a table overlooking the Beautiful People parading on the beach and the deepest blue of the sea and the sky… The Provençal picture is complete with a bottle of pale, pretty, and pert rosé, hiding in the shade, cooling and cleansing with its delicate strawberry and grapefruit.

Château Minuty M de Minuty Rosé, Provence, France
12.5% ABV $$ Ro

15 Graduation

Graduation is where the adult world really begins. Wherever you go from here, and however you spent your college years, you are on your own now. As you come out of the ceremony, freshly printed degree in hand, some part of you will be drunk on the pure potential of life, the dizzying sense that anything is possible. Of all the landmark moments in your life, this is the one where you can dare to dream a little, to allow yourself the feeling that the world is there for the taking. This is the time, too, when all those long hours in the library and lecture theater, not to mention those summer-vacation internships and late nights working up your résumé to a finely tuned weapon of personal salesmanship, are, you hope, about to come into their own. All the same, there's a part of you that looks back on the past four years and wonders if life could ever be that much fun again. You've met people who you know will be lifelong friends, but how often will you see them when you all head off to your new, adult lives? Now is not the time for doubts though, for the future or the past. Your final night at college is all about the present—a time to grab a bottle of something as young and lively as you are, with the immediate aromas and vibrant flavors that make it perfect for celebrating the here and now.

> *"Go confidently in the direction of your dreams. Live the life you have imagined."*
>
> Henry David Thoreau

BODEGAS LAS ORCAS DECENIO JOVEN RIOJA

FROM Rioja, Spain
STYLE Fruity Red
GRAPE VARIETY
Tempranillo
PRICE $
ABV 13%

RIOJA HAS A REPUTATION for making wines that only come into their own with time, with long aging in both barrel and bottle before they are even released. Beyond the crianza, reserva, and gran reserva wines, however, there is another side to this great Spanish region: *joven* (young) wines made with little (as in this instance) or no oak and emphasizing the lively, freshly picked fruit rather than the coconut and savory flavors of wood aging. From a century-old bodega enjoying a renaissance, this is both joyously juicy and suave.
Drink it with: *Informal tapas food such as chorizo, patatas bravas, or fava-bean stew.*

A ROSÉ FULL OF LIFE

Rosé wine isn't built to last; it's a wine for drinking in the year following the vintage when the fruit is at its most vivacious. Though it makes very good red and white wine, too, Château de Sours is unusual for Bordeaux in being better known for its rosé, which is lifted with fragrant strawberries and cream.

Château de Sours Rosé, Bordeaux, France
12% ABV $ Ro

A FIZZ FULL OF FUN

The gentle floral aromatics and sweetly crisp apple and pear fruit of the northeastern Italian sparkling wine Prosecco are at their best in their youth. Sticking them in the cellar for too long doesn't improve them. This example's literal and metaphorical effervescence certainly fits the mood today.

Canevel Prosecco di Valdobbiadene Extra Dry, Italy
11% ABV $$ SpW

AN EXUBERANT WHITE

While some Sauvignon Blanc, particularly if it's been blended with Semillon and aged in oak, will improve with time, for the most part (and this pulsating, passion-fruited example is no exception) it is the sheer verdant exuberance that we're after, and that fades after the first flush of youth.

Villa Maria Private Bin Sauvignon Blanc, Marlborough, New Zealand
13% ABV $ W

UN VIN DE PLAISIR

The Fronton appellation provides the everyday drinking reds for the lively nearby city of Toulouse, with its large student population. Made largely from the spicy, peppery Négrette, they have a crunchy dark-cherry fruitiness, a twist of aniseed, and a youthful drink-me-now brightness.

Château Plaisance Le Grain de Folie, Fronton, France
13% ABV $ R

TO KEEP, OR TO DRINK

Most wine is designed to be drunk within a year of purchase. But there are wines that do respond to being kept in a cool, dark place at an even temperature (59°F [15°C]) for years. Not everyone enjoys older wines, but if you're intrigued by the prospect, styles with a track record include top reds from Bordeaux and California, Vintage Port and Champagne, Pinot Noir and Chardonnay from Burgundy, Nebbiolo from Piedmont, Syrah/Shiraz from the Rhône and Australia, German Riesling, and Loire Chenin Blanc.

21st Birthday

THIS DAY—IF WE'RE BEING HONEST, and no matter what the law has to say on the matter—is unlikely to mark your first sip of wine. But it is a rare 21-year-old who will have developed wine expertise by the time of their official coming of age. Whoever's doing the buying for this celebration, then, might be tempted to think, "What the hey. No need to go overboard here. I (or they) won't notice the difference anyway, so why buy something decent? Pearls before swine and all that." Tempting, but a missed opportunity: This is an initiation into adulthood, after all, and wine is one of adulthood's great pleasures, so why not start off as you mean to go on, and buy something just a little special? It doesn't have to be—in fact, it really shouldn't be—anything challenging or out of left field; no novice wine drinker ever took well to the combination of searing acidity and high levels of mouth-drying tannin found in young Barolo from northwest Italy, for example. Generous fruit flavor, maybe leavened with a barely perceptible dose of sugar, generally goes down well, however, and few wines do that better than the white wines of Alsace, in eastern France.

"Growing up is losing some illusions, in order to acquire others."

VIRGINIA WOOLF

HUGEL GENTIL CLASSIC

FROM Alsace, France
STYLE Aromatic White
GRAPE VARIETY
Blend
PRICE $$
ABV 12%

AS AN INTRODUCTION TO WINE for the neophyte, or for the more experienced drinker who has yet to discover Alsace, the venerable Hugel estate's blend of five of the grape varieties used (generally on their own) in Alsace is hard to beat. It has a floral bouquet that calls to mind spring blossom, then a little gingery spice and some grapey and peachy fruitiness, and, as its name suggests, a kindly softness of texture.

Drink it with: *This versatile wine will stretch from white meat to meatier fish (it may have a little too much going on for seafood)—and even, thanks to those notes of gingery spice and subtle sugar (sweetness is a great foil for chili) mild Southeast Asian flavors.*

BUDGET CHOICE

Roses, litchis, ginger… While not everybody loves it forever, there isn't a person in the world who hasn't been won over by the sheer perfumed intensity and slightly oily texture of their first sip of the exotic "Gewurz" grape variety.

Cave de Turkheim Gewurztraminer, Alsace, France
12% ABV $ W

MONEY'S-NO-OBJECT CHOICE

Only made by the Trimbach family in the very best vintages, from the Riesling grape variety, Frédéric Emile is remarkable for its concentration of flavor, a mix of the northern European orchard (blossom and apples) and Asian cuisine (lime, lemongrass).

Trimbach Cuvée Frédéric Emile Riesling, Alsace, France
12.5% ABV $$$$ W

BEGINNER'S RED

"No wimpy wines" is the motto of the Ravenswood winery in Lodi County, and this consistent Zinfandel complies from vintage to vintage, with an abundance of blueberry and blackberry fruit, as well as a softness of tannin and plumpness of texture that make it very easy to like.

Ravenswood Lodi Zinfandel, Lodi County, California, USA
14.5% ABV $ R

A YOUNG PERSON'S GUIDE TO BUBBLES

There's a sharp, almost austere acidity in many Champagnes that doesn't always appeal to drinkers just starting out, but the demi-sec style balances that with a little more sugar than your standard brut, making it a great starter fizz—not to mention an excellent match for birthday cake.

Champagne Veuve Clicquot Demi-Sec Champagne, France
12% ABV $$$ SpW

17 At the Beach

WHY ARE WE DRAWN to the beach? Why, as I write this on a cold winter's morning, do these two little words draw an almost painful sigh of longing? The beach means escape—that's part of it. We feel it the moment we see the sea, our breathing falling in step with the rhythm of the waves, deep and slow, as our minds are drawn into the blue, to the places and lives beyond it, the promise of a better life, perhaps, somewhere over there. There's nostalgia, too, of course: all those childhood memories of our families at their happiest, the sand-castling, rock-pooling, sunscreen-smelling moments forever preserved in honeyed Instamatic tones. Most of all, perhaps, there is that delicious feeling of freedom, of liberation from the everyday—you can't be formal in a swimsuit, you can't feel stressed out in a deck chair. Even on a Northern European beach, cowering behind a windbreak, buffeted by Arctic winds, there is a mind-scrubbing exhilaration that comes with feeling part of nature at its most elemental. As with people, so with the vine: The sea is the great climatic moderator, bringing its cooling influence to wine-growing regions from Bordeaux to Bolgheri, from New Zealand to coastal California, slowing the pace of the grape's ripening and helping give the wines their lift and life.

> *"To me the sea is a continual miracle;*
> *The fishes that swim—the rocks—the motion of the waves—the ships, with men in them.*
> *What stranger miracles are there?"*
>
> FROM *"LEAVES OF GRASS"* BY *WALT WHITMAN*

VIÑA LEYDA RESERVA SAUVIGNON BLANC

FROM Leyda, Chile
STYLE Crisp Dry White
GRAPE VARIETY
Sauvignon Blanc
PRICE $
ABV 13.5%

OVER THE PAST COUPLE OF DECADES, Chilean winemakers have been increasingly drawn closer to the coast in a bid to plant grape varieties that respond better to cooler climates. One of the key producers in this move has been Viña Leyda, pioneer of the eponymous valley near the Pacific Ocean. In the first decade or so of its existence, it has already established itself as one of the country's best producers of Pinot Noir and Sauvignon Blanc. Nervy acidity, a herbal, nettle-like character, and lemon-and-lime refreshment are the hallmarks of this dry white, a wine that may well have been designed with a post-beach seafood meal in mind.

Drink it with: *In long, thin Chile, you're never very far from the coast and the seafood bounty of the Pacific. Razor clams are a particular specialty and the perfect accompaniment for this crisp, clear wine.*

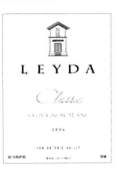

A SOUTH AFRICAN SUNDOWNER

The Cape's answer to Chassagne-Montrachet, Hamilton Russell's Chardonnay has a finely focused clarity and a tension that is explained, at least in part, by the estate's proximity to the Atlantic Ocean in the southerly tip of the continent. There's richness of fruit here, too, in a deftly oaked, restrained white.

Hamilton Russell Chardonnay, Hemel-en-Aarde, South Africa
13% ABV $$ W

THE TASTE OF THE SEA

The Manzanilla style of Sherry produced in the bodegas of Sanlúcar de Barrameda has a saline tang that is derived to some degree from by the influence of the salty air blowing in from the nearby Atlantic. This popular example is airy, crisp, and great with seafood when chilled.

Barbadillo Solear Manzanilla Sherry, Jerez, Spain
15% ABV $ F

THE BEACH IN WINTER

A tumbledown shack of a restaurant, warmed by a rickety stove, serving cheap, plentiful, delicious seafood as the sea throws its spray against the windows. You want a wine with a little more density than the whites of summer to keep you warm, but it must be crisp and light enough to drink with the fish. This perfumed Gamay may not hail from the seaside, but here it feels just right.

Robert Sérol Vieilles Vignes, Côte Roannaise, France
12.5% ABV $ R

RIGHT ON THE BEACH

This is beach wine at its most literal, made from grapes grown on vines planted in sand dunes in the tiny Portuguese appellation of Colares near Lisbon. It's not an easy wine to get hold of outside the country, but its flavors are as fascinating as is its production: red fruit, grippy tannins, and bracing acidity.

Manuel José Colares, Portugal
12.5% ABV $$$ R

Coming-Out Party

18

THE PLUMED AND BEJEWELED SOCIETY MATRONS of the 19th century never dreamed that the term for formal introductions of their daughters of marriageable age would be co-opted by the gay community. But "coming out," whether as a splashy public bash or an intimate communication with loved ones, is the ultimate introduction to society —the debut of a person who has been able to abandon pretense and embrace his or her true self. That family and friends have become more welcoming of this rite of passage is a sign of great progress—itself worthy of fêting. And unlike debutante balls, coming out is a personal, deeply felt experience, from timing to manner of announcement to type of celebration. For the unashamed, unabashed proclamation of your individuality that is the coming-out party, you may simply want to opt for wines that you like, wines with no discernible message or reflection of the occasion and its "meaning." Alternatively, you might want to find wines that seize the moment, saying, "I'm in control of my destiny. I am proud of who I am. I'm going to have the party I want, because my life, from now on, will be lived honestly and openly!"

"Heterosexuality is not normal, it's just common."

DOROTHY PARKER

KIM CRAWFORD PANSY! ROSÉ

FROM Marlborough, New Zealand
STYLE Off-Dry Rosé
GRAPE VARIETY Merlot
PRICE $$
ABV 13%

WHEN I FIRST HEARD about this rosé, I was taken aback by what I thought was its astounding crassness: a wine made by straight people, cynically targeting the gay bars of Auckland and Sydney with the implicit, patronizing assumption that "those gay guys just love anything pink." A little more research, however, and it turns out that the wine was intended as a—*ahem*—tongue-in-cheek thank-you to the gay community who had supported the winery in some tough times. At the light-red end of the rosé spectrum it works just right for a party: uncomplicatedly berry fruited and a little (but not too) sweet.

Drink it with: *It isn't designed as a food wine, but that subtle sweetness works with spicy buffet foods.*

BUDGET PINK

The hardy Garnacha grape variety produces a slightly more robust style of dry rosé in the Navarra region of northeast Spain, just next door to Rioja. Bodegas Ochoa's version is both crisper and more subtle than most, with a freshening streak behind the candied strawberry fruit.

Bodegas Ochoa Garnacha Rosado, Navarra, Spain
12.5% ABV $ Ro

MONEY'S-NO-OBJECT CHOICE

Rosé isn't generally expensive—it's still seen by many as a kind of bastard offspring of white and red and not taken all that seriously. Château d'Esclans is an exception in both respects, and this classically pale Provençal pink has the elegance and subtly insinuating flavors of a top white wine.

Château d'Esclans Whispering Angel, Provence, France
12.5% ABV $$$$ Ro

THE PLATONIC CHOICE

Greek philosophers wrote some of the most compelling tributes to same-sex love, and the symposia where they discussed their ideas were fueled by wine. You can pay homage to the tradition with this sumptuous, peach-scented white from Macedonia.

Domaine Gerovassiliou Malagousia, Epanomi, Macedonia, Greece
13% ABV $$ W

THE SPARKLING CHOICE

Laurent-Perrier's pink Champagne has a justifiably high reputation as one of the best in the region. Made entirely from red (Pinot Noir) grapes, it is gently aromatic with pure cranberry and strawberry fruit and a caressing mousse.

Laurent-Perrier Cuvée Rosé Brut Champagne, France
12.5% ABV $$$ SpRo

ROSÉ: NO HALFWAY HOUSE

With the exception of many producers in France's Champagne region, very few rosés today are a blend of red and white wines. Most are made by pressing red grapes and leaving the juice in contact with the skins for a short time. They are then treated like a white wine, with a cold fermentation in stainless-steel tanks.

19

At a Seafood Restaurant

THE LEMON WEDGE IS AN AUTOMATIC ADDITION to any dish of white fish or seafood—so much so, as the British food writer Niki Segnit says in her exhaustive but never exhausting book on matching ingredients *The Flavor Thesaurus*, that the fish can look a "little lonely" without it. As Segnit goes on to say, there are sound reasons for having it; it's not simply a colorful garnish. The sourness of the lemon emphasizes the sweetness of the fish, as well as disguising some of the more challenging marine odors, and cutting through the fat in traditional fish and chips, tempura, or other fried fish. Much the same can be said of the white wines that we usually choose to accompany fish and seafood. The ones that work best approximate the lemon in providing a citric condiment. These are dry wines, high in the tart malic acid that naturally forms in grapes; direct, even a little austere, rather than floaty, fat, or elaborate. They tend to come from cooler climates, either in places near the northern and southern limits of wine's 28–50° latitudinal spread or in vineyards cooled by ocean or mountain breezes. And while they're almost always white, don't discount lighter pinks or even, when the fish is particularly fleshy and rich, a light cool-climate red.

"You needn't tell me that a man who doesn't love oysters and asparagus and good wines has got a soul, or a stomach either. He's simply got the instinct for being unhappy."

HECTOR HUGH MUNRO ("SAKI")

DOMAINE SAMUEL BILLAUD CHABLIS

FROM Chablis, France
STYLE Crisp Dry White
GRAPE VARIETY
Chardonnay
PRICE $$$
ABV 12%

CHABLIS AND SEAFOOD is such a classic match, it would be a surprise not to find at least one bottle offered on a fish restaurant's wine list. It can be very disappointing—bland, dilute, tart—but once you've had a good one, its popularity makes perfect sense. It has the cut and flash of steel, the tang of lemon and green apples, a mineral refreshment that make it quite unlike any other Chardonnay. In the classic style without oak influence, winemaker Samuel Billaud's wines have an extra level of intensity, purity, and electric energy.

Drink it with: *Like the fish without that wedge of lemon, this wine would be lonely without oysters, mussels, or grilled white fish.*

BUDGET CHOICE

From the estuary of the Loire river where it meets the Atlantic around the maritime city of Nantes, Muscadet is another French wine that is all but synonymous with seafood, particularly oysters. Bone-dry, the best have an almost yeasty, iodine tang and a blast of lemon citrus that cleanses and invigorates.

Château du Cléray Muscadet Sèvre et Maine Sur Lie, Loire, France
12.5% ABV $ W

SHELLFISH

As well as providing abundant seafood to the region, the Atlantic has a cooling influence on the climate in the Galicia region of northwest Spain, helping bring a crisp, salty edge to wines made from the aromatic white grape variety Albariño, topped with white-peach and floral notes.

Palacio de Fefiñanes Albariño Rías Baixas, Galicia, Spain
13% ABV $$ W

RED FISH

One of Beaujolais's ten named villages, or crus, Brouilly produces lively, charming reds with pretty summer berry fruit, a burst of cherry-like acidity, and very light tannins. They are at their best after being chilled for a half-hour or so and accompanied by salmon or trout.

Château Thivin Côte de Brouilly, Beaujolais, France
12.5% ABV $$ R

PINK FISH

Best known for its grassy, crisp white Sauvignon Blanc wines (which also make a fine match for fish), the Sancerre appellation makes delicate, pretty reds and rosés from Pinot Noir, which echo the color and complement the flavors of salmon, their luminous acidity cutting through the fat.

André Dezat Sancerre Rosé, Loire, France
12.5% ABV $ Ro

RED WINE WITH FISH

Delicate white fish and seafood need red wine like they need a bicycle. They don't need heavy, oaky whites either: Both styles overwhelm the subtlety of the fish. Research by Japanese scientists has also suggested that the high tannins of some red wines are responsible for that jarring metallic clang in the mouth when it's paired with some seafood. But unoaked, light reds high in acid and low in tannin, like Gamay, Pinot Noir, and traditional Barbera, go well with meatier fish such as tuna, salmon, and swordfish.

20

Bachelorette Party

YOU KNOW, BECAUSE IT ALWAYS HAPPENS when a big group of friends gets together for a big night out, that your mood is likely to pass through three stages tonight. You'll start off feeling sensible enough, if a little nervous about what you might get up to on this, your Last Night of Freedom. Then your friends will arrive, and they'll be in the mood for jokes in varying shades of blue, with someone inevitably bringing along some kind of comedy contraceptive or bizarre item of underwear that you can all have a giggle about. They might even make you model them. It's all part of the ritual. Things will then get progressively sillier as the drinks slip down and you head off for dancing and, yes, more drinks, at which point, almost imperceptibly, the mood will segue from silly to sentimental, and the earnest, slightly garbled proclamations of eternal friendship, the tough love, and the truth-telling will begin. This is the dangerous time when, if you're not careful, the frivolity and fun tip over into the recriminatory and the maudlin. Best be prepared: You're going to drink cocktails but maybe something a little less heavy than the usual. If you're set on a "big" night, cocktails made from wine rather than strong liquor won't entirely spare you from the consequences (only your internal moderator can do that), but it may just help keep the night from teetering toward a fractious scene from *Bridesmaids*, letting you head to your wedding day with most of your friendships intact.

"Marriage is a great institution, but I'm not ready for an institution yet."

MAE WEST

ADRIANO ADAMI GARBEL PROSECCO DI TREVISO BRUT

FROM Veneto, NE Italy
STYLE Sparkling White
GRAPE VARIETY Glera
PRICE $
ABV 11.5%

PROSECCO FROM NORTHEAST ITALY is a very versatile cocktail ingredient. In Venice, the nearest big city to where this sparkling wine is made, the locals mix it with the bitter red apéritif Aperol and a little soda water to make a Spritz (a good substitute for a Negroni), with peach juice for a Bellini, and with orange juice for a Mimosa (the latter two are both worth considering in lieu of vodka-and-fruit-juice cocktails like the Cosmopolitan). You can also get creative with Prosecco and spirts such as vodka (but those will, of course, be much more powerful in terms of alcohol). Whatever you're making, you don't really need to go for the highest quality here, since subtle flavors won't be apparent once the drink is mixed. But neither do you want the bargain basement, which will lead to a tart, bitter end result. Besides, not everyone wants a cocktail, and a glass of Adriano Adami's example is a very perky, fragrant apéritif all on its own.

Drink it with: *Go for a few canapés—anything from potato chips or nuts to smoked-salmon blinis and Asian-inspired chicken skewers.*

FOR A KIR

You'll need one part crème de cassis (Gabriel Boudier makes a very good version of this black-currant liqueur) to mix with five parts white wine (a decent example of the local Aligoté) to make this classic Burgundian apéritif. Using sparkling wine transforms the drink into a Kir Royale.

Olivier Leflaive Bourgogne Aligoté, Burgundy, France
12% ABV $ W

FOR A CHAMPAGNE COCKTAIL

Place a sugar cube in a teaspoon full of Angostura Bitters. Allow the cube to soak up the bitters, then place it in a Champagne flute. Pour over a measure of Cognac such as Delamain, then fill the glass with a decent, inexpensive Champagne.

Champagne Nicolas Feuillatte Brut NV, Champagne, France
12% ABV $$$ SpW

FOR SANGRIA

This thirst-quenching Spanish fun fuel requires three parts fruity Spanish red wine, two parts lemonade, one part freshly squeezed orange juice, plenty of ice, some mint, and some slices of orange and lemon.

Campo Viejo Rioja, Spain
12.5% ABV $ R

STRAIGHT UP, NO CHASER

Finally, for the cocktail-averse, this is a great, affordable white wine with a richness of apple fruit and a cushion of sugar that make it great for drinking on its own. But it also has a tangy snap of acidity to help it go with fish, chicken, or pork.

Ken Forrester Chenin Blanc, Stellenbosch, South Africa
13% ABV $ W

First Job

21

AT FIRST IT FELT LIKE YOU WERE JUST PRETENDING, acting out the part of the grown-up on the way to the office in a business suit and squeaky shiny shoes. And since you'd arrived two hours before you were due to start (just in case), you had plenty of time to get into character in the coffee shop across the street. Too much time, as it turned out, too much coffee, and as 9:00 a.m. rolled around and you made your way through the doors into the frankly terrifying new world of work, you were a jittering, jabbering wreck. Not since you used to come downstairs as a child to interrupt your parents' dinner parties had you felt so conspicuously young, so alone in an adult world. It didn't help that your boss was so nice to you when you finally made your presence known. *Get a grip*, you said under your breath, and you did, just about. The tasks she gave you were, you both knew, the most gentle and menial she could have found. But they were *your* tasks, and this was *your* job, and it would be *your* paycheck at the end of the month. The fact is, you really are a grown-up now, even if it doesn't quite feel like it. And you can unwind like a grown-up, too, in a bar or at home, with a glass of wine, a fully paid-up member of society—even if you haven't yet been paid. The wine shouldn't be too taxing on the intellect or the wallet, but enjoyable enough to mark the occasion and make you feel the work will be worthwhile. Happily, there are many regions in both the Old and New Worlds that can supply exactly that.

"I always arrive late at the office, but I make up for it by leaving early."

CHARLES LAMB

BODEGAS JUAN GIL EL TESORO MONASTRELL/SHIRAZ

FROM Jumilla, Spain
STYLE Fruity Red
GRAPE VARIETY
Blend
PRICE $
ABV 14%

WHETHER WE'RE FEELING exhilarated or out of our depth, most of us have one thing in common when we start our first job: We're broke until our first paycheck comes in. That first post-work bottle of wine is going to have to leave a little change from a $10 bill in a store, then, and Spain's southeastern Jumilla region is one of the best places in the world at producing wines at that price level. The Monastrell grape variety, known elsewhere as Mourvèdre or Mataro, is the king in these parts, often grown on old vines and providing spicy, full-bodied reds with a level of concentration that you would expect to find in bottles several times the price. If you can't find this specific bottling, which also includes a little Shiraz for added plumpness, Bodegas Juan Gil is quite a large and consistently good operation, with many excellent, well-priced labels.

Drink it with: *You're unlikely to have the time, budget, or mental space for elaborate cooking tonight, but this wine will enliven that frozen pizza or pasta with a basic Bolognese sauce.*

WAITING-TO-GET-PAID RED

Bodegas Salentein produces a clutch of excellent red and white wines from its vineyards in the high-altitude Uco Valley in the foothills of the Andes, a new region that it helped pioneer in the 1990s. The quality carries over into its bargain entry-level wines, such as this juicy, fragrant, plummy Malbec.

Bodegas Salentein Portillo Malbec, Mendoza, Argentina
14% ABV $ R

WAITING-TO-GET-PAID WHITE

The Perrin family are key players in France's Rhône Valley, and the wines they make at Château Beaucastel in Châteauneuf-du-Pape are among the region's most highly regarded. This delightful orchard-fruit and blossom-scented crisp dry white, and its companion red, are both excellent value.

Perrin & Fils La Vieille Ferme Blanc, Côtes du Luberon, France
13% ABV $ W

FIRST-DAY FIZZ

Fizz is the vinous language of celebration, and after surviving your first day at work, you certainly have something to celebrate. But you're not on Champagne levels of income yet. This Spanish sparkler, made in the same way as Champagne, offers crisply apple-scented bubbles on a budget.

Bodegas Sumarroca Cava Brut Reserva, Catalonia, Spain
11.5% ABV $ SpW

BLOW THE FIRST PAYCHECK

If you're asking yourself why you would want to drink cheap wine on a night when you've finally made it into paid employment, here's something a little smarter to stick on the credit card without eating too much into next month's salary. This red is truly soothing, with its layers of eucalyptus-scented black-currant fruit.

Katnook Estate Founder's Block Cabernet Sauvignon, Coonawarra, Australia
13.5% ABV $$ R

By the Pool

22

IT'S THE HEIGHT OF SUMMER, SCHOOL OR WORK IS OUT, and the cool blue of the pool beckons. In this hazy, lazy mood, the drink we seek should meet three demands: It must fit the vibe. It must refresh. And, given the heat and the time of day, it must be light in alcohol. The drink that fits all these needs most closely is a style of wine that has surged in popularity in recent years, thanks in part to the endorsement of a number of hip-hop stars (many of whom can be seen drinking it while extolling its virtues in poolside videos): gently fizzy, gently sweet Moscato. The name is taken from the Italian name for the grape variety otherwise known as Muscat, a variety that is known for reproducing the flavors of the grape, rather than associations with other fruits (such as black currants in Cabernet Sauvignon, or passion fruit in Sauvignon Blanc). The style originates, and is still at its best, in northwest Italy (Moscato d'Asti), where the best producers leaven the sweetness with sufficient acidity and a beguiling floral dimension. But it has caught on in California and Australia, too, and, with many examples clocking in at just over 5 percent alcohol, it's the sort of thing you can drink all day, maybe accompanied by (or even transformed into) a fruit sorbet, as you dream the afternoon away.

"Summer afternoon—summer afternoon; to me those have always been the two most beautiful words in the English language."

HENRY JAMES

CERUTTI MOSCATO D'ASTI SURI SANDRINET, CASSINASCO

FROM Piedmont, Italy
STYLE Sparkling Sweet White
GRAPE VARIETY Muscat
PRICE $$
ABV 5.5%

THERE'S AN EXUBERANCE to the best Moscato d'Asti that never fails to raise a smile. In aroma, this wine feels closer to unfermented juice than to an alcoholic beverage: It's all perfumed Muscat grapes and spring blossom. On the palate, it is gently spritzy and sweet but cut with a clean blade of citrus acidity that keeps it from feeling cloying. Perhaps most crucial of all for poolside sipping, however, is the alcohol. At just 5.5%, it can be enjoyed without knocking you into the pool and out for the rest of the day.

Drink it with: *The Italians enjoy Moscato d'Asti with fruit-based desserts, and the combination of sweetness and gentle acidity sits beautifully with a bowl of strawberries.*

MULTIPLATINUM ARTIST

The vast Gallo vinous-industrial complex comes in for a lot of justified stick, but some esteemed colleagues persuaded me to taste this multiplatinum-selling sweetie without prejudice, and I was glad they did. It's an uncomplicated, undemanding splash of grapey, peachy fruit salad.

Gallo Barefoot Bubbly Moscato, California, USA
8.5% ABV $ SpW

JACUZZI BLING

Despite an unfortunate spat with the man who was once its most vocal proponent, Jay-Z, Cristal remains the drink of choice for the boastful and brash Jacuzzi-dweller. It is worth boasting about, too, and not just because of its price. It's a simply scintillating Champagne that can age for decades.

Champagne Louis Roederer Cristal Champagne, France
12.5% ABV $$$$$ SpW

A BUBBLY RED

Like Moscato d'Asti, Brachetto d'Acqui is a gently sweet, gently fizzy low-alcohol Piedmontese specialty. The difference is that it's made from a dark-skinned grape into a rosé or, here, a red that is like a fistful of fresh, drippingly ripe strawberries and raspberries.

Araldica Alasia Brachetto d'Acqui, Piedmont, Italy
5.5% ABV $$$ SpR

BY THE COUNTRY-CLUB POOL

If one were looking to cultivate a more restrained poolside vibe, something more in keeping with a country club, one would get terribly tight on gin and tonic. Or one could do what the posh British community in Porto, Portugal, does, replacing the gin with a white Port for a slightly less heady alternative.

Taylor's Chip Dry White Port, Douro, Portugal
20% ABV $ F

23

The Unexpected Guest

SOMETIMES, YOU SEEK OUT A WINE for a specific purpose. It might be that you're looking for something to match a dish, or maybe you're looking for a bottle that is particularly apt for the occasion or the people you're drinking it with. Helping you choose those wines is, of course, the very purpose of this book. However, there is another kind of wine that plays a slightly less glamorous role. It's the backroom boy, the understudy, the quietly industrious worker who unobtrusively goes about whatever is asked of them. These are what are generally referred to in wine-merchant shorthand as everyday wines or, if you're feeling particularly grand, house wines. They are the faithful bottles that you can afford to buy by the case to fill the kitchen wine rack: a red and a white that you never tire of drinking, that you can call on for a small party or a hasty meal after a late night at the office, or in this instance, when a friend calls round unexpectedly. There is something unfussy about these wines; their flavors and textures cannot be too shouty, sharp, or rich. They're versatile because they are, above all, refreshing and drinkable, which is why in France, they call them *vins de soif* (literally, "wines for thirst").

"If it were not for guests all houses would be graves."

KAHLIL GIBRAN

FRANCESCO BOSCHIS PIANEZZO DOLCETTO DI DOGLIANI

FROM Piedmont, NW Italy
STYLE Fruity Red
GRAPE VARIETY Dolcetto
PRICE $$
ABV 13%

IN PIEDMONT, WINES MADE FROM the Dolcetto grape variety are part of everyday life, their black-cherry and summer-berry-compote juiciness being the basic accompaniment to lunch and dinner at any time of the year. They can be rather rustic and tart (rendering the name, which means "little sweet one," something of a misnomer), but the best producers, such as Francesco Boschis in the Dogliani area, make it with more seriousness and care, yielding wines with a bit more texture, complexity, and purity, though always staying true to the variety's naturally exuberant fruit.

Drink it with: *Whatever you have in the fridge is fine, but this is particularly good with Parma ham or Italian salami, or a bowl of simple pasta.*

VIN DE SOIF ROUGE

This light and utterly drinkable red wine made from Pinot Noir and Gamay by Thierry Puzelat—a noted Loire winemaker with a sensitive, natural style—is refreshing but not at all facile. It feels gentle, soft, and fresh, but there's a little game and earthiness, too, amid the red-berry fruit.

Clos du Tue-Boeuf Cheverny Rouge, Loire, France
13% ABV $$ R

VIN DE SOIF BLANC

From one of Bordeaux's bigger firms, Dourthe, comes an ever-reliable white that is crisp and clean and punchy, with a grapefruit tang and just a little of that green, herbaceous quality that distinguishes Sauvignon Blanc. This is fuel for both the last-minute lunch and the early-evening chat.

Dourthe La Grande Cuvée Sauvignon Blanc, Bordeaux, France
12.5% ABV $ W

AN ALL-PURPOSE ROSÉ

From the Tavel appellation in the southern Rhône Valley dedicated solely to rosé wines, this is quite robust, even chunky in style, on its way to being a light red wine. It has good acidity and just a little grip as it works on your tongue, which gives it great versatility with food (fish, meat, or cheese), though the vibrant ripe strawberry fruit is attractive on its own.

Domaine Pélaquié Tavel Rosé, Rhône, France
13% ABV $$ Ro

FOR THE LATE-NIGHT CALL

For those times when a friend calls in just as you're winding down for the evening— usually to talk through something of great importance to them (if not always you)— this is a red wine with a little more depth and presence from northwest Spain. It is layered with dark fruit and spice, but, unoaked, it is full-flavored without being a bruiser.

Bodegas Monteabellón Avaniel, Ribera del Duero, Spain
14% ABV $$ R

24

At a Mexican/Tex-Mex Restaurant

THE CHILI IS THE KEY TO MEXICAN CUISINE. But that's not as straightforward a statement as it first seems. Just as the Inuit are reputed (possibly apocryphally) to have 50 words for snow, so the Mexicans have dozens of different types of chilies, each of which is appreciated for its aroma and flavor as much as its degree of heat: jalapeño, serrano, chilaca, guajillo—the list runs to 200 or more; and then there's the chipotle, the smoked, matured jalapeño with its sweetly smoky flavor. Whatever the variety, the chili finds its way, in some form or another, into most Mexican savory dishes, whether as the base of a complex, spiced mole sauce, as part of a marinade for meat or fish, or providing the kick in a tomato salsa. It's also an important ingredient in the cross-border fusion dishes that represent most non-Mexicans' idea of the country's national cuisine: the Tex-Mex of burritos, tacos, tortilla chips, guacamole, and chili con carne. Whether you're having a traditional dish of Oaxacan black mole or a volcano taco in a Mexican-themed chain restaurant, however, it's that fiery heat that presents the biggest test for your choice of wine, though a little hunting around shows the grape can offer alternatives to the traditional beer, Tequila, and mescal.

"Chilies, like love, are unpredictable. You can never tell how spicy they will be until you taste them."

DIANA KENNEDY

DE MARTINO LEGADO RESERVA CARMENÈRE

FROM Maipo, Chile
STYLE Rich, Powerful Red
GRAPE VARIETY Carmenère
PRICE $$
ABV 14.5%

A FEW YEARS AGO, the marketing body for Chilean wine embarked on a promotional campaign extolling the virtues of serving wines made from local specialty variety Carmenère with curry. It was a counterintuitive idea—most expert advice pairs spicy food with off-dry whites. But they were on to something. There's a leafy, herbal twang to these sometimes powerful reds that goes particularly well with spicy, aromatic meat dishes, and this smooth, plummy, subtly herby example from De Martino is no exception.
Drink it with: *Works well with any meat-based Mexican or Tex-Mex dish, such as beef fajitas, chili con carne, or chicken in mole sauce.*

WITH CEVICHE

In a ceviche, raw fish or seafood is "cooked" by marinating it in lime and lemon in the fridge and is served, like a salsa, with chopped tomato, cilantro, and chili. The pristine dry Rieslings of Australia's Clare Valley, with their pinpoint lime zestiness, offer the perfect foil for a dish that is popular throughout Latin America.

Pikes Traditionale Dry Riesling, Clare Valley, Australia
12.5% ABV $$ W

WITH GUACAMOLE

Guacamole has a creamy, almost fatty feel, as well as varying degrees of chili spice and herbs (cilantro), depending on the recipe. That calls for a white with a little bit of weight, good aromatics to go with the herbs, and good acidity to cut through the richness. This peachy, floral Argentinian specialty passes the test.

Susana Balbo Crios Torrontés, Cafayate, Salta, Argentina
13.5% ABV $ W

WITH TOMATO AND CHILI DISHES

Chili and tomato, key ingredients in Mexican cuisine, can play havoc with wine. Provided the chili is not super-hot, however, something in the robust tanginess of a decent cheap Chianti works with the acid of the tomatoes, while the herbal note echoes cilantro.

Melini Chianti, Italy
12.5% ABV $ R

WITH FAJITAS

Tex-Mex it may be, but fajitas are now a fixture of Mexican restaurants, and the sizzling spicy strips of grilled beef or chicken served in a taco call for a full-flavored, robust red with a sweetness of fruit to cushion the spice. This ripe and juicy but cooling Garnacha fits the bill.

Bodegas Nekeas El Chaparral de Vega Sindoa, Navarra, Spain
14% ABV $ R

ON THE LIST AT PUJOL

Voted as one of the world's 50 best restaurants, Mexico City's Pujol proves that Mexican cuisine can be haute as well as artisanal, with its refined modern spin on the likes of fried frogs' legs, Yucatan pork confit, and tortilla soufflé. The drinks list is big on local wines, with Mexican producers rarely seen outside the country, such as Mogor-Badan and Vinícola Fraternidad, taking their place alongside a broad selection that is strong on the USA, Chile, Argentina, and Spain, as well as French classics.

25

The Difficult Neighbor

FIRST THERE WAS THE LEAF BLOWER INCIDENT that Saturday last October, when your neighbor Bob rose just after dawn to clear his lawn with his latest toy, wrenching you from your weekend sleep-in and leaving the drive you'd raked the previous evening looking once more like a forest floor. Then there was the Great Birthday Baseball Robbery, the home-run ball hit by your son over center field (Bob's fence) on his tenth birthday. Since then, things have only got worse, an accumulation of increasingly irritating and embarrassing events: the Mysteriously Moving Fence, the Total Plumbing Disaster . . . relations are at an all-time low. Something has to be done to bring about détente. You don't want a confrontation, but neither do you want to move house. Swallowing your pride, you ask Bob over for a piece of home-baked "friendship cake" and a glass of that most emollient of drinks: a golden, honeyed dessert wine. It may not transform him into the neighbor from heaven, but it's a nectar so luscious, so unctuously close to ambrosia, it must surely sweeten the mood of even this most difficult of men.

> *"When envoys are sent with compliments in their mouths, it is a sign that the enemy wishes for a truce."*
>
> SUN TZU, THE ART OF WAR

CHÂTEAU DE SUDUIRAUT LIONS DE SUDUIRAUT SAUTERNES

FROM Bordeaux, France
STYLE Sweet White
GRAPE VARIETY Blend
PRICE $$
ABV 13%

THE SAUTERNES REGION of Bordeaux is home to the world's most celebrated sweet wines. They get their intense sweetness from being left on the vine after the grapes used for dry wines and from being attacked by the fungus *Botrytis cinerea*, which acts to concentrate the accumulated sugars. This wine was conceived by producer Château Suduiraut as a lighter, less unctuous, but still decadent alternative to its celebrated grand vin, one of the top handful in the region. With fresh apricot and honeyed dried citrus, it's tangy, clean, bright, and long.

Drink it with: *A classic French tarte aux pommes, but best call it apple pie—you don't want your neighbor thinking you're trying to intimidate him with your fancy ways.*

BUDGET CHOICE

The Limarí Valley north of Santiago is one of Chile's most exciting wine regions. It has a dry, desert-like climate but with cooling breezes that act like air-conditioning for grapes, helping them preserve freshening acidity that, in this wine, brings lift and life to a floral, peachy, joyful sticky.

Viña Tabalí Late Harvest Muscat, Limarí, Chile
12.5% ABV $ SW

A SWEET GERMAN

High natural acidity makes the Riesling grape variety ideally suited to making sweet wines (*see below*), and as well as dry styles, the energetic Johannes Leitz makes a bewildering array of different examples each vintage. This one has a delectable hit of sour apple amid the sweet peach and blossom.

Leitz Rudesheimer Klosterlay Riesling Auslese, Rheingau Germany
10.5% ABV $$ SW

A LITTLE DRIER

If your neighbor's tooth isn't quite as sweet as you'd thought, then this off-dry white may be a better bet. It still has a persuasive richness and density, with quince, peach, and cinnamon and ginger spice, but without the viscous, syrupy feel.

Trimbach Pinot Gris Reserve, Alsace, France
13% ABV $$ W

IF IT HAS TO BE RED

A kind of southern French answer to Port, this sweet fortified red wine has an appeal that rests in its brightly presented dark fruit—blackberries and black cherries dipped in chocolate, with a smoky, peppery edge.

Mas Amiel Maury, Roussillon, France
16% ABV $$ R

THE BALANCE OF SUGAR AND ACID

Just as Coca-Cola would be unbearably sickly without its generous dose of citric acid, so sweet wines lacking in natural acidity feel flabby and are hard work to drink. The acidity serves to balance and even mask the sweetness; the high levels of acidity in some off-dry wines, which contain just a few grams of sugar per liter (Sauternes will usually have around 130 g per liter), means they can taste completely dry.

26

Rehearsal Dinner

WHEN YOU'RE PLANNING A WEDDING, and perhaps feeling a growing sense of panic as the costs spiral, a rehearsal dinner can seem like an unnecessary expense. Certainly, if you happen to be the groom's father, you might, in your grumpier moods, suggest that your son and his fiancée take a look at how they do things in Europe: no rehearsal dinner there; they get it all done concisely in one hit. But that would be more than a little churlish. When couples look back on their wedding in later years, it's often the rehearsal dinner that they remember most fondly. Even if it's taking place in a gourmet restaurant, the rehearsal dinner has a relaxed informality compared with the big day itself. The scale is more human, more intimate, and because it's usually just the couple's close friends and family, there's less pressure on the bride and groom to "perform." The toasting (and roasting) adds to the feeling of spontaneity. There are no set-piece speeches as there will be on the big day. The couple are free to relax and enjoy a glass or two of something classy, classic but fruity and accessible, and, if not cheap, then not too expensive—this is just the rehearsal after all.

*"Let us celebrate
the occasion
with wine
and sweet words."*

PLAUTUS, ASINARIA

DOMAINE VINCENT CARÊME ANCESTRALE PÉTILLANT

FROM Vouvray, France
STYLE Sparkling
Off-Dry White
GRAPE VARIETY
Chenin Blanc
PRICE $$
ABV 13%

THE CHAMPAGNE can wait until tomorrow, but you'll still want something to toast with tonight, and this gently sparkling fizz from the Loire is an utterly charming alternative to the more expensive bottles from farther north and east in France. Unlike the classic Champagne method, where the dead yeast cells of the second, fizz-giving fermentation are taken out before the bottle is recorked for sale, the *ancestrale* method, which is making a small resurgence in France, leaves the yeast in the bottle. That means it might be a little cloudy, like bottle-conditioned ales, but the flavor in Vincent Carême's example is crystal clear, the texture and bubbles fluent, and the little touch of sweetness very appealing to those who find Champagne too austere.

Drink it with: *There's just enough sweetness here to pair it with light fruit desserts. Its fine acidity also makes it a great match for soft cheeses.*

REHEARSAL WHITE

The Dão region of central Portugal tends to be overshadowed by the neighboring Douro Valley, but the prices of its top wines are absurdly cheap. Quinta dos Roques certainly qualifies as one of region's best, and this complex white from the local Encruzado, by turns nutty, fruity, herbal, and mineral, knocks spots off many a pricier white Burgundy.

**Quinta dos Roques
Encruzado,
Dão, Portugal**
13% ABV $$ W

REHEARSAL RED

Barbaresco may be too expensive for a mere rehearsal, and it may also be a little too powerful, but a red made from the same grape from younger vines in the same region, though designed for youthful drinking, could be just the ticket. Indeed, this cherry-and-rose-scented wine could grace the table at any Italian wedding feast.

**Sottimano
Langhe Nebbiolo,
Piedmont, Italy**
13% ABV $$ R

REHEARSAL ROSÉ

Sancerre is famously the home of green and pleasant Sauvignon Blanc white wines, but it also does a fine line in Pinot Noir, as both light, elegant reds and crisp, softly scented rosés. Pascal Jolivet makes all three, and his rosé is delicate, quicksilver, and shot through with the flavors of wild strawberries.

**Pascal Jolivet,
Sancerre Rosé,
Loire, France**
12.5% ABV $$ Ro

REHEARSAL DESSERT

It's unlikely that you'll be having a heavy dessert the night before a wedding—something involving fruit would make more sense than chocolate, for example —and this light but lusciously sweet German white, with its dancing lime acidity, ripe apricot, and mandarin, is a graceful way to send you off to bed.

**Meulenhof Erdener
Treppchen Riesling
Auslese Alte Reben,
Mosel, Germany**
8.5% ABV $$ SW

27

Weekday Night at Home

ON DAYS LIKE TODAY, all you really want to do is get home. Like today, tomorrow's going to be busy—tomorrow's always busy—but tonight at least you have nothing pressing to do, nothing special planned. You'll watch a bit of TV, maybe flitter about on the Internet, or climb into bed or the bath with a book. All that remains to do before you reach your longed-for terminus is a brief stop at the grocery store to pick up something quick and easy to cook: pasta and a jar of sauce, a pizza, or even something pre-prepared from the deli counter. And a bottle of wine—you'd definitely like a couple of glasses to help take you down through the gears. You're not looking for the finest wines known to humanity. You don't want to agonize over your choice. You're looking for something simple, undemanding, and, perhaps above all, cheap, without straying into the scary-looking, two-buck strong medicine that lurks on the bottom shelf. Honest, affordable *vin ordinaire* from southern France, Italy, or Iberia—modest everyday wines that lift us, however briefly, from the routine of our everyday lives.

"Wine makes every meal an occasion, every table more elegant, every day more civilized."

ANDRÉ SIMON

CHÂTEAU DE PENNAUTIER CABARDÈS

FROM Languedoc, France
STYLE Spicy Red
GRAPE VARIETY Blend
PRICE $
ABV 12.5%

YOU WOULDN'T, EVEN IF YOU had the funds to do so, want to eat Michelin-starred food every night. Quite apart from what it would do to your waistline, fine dining requires too much attention, is too rich and complex, for tired minds. Similarly, nobody, not even an oenophile with a bottomless cellar of fine bottles, wants to drink serious wines all the time. There are moments when a simple, even slightly rustic *vin de table* fits the mood better than a refined, sophisticated *vin de garde*. It would be doing this Rhône-meets-Bordeaux southern French blend a disservice to call it simple, but with its crunchy blackberry fruit, cedar spice, and cooling note of freshness, it's definitely one for drinking happily rather than thinking about endlessly.

Drink it with: *Your midweek meat dish of choice, whether that's spaghetti Bolognese, meatloaf, or grilled lamb chops.*

MIDWEEK MIDSUMMER

Vermentino has been enjoying a renaissance across the Mediterranean basin, including the south of France, where it is also known as Rolle. Domaine Les Yeuses's absurdly well-priced version is perky and pithy, with a pulse of lemon-lime acidity and a slightly rounded feel in the mouth. Sip it on its own or with fish.

Domaine Les Yeuses Vermentino, IGP Pays d'Oc, France
12% ABV $ W

MIDWEEK MIDWINTER

The British Symington family is behind some of the world's best and best-loved Port brands. However, like many in the Douro Valley, they've turned their hand to table wines as well over recent years. Their house red is full of plum, damson, and black cherry, and it fits the bill with winter casseroles.

Altano Douro Red, Portugal
13.5% ABV $ R

MIDWEEK PASTA-BASHER

The Primitivo grape variety shares its DNA with Zinfandel, and it has a similarly full-throated, black-fruited exuberance, which is in full effect here. Offering terrific value for the level of concentration, this juicy wine works with tomato-based pasta sauces, red meat, pizza, or the TV.

A Mano Primitivo, Puglia, Italy
13.5% ABV $ R

MIDWEEK TREAT

The Ataraxia estate takes its name from the Greek for a relaxed or tranquil state of mind, and its cool-climate Cape Chardonnay is capable of leading you to somewhere approximating that mood. It mixes the brisk and the crisp with layers of tropical fruit and subtle toasty flavors.

Ataraxia Chardonnay, Western Cape, South Africa
13.5% ABV $$ W

28

Wedding

It seems straightforward: two people making a public declaration of their love and commitment to each other, followed by a bit of a party. But the decision to get married is just the beginning, your entrée to an industry so vast that it makes the economy of some small countries look like folksy local businesses. It has its own press, its own bureaucracy, its food suppliers, travel agents, artisans . . . At first you may resist, insisting that you only ever wanted a simple ceremony, a few close friends and family—nothing fancy. But it's not just the two of you now; both sets of parents have been preparing for this event for years, perhaps even before either of you was born. As the big day gets closer, it increasingly feels like your arrival home each night signals the start of another working day at a particularly busy office. Your weekends become an endless cycle of meetings with florists, musicians, organic candle specialists. Exhausted, you wave through every suggestion. All except one. It's your party and you'll be damned if you're going to let anyone else tell you what to drink. Bring on the Champagne!

"I was married by a judge. I should have asked for a jury."

Groucho Marx

CHAMPAGNE GOSSET GRANDE RÉSERVE BRUT

FROM Champagne, France
STYLE Sparkling White
GRAPE VARIETY Blend
PRICE $$$$
ABV 12.5%

GOSSET IS PERHAPS THE LEAST KNOWN of the club of big brands, once known as *les grandes marques*, that dominate Champagne production. But while the oldest wine producer in the region (like the rest of Champagne, it made still wines until the 18th century) deserves wider renown, its under-the-radar status does make it an attractive choice if you want to stamp a bit of your own personality on your wedding day. It also happens to be one of the best Non-Vintages around, rich, full in flavor, with a bell-like clarity.

Drink it with: *When it comes to the toasting, you won't be thinking about food, but if you choose this Champagne for the reception apéritif, it works very well with most canapés.*

A TOAST FOR ALL

Le Mesnil-sur-Oger is one of Champagne's highest-rated grand cru villages for growing Chardonnay, and those grapes find their way into some of Champagne's starriest bottles. The wines of local cooperative, Le Mesnil, however, offer the charm and richness of the village at relatively (this is Champagne) affordable prices.

Champagne Le Mesnil Blanc de Blancs Grand Cru, Champagne, France
12.5% ABV $$$ SpW

A TOAST AT THE TOP TABLE

A very dear and generous friend brought a bottle of this intricate, deceptively powerful, feather-textured Champagne to the author's own wedding party, which makes this a very personal choice, not to mention Wall Street–bonus expensive if you wanted it for the whole room. But would it be wrong to squirrel a bottle away for the top table, or even your hotel suite?

Champagne Henriot Cuvée des Enchanteleurs, Champagne, France
12% ABV $$$$$ SpW

WEDDING-DINNER WHITE

This top producer, Domaine Chavy-Chouet, makes this Chardonnay of great finesse and thrilling intensity from vines just outside Puligny-Montrachet (which is why it's officially "only" Bourgogne). It's the equal of many a wine featuring the famous village name on the label (including those made by Chavy-Chouet) but comes at a fraction of the cost. A very stylish match for fish or chicken.

Domaine Chavy-Chouet Bourgogne Blanc Les Femelottes, Burgundy, France
13% ABV $$ W

WEDDING-DINNER RED

Margaret River is Western Australia's answer to Bordeaux, specializing in red wines made from the same grape varieties in a not-dissimilar climate. This sleek, stylish example has layers of cassis fruit and cedar (classic Bordeaux flavors) but is more generous and less astringent than similarly priced equivalents from the French region, which should mean it appeals to all, rather than some, of your guests.

Cape Mentelle Cabernet/Merlot, Margaret River, Western Australia
14.5% ABV $$ R

29

At an Italian Restaurant

FOR MOST ITALIANS, wine is, to all intents and purposes, a food. A meal would not be a meal without a glass or two of *vino*: in Italian culinary culture, the two are intimately related: The whole raison d'être of Italian wine is to act as an accompaniment to food, even if the reverse—that food is there to act as an accompaniment to wine—isn't (quite) true. That means that wine in Italy, even more than in France, is created with food in mind. Drunk on their own, Italian wines of all colors tend to feel more acidic, its reds more astringent with more of that rough grip of tannin, than wines from, say, California or Australia, which seem softer and more generous when you're having them by the glass. Once you have before you a bowl of pappardelle pasta with a rich wild-boar or hare ragù from Tuscany, however, that rather tart, mean-seeming glass of the local Chianti Classico suddenly seems a lot more appealing, the high acidity of the tomato-based sauce and the fat of the meat the perfect counterpoints to the acid and tannin in the wine. That's just one example, but the beauty of Italian wine and food, with its seemingly infinite regional variations, is that there are thousands more pairings of local dishes and local wines, refined over generations, for you to try.

"I feast on
wine and bread,
and feasts they are."

MICHELANGELO

FONTODI CHIANTI CLASSICO

FROM Tuscany, Italy
STYLE Powerful Red
GRAPE VARIETY
Sangiovese
PRICE $$
ABV 14%

THE QUINTESSENTIAL ITALIAN red-wine region is perhaps as familiar for its traditional *fiasco* bottles, used as candle holders by a million *trattorie*, as for the somewhat rustic liquid they once contained. But the red wines of Chianti in Tuscany, particularly when produced in the Classico zone at the heart of the region, can be refined and elegant, too. Certainly those are the adjectives most commonly used about Fontodi's wines, which have a striking purity to them, made in a modern way without sacrificing the traditional character of the local Sangiovese variety. This 100 percent Sangiovese feels brisk and tangy, with finely gripping tannins and flavors of cherry, oregano, and tobacco leaf.

Drink it with: *Tuscan food is all about the strong, simple flavors of high-quality natural ingredients: powerful olive oil (Fontodi makes a great example), fresh ripe tomatoes, herbs such as basil and oregano, pappardelle egg pasta with rich meat ragù, and—the perfect match for this classy Chianti—a Florentine T-bone steak.*

FOR FRUTTI DI MARE

Made from the Cortese grape variety in the southeast of Piedmont, Gavi is a popular choice along the coast in this part of northwest Italy, and you can see why. It has a kind of Alpine-stream clarity and minerality, a lick of preserved lemon and herbs, and crisp green-apple bite that demands seafood.

Broglia Villa Broglia Gavi, Piedmont, Italy
12.5% ABV $$ W

THE UPSCALE TRUFFLE DINNER

Piedmont in northwest Italy draws chefs and foodies from around the world in autumn to take in the delights of the treasured white truffle. A dish made with the delicacy and served with an ethereal local red wine made from the Nebbiolo variety, which takes on similar aromas as it ages, would be a match made in heaven.

Bruno Giacosa Barbaresco Asili, Piedmont, Italy
14% ABV $$$$$ R

THE SYLISH WHITE

From an estate nestled high up in the Apennines in east-central Italy's Marche region, this is a remarkable white wine showcasing the potential of a grape variety that is generally regarded as a little workaday. Here, though, layers of peach, apricot, and Verdicchio's distinctive nutty flavors give a textured, immaculate white that matches poultry or rabbit, as well as fish.

La Monacesca Mirum Verdicchio di Matelica Riserva, Italy
14% ABV $$$ W

IN THE PIZZA RESTAURANT

If you were lucky enough to be in a restaurant serving authentic Sicilian food, this supple light red blend of Nero d'Avola and Frappato, with its flavors of strawberry and blood orange and its silky feel, would fit just right with the popular local dish *farsumagru* (veal stuffed with meat and hard-boiled eggs), but it hits the spot with a more run-of-the-mill pizza, too.

Planeta Cerasuolo di Vittoria, Sicily, Italy
13% ABV $$ R

30

Bad Day at the Office

THERE ARE DAYS IN YOUR WORKING life when you wish you'd never got out of bed. You might have left home in the morning with a spring in your step, or you might already have an inkling of what's to come when the car fails to start or the bus doesn't show up—but once you've arrived at your workplace, you just know that nothing's going to go to plan that day. Your clients complain. Your boss is in a rage. Your co-workers are tetchy. A small mistake is taken as evidence of your monumental incompetence. A friendly aside is taken out of context and perceived as a snarky put-down. And then, to cap it all, the coffee machine backfires all over you, and the computer just won't stop saying no! On days like these, home time cannot come soon enough, and a little Simon & Garfunkel plays in your inner ear: home where your thought's escaping, home where your music's playing, home where the Merlot's waiting, silently for you. Soft, plump, generous Merlot is wine as comforting balm— the wine world's equivalent of a long, hot bath with soft music, candles, a good book, a bar of chocolate… Whatever it takes to wash that day right out of your hair.

"Work is the curse of the drinking classes."

OSCAR WILDE

L'ECOLE NO. 41 COLUMBIA VALLEY MERLOT

FROM Washington State, USA
STYLE Rich Red
GRAPE VARIETY Merlot
PRICE $$$
ABV 14%

WINE PRODUCTION IN WASHINGTON STATE only really began to take off in the late 20th century, but it already has a deserved reputation for producing some of the world's best reds from Merlot, a grape variety that originally hails from Bordeaux, France. From one of the state's top, pioneering producers, this is the perfect introduction to Washington's charms: layers of black and red fruit, smoothly presented with fine tannins, and a quality of brightness that is the hallmark of all Washington's best wines.

Drink it with: *Your comfort food of choice—and as a Brit, that would be the mashed-potato-topped lamb mince of shepherd's pie; for Americans, it would more likely be meatloaf. But there is power and depth enough in this wine to handle most red-meat dishes, such as steak, burgers, and roasts.*

BUDGET BALM

Chilean Merlot is a ubiquitous budget choice in supermarkets around the world, much of it defiantly ordinary and unexciting. But this, from one of the country's leading producers, is a cut above, with its depth of juicy plum and blackberry fruit.

Santa Rita 120 Merlot, Central Valley, Chile
14% ABV $ R

THE EXTRAVAGANT CHOICE

Along with St-Emilion, Pomerol in Bordeaux is where Merlot reaches its greatest heights—nowhere higher than at this magnificent estate, where, with a little help from the Cabernet Franc variety, it achieves a scintillating, perfumed, silky elegance. This wine can turn a bad day into a great one.

Vieux Château Certan, Pomerol, Bordeaux, France
13.5% ABV $$$$$ R

IF YOU DON'T DO MERLOT

If you've been put off by the many inferior Merlots out there, then Pinot Noir made at the plumper, riper end of the spectrum can offer a similarly luxuriant brand of escapism. Saintsbury's sun-filled example will certainly soothe stressed-out nerves.

Saintsbury Carneros Pinot Noir, Carneros, California, USA
14% ABV $$$ R

THE WHITE-WINE DRINKER'S BALM

This is a richer style of Chardonnay from a Burgundy producer working in the Ardèche region, farther south in France. It has a mellow, luscious feel, with no rough edges—the kind of wine you can sink into but without the sawdust and butterscotch sweetness of many oak-aged Chardonnays.

Louis Latour Ardèche Chardonnay, PDO Ardèche, France
13% ABV $ W

Fourth of July

31

FOR SOME PEOPLE, THE FOURTH OF JULY is an uncomplicated celebration of patriotism. It's a day to remember all the things that make them proud to be an American—from the lofty concepts of freedom and democracy embodied in the Declaration of Independence to the more everyday by-products of life, liberty, and the pursuit of happiness: baseball, hotdogs, and hamburgers; country, jazz, and rock 'n' roll. Then there are people for whom national pride can never be uncomplicated—people who see themselves as citizens of a world without borders, who feel no stirring as yet another rendition of "The Star-Spangled Banner" wafts across the streets, unless it happens to be Jimi Hendrix's countercultural counter-blast. Still, they would have to agree that a national holiday in high summer is no bad thing. And as they drink bottles from across the USA at the barbecue, street party, or firework parade on a day that most Americans will spend outside—whether the wine is Napa Cabernet Sauvignon or Santa Barbara Pinot Noir, Finger Lakes Riesling or Oregonian Pinot Gris—even they might begin to feel something a little like national pride.

"By making this wine vine known to the public, I have rendered my country as great a service as if I had enabled it to pay back the national debt."

THOMAS JEFFERSON

STAG'S LEAP WINE CELLARS SLV CABERNET SAUVIGNON

FROM Napa, California, USA
STYLE Powerful Red
GRAPE VARIETY
Cabernet Sauvignon
PRICE $$$$$
ABV 14.5%

A LANDMARK BOTTLE in the history of American wine, the debut (1973) vintage of Stag's Leap's SLV was the top-scoring red wine in a blind tasting organized by British wine merchant Steven Spurrier in 1976, the 200th anniversary of American independence. Known as the Judgment of Paris, and the subject of both a best-selling book and a Hollywood movie, the tasting pitted the best bottles of Bordeaux and Burgundy against the best of California, and, to the chagrin of the mainly French judges, a California white and red came out on top. The resulting publicity, prompted by an article in *Time* magazine by reporter George Taber, did wonders for the burgeoning Californian industry's self-confidence, proving that it could match the very best in the world—its vinous independence, if you like. Estate founder Warren Winiarski may have sold the estate to a partnership between Washington State's Chateau Ste-Michelle and Italy's Piero Antinori, but the wine remains a Napa classic: ripe but balanced, suave but savory, and capable of long aging—a very fine wine for the patriotic and the skeptic alike.

Drink it with: *The Fourth of July is a day for the smoking grill, and this red would handle a charred steak beautifully.*

PATRIOTISM ON A BUDGET

A great value from a pioneering producer in Washington State's Red Mountain AVA (though the grapes here are sourced from across the wider Columbia Valley), this blend of Cabernet Sauvignon, Merlot, and Syrah (hence the name) is smoothly structured and bright with black-currant fruit: great for the grill.

Hedges CMS Red, Columbia Valley, Washington State, USA
14% ABV $ R

FIREWORK WHITE

A full-on take on the Viognier grape variety, this has a riotously aromatic nose of peaches, tropical fruit, and white flowers, and a bouncy, juicy fruit-salad palate, making it a fun wine to sip with the fireworks popping and smoking in the night sky.

Smoking Loon Viognier, California, USA
13% ABV $ W

A VERSATILE WHITE

Inspired by the way Pinot Gris is made in Alsace rather than by the way its synonym Pinot Grigio is made in Italy, this is a rich and weighty white. Quite forceful with its peach Danish pastry flavors, but cut with enough citric vim to refresh, it's a white wine that will stand up to food from the grill.

Duck Pond Cellars Pinot Gris, Willamette Valley, Oregon, USA
13.5% ABV $$ W

THANK YOU KINDLY, SIR. GOOD-BYE!

Limeys do make wine. Not very much, it's true, but the sparkling wines produced in the south of England share many of the virtues of Champagne. Nyetimber, now Dutch-owned, is one of the best, and its incisive Classic Cuvée is a magnanimous way of commemorating the day the USA left the UK behind.

Nyetimber Classic Cuvée, West Sussex, UK
12% ABV $$$ SpW

New Job

32

NERVES? HOW COULD THERE NOT BE? Everyone here seems to know what they're doing. They're busy, professional, comfortable—they belong. Whereas you, in your brand-new unfamiliar clothes, feel different, not quite yourself. You're introduced to everyone, and they seem friendly enough, but they're wary, too: "How do you fit in?" they seem to be asking behind the smiles. "Are you going to be an ally or a competitor, a team player or a lone wolf?" Of course, you're asking the same questions yourself. You can't help comparing everyone to your old colleagues, some of whom became—and will remain—good friends. Did you make the right move? Did you really need to leave the old place after all? And then you write your first email from your new account, get started on your first assignment, share your first joke, and you remember the excitement you felt when you first saw the job advertised. The time whizzes by, and before you know it, the day is through. Back home, you've earned the right to unwind. You want something undemanding to soothe and cleanse. A cool glass of Sauvignon Blanc awaits, its first sip releasing that sigh of satisfaction that only a hard day's work can provide.

> *"The best way to appreciate your job is to imagine yourself without one."*
>
> OSCAR WILDE

BLIND RIVER MARLBOROUGH SAUVIGNON BLANC

FROM New Zealand
STYLE Aromatic Dry White
GRAPE VARIETY Sauvignon Blanc
PRICE $$
ABV 13%

SAUVIGNON BLANC from the Marlborough region, on the north of New Zealand's South Island, produces one of the world's most distinctive wine styles: all explosive gooseberry, passion fruit, and green flavors (asparagus, bell pepper, grass). The style, once so new and unusual, is perhaps in danger of becoming a little formulaic today. When it's good, however—as this example from the family-owned Blind River undoubtedly is—Kiwi Sauvignon has a vital, verdant quality that goes straight to the brain's pleasure center, quenching the thirst and cleansing the mind like no other wine.

Drink it with: *Seafood, of which there is an abundance in New Zealand, is the obvious foil for Sauvignon Blanc's naturally high acidity. The Sauvignon acts like a lemon to balance the sweetness of the fish, but the flavors are robust enough to cope with a little Asian spice, too—a dish of shrimp with a little chili, coriander, and ginger, say, or white fish with a peri-peri sauce.*

BUDGET CHOICE

Chilean winemakers have spent the past decade or two moving toward either the sea or the mountains to find cooler sites that are better suited for making crisp white wines such as Sauvignon Blanc. From a site near the Pacific Ocean, this has a bracingly clean citrusy tang.

Casa Silva Cool Coast Paredones Sauvignon Blanc, Colchagua, Chile
13% ABV $$ W

FOR THE BIGGER PAY PACKET

There may be no second acts in American life, but Kevin Judd's Greywacke operation proves there is in New Zealand wine. From the founder of Cloudy Bay's outstanding new operation comes a Sauvignon that defies the clichés with pithy grapefruit, minerals, and a piercing purity.

Greywacke Wild Sauvignon, Marlborough, New Zealand
13% ABV $$$ W

AFTER-WORK RED

Beaujolais, to the south of Burgundy, is the go-to place for refreshing, light red wines; the region's very name is a kind of shorthand for the style. Produced from the Gamay grape, this has the sappy succulence of just-ripe blackberries.

Henry Fessy Beaujolais-Villages, France
13% ABV $ R

SPANISH REFRESHMENT

Overfamiliarity with Sauvignon's distinctive flavors has bred contempt in some quarters. But if you crave the mix of aromatic fruit and febrile acidity paired with a different flavor spectrum, Galicia's Albariño, with its peachy fruit and slightly salty edge, has the same cleansing effect.

Castro Celta Albariño, Rías Baixas, Galicia, Spain
13% ABV $ W

33

Honeymoon

HONEYMOON: The very word conjures up an image of a golden glow, and that is how many of us feel in the first few weeks of marriage. The nerves and then excitement of the wedding have passed, and now the reason for all the fuss can at last unfurl, undisturbed by the demands of family and friends—a new world with your loved one; married life. However new or long established your relationship, and wherever you may choose to go (not all of us settle on sun, sea, and sand), the mood is languorous, lazy, peaceful; your senses are fully awake, the only calls on your attention the welcome sight of your beloved and the things you see through each other's eyes. It's an idealized vision, maybe, but then, why even enter marriage without just a little idealism? The future may be uncertain, but your love…? Well, as the song playing on a loop in the resort bar puts it cheesily but correctly, you know that much is true. On your hotel balcony, you pour wines that, as the sunlight catches the glass, also have that golden glow: the products of a harmonious union of oak and grape, sensuous in texture, rich in flavor, but alert, alive—Chardonnay.

"Our honeymoon will shine our life long: its beams will only fade over your grave or mine."

FROM JANE EYRE
BY CHARLOTTE BRONTË

AU BON CLIMAT BIEN NACIDO CHARDONNAY

FROM Santa Maria Valley
California, USA
STYLE Dry White
GRAPE VARIETY
Chardonnay
PRICE $$$
ABV 13.5%

JIM CLEMENDEN OF AU BON CLIMAT makes Chardonnays that are a million miles away from the clichéd oak-bombs that have marred the grape variety's reputation. This one has Clemenden's trademark balance of fruit richness, flinty minerals, and a racy freshness, while the use of oak is supporting rather than dominant—a very classy example of modern California Chardonnay.

Drink it with: *One of the great things about Chardonnays like this are their food-matching versatility. This one has the balanced acidity to go with fish, as well as the weight and richness to stand up to white meat and mushroom sauces.*

ELEGANCE ON A BUDGET

This winery, run by an expat British couple, is based in the Limoux appellation, in the foothills of the Pyrenees. Limoux is a kind of southern French embassy of Burgundy, producing elegant Chardonnays that have the flavors and feel of an autumnal orchard.

Domaine Begude Terroir Chardonnay, Languedoc, France
13% ABV $ W

THE QUIET AUSTRALIAN

Just as many California Chardonnays have been on a fat-busting diet, so Australians, too, have learned the virtues of restraint over the past decade or so. Yabby Lake makes some of the best of this new leaner style, with a drum-skin tautness and a mineral complexity.

Yabby Lake Single-Vineyard Chardonnay, Mornington Peninsula, Australia
13% ABV $$$ W

HONEYMOON CHAMPAGNE

If you see "blanc de blancs" on a Champagne label, it means the wine has been made entirely from Chardonnay. Taittinger's top cuvée is one of the greatest expressions of the style, a voluptuous but laser-guided wonder that isn't cheap but is a very fine way to start married life.

Champagne Taittinger Comtes de Champagne Blanc de Blancs
12.5% ABV $$$$$ SpW

LATIN LOVE

Chardonnay is not the only white grape variety that responds well to the ministrations of an oak barrel. Rioja's Viura, for example, tends to be rather neutral without it, but in this modern example, it develops a voluptuous texture and tropical-fruit richness.

Finca Allende Rioja Blanco, Spain
13.5% ABV $$ W

ABC

With producers the world over looking to mimic the success of Australia and California, Chardonnay became a victim of its own success during the 1980s and 1990s. A tide of formulaic buttery, creamy imitations flooded the market, and the fashion-conscious declared that they'd rather drink ABC—Anything But Chardonnay. Recent times have seen producers looking more to the model of restraint offered by Burgundy, however, and the grape is enjoying a renaissance from New Zealand to Sonoma.

34

Saturday Night in with Friends

THE RESTAURANT MARK-UP, which generally makes wines about three times the price they would be in a store, can be a little frustrating, to put it mildly, when you go out. But it does give you the opportunity for a bit of reverse psychology if you're entertaining at home. You can tell yourself that paying the same for a bottle in a store that you'd pay in a restaurant gets you three times the quality. It doesn't always work out that way: Quality and price don't necessarily follow each other exactly on a graph. Things like reputation, fashion, exchange rates, and different costs of production (land and labor costs are cheaper in, say, Chile, than they are in Champagne, for example) all have their say in what makes one wine more expensive than another. Still, a Saturday night dinner at home with friends is an excuse to go up a level or two on your weekday bottles. It's also a chance to try something new and different, to explore a region, variety, or style you've not tried before, and maybe dabble in a bit of food-and-wine matching, though not the kind of formal fuss you'd get at a restaurant—you're not about to get prescriptive and say you must have this with that. This is a relaxed occasion, and the wines, as they always should be, are there for one main purpose: to get the conversation flowing, helping bring you and your fellow drinkers closer together.

"The discovery of a good wine is increasingly better for mankind than the discovery of a new star."

LEONARDO DA VINCI

MEYER-NÄKEL BLAUSCHIEFER SPÄTBURGUNDER

FROM Ahr, Germany
STYLE Elegant Red
GRAPE VARIETY
Pinot Noir
PRICE $$$
ABV 14%

WHEN MOST OF US THINK of German wine, chances are we think of white wine and the Riesling grape variety. But the country also makes rather a lot of red wines. The best are made from Pinot Noir (Germany is the world's third-largest producer of the variety, known there as Spätburgunder, after France and the USA), and while they're not cheap, they're getting better all the time, comparable in quality and style to the bottles produced to the west in France's Burgundy. The Ahr Valley to the south of Cologne is the home of many of Germany's top red bottles, and Meyer-Näkel is one of the region's stars, as this silky, racy, freshly red-berried delight with cooling mineral notes amply shows.

Drink it with: *This is ideal for game birds such as grouse, pheasant, partridge, pigeon, and duck.*

A RISING CROATIAN STAR

There's nothing new about wine production in Croatia (they've been at it since the earliest Ancient Greek settlers), but the industry has come on dramatically since the fall of Yugoslavia and the Balkan Wars. This Malvazija from the Italianate Istrian peninsula is no mere curiosity, with its punchy but refined mix of herbs, minerals, apricots, and almonds.

Kozlović Malvazija, Istria, Croatia
13.5% ABV $$ W

A LESSER-SPOTTED GALLIC WHITE

Pacherenc du Vic Bilh comes from the same area of Gascony in southwest France as the tannic, muscular red wines of Madiran. Alain Brumont is a master of both styles, as is apparent in this richly exotic but invigorating dry white, where mango and pineapple are cut with a burst of grapefruit.

Château Bouscassé Jardins, Pacherenc du Vic Bilh, France
12.5% ABV $$ W

THE NEXT LEVEL

Chile's largest producer Concha y Toro is familiar to most as the name behind the widely stocked and consistently good-value Casillero del Diablo brand. But it also makes a range of more serious upscale bottlings for when you have a bit more to spend. This suavely brooding, black-fruited powerhouse is one of the peaks.

Concha y Toro Don Melchor Cabernet Sauvignon, Puente Alto, Maipo, Chile
14% ABV $$$$ R

SWEETLY EXOTIC

The Sherry-like fortified wines produced in the area around the towns of Montilla and Moriles in Andalusia are usually overshadowed by those produced around "Sherry Central" in Jerez, but they can be just as good. This extremely sweet and viscous dark molasses-like elixir is wonderful poured over vanilla ice cream—or as a dessert in itself.

Alvear Pedro Ximénez de Añada, Montilla-Moriles, Spain
16% ABV $$ F

At a Spanish Restaurant

THE INTERNATIONAL REPUTATION OF SPANISH FOOD has been transformed over the past couple of decades. Today its top chefs and restaurants are regularly ranked at the pinnacle of global fine dining, while the tapas bar has become a familiar feature of cities around the world. The poster boy of the *nueva cocina* was Ferran Adrià, the Catalan wizard behind the now-closed El Bulli restaurant. Adrià pioneered the intricate, playful, surrealistic style of cooking known as molecular gastronomy, with its foams, spheres, and counterintuitive combinations (such as white asparagus with virgin olive oil capsules), and inspired a generation of chefs at home and overseas. But for the vast majority of people, it's the Spain of the tapas bar that is most familiar, with traditional dishes such as smoky paprika-scented chorizo, calamari, Serrano ham, patatas bravas, and sardines soaked in lemon.

"Hunger is the best sauce in the world."

FROM DON QUIXOTE
BY MIGUEL DE CERVANTES

Spain's diverse modern wine scene offers bottles for both ends of the spectrum—and from the many new-wave producers reviving unfashionable areas with modern techniques, to the arch-traditionalists of Rioja and Jerez, its international reputation has also never been higher.

GONZÁLEZ BYASS TÍO PEPE FINO SHERRY

FROM Jerez, Spain
STYLE Fortified
GRAPE VARIETY
Palomino
PRICE $
ABV 15%

FROM SEATTLE TO SALAMANCA, rare is the tapas bar that doesn't stock a bottle of Tío Pepe. But are they serving it right? Many people have been turned off Sherry for life after a tiny thimble-full of warm, stale Fino from a bottle kept on the back bar for months. But really it should be thought of as it is in Spain: as a white wine, chilled and served in a decent-sized wine glass from a freshly opened bottle, whereupon it is transformed into a yeasty-savory, salty-fresh, thirst-quenching food partner and one of the best-value and most consistent wines around.

Drink it with: *The lighter Fino style of dry Sherry is a joy with tapas such as garlicky seafood, nuts, and dried hams.*

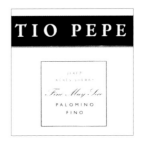

MODERN TAPAS RED

Made from the swarthy Mediterranean grape variety Carignan grown in the Montsant region close to the much more famous (and expensive) Priorat, this is an explosively fruity and juicy unoaked red with an inky, earthy, and black-fruited character for sipping with chorizo or Serrano ham.

**Celler El Masroig
Solà Fred,
Montsant, Spain**
14% ABV $ R

CLASSICAL RED

López de Heredia is a grand old name in Rioja that has remained true to its traditional methods of long barrel and bottle aging even as others there have changed. The wines are stately and complex, the red gran reserva taking on flavors of truffle, leather, and tobacco: a fine match for pork.

**López de Heredia
Viña Tondonia Rioja
Gran Reserva, Spain**
13.5% ABV $$$$ R

A TASTE OF GREEN SPAIN

The cooler, wetter, Atlantic-influenced Galicia in northwest Spain is home to the country's most intriguing, aromatic whites—wines that go so well with the abundant local seafood. Made from the Godello variety, this is a textured floral white with a mineral raciness.

**Bodegas Valdesil
Godello sobre Lías
Valdeorras, Galicia, Spain**
13% ABV $$ W

A CAVA CUT ABOVE

Cava is frequently cheap and cheerless, but Gramona operates in a different league to most producers, and this fizz justifies its loftier price with the sheer concentration of its citrus-peel and floral character and its tingling verve and clarity.

**Gramona III Lustros
Cava Gran Reserva,
Spain**
13% ABV $$$ SpW

EL BULLI: CELLAR FOR SALE

To help fund the transition of El Bulli from a restaurant to a center of culinary research, chef Ferran Adrià put its wine cellar up for sale. The sale included 2,000 Spanish wines and old vintages of some of the country's most treasured reds, such as Vega-Sicilia Único and Valbuena and Pingus from Ribera del Duero, Bodegas Artadi's Grandes Añadas and Pagos Viejos from Rioja, and a cluster of big names from Priorat, such as Clos Erasmus, Clos Mogador, and L'Ermita. The sale fetched several million dollars.

36 Courting the Client

FOR MANY OF US, being offered the wine list at a restaurant is a source of fear rather than fun, even when we're with our friends or family. At a business dinner, particularly when there's an important deal or contract on the table, that fear is magnified by the consequences of getting things wrong. Consulting the sommelier, generally a sensible option in a restaurant, may not do when you're trying to project a decisive image. Paying too much will make you (or rather your company) look profligate; paying too little may make the opposite impression. To complicate the issue further, you want something that people will actually want to drink and enjoy—you want them to feel comfortable, not challenged—and it's likely, too, that everyone will order different food. There is no wine that can meet all those requests, but the safest bets are the light but succulent reds of Beaujolais, to the south of Burgundy, France. These are wines that steer a course between all those competing demands: matching both fish and meat; red but light enough to appeal to white-wine drinkers; chic without being *cher*.

> *"The natural effect of good eating and drinking is the inauguration of friendship and the creation of familiarity, and when people are a trifle warmed by wine they often disclose secrets of importance."*
>
> FROM L'ART DE NÉGOCIER AVEC LES PRINCES BY FRANÇOIS DE CALLIÈRES

DOMAINE COUDERT CLOS DE LA ROILETTE FLEURIE

FROM Beaujolais, France
STYLE Light Red
GRAPE VARIETY
Gamay
PRICE $$$
ABV 12.5%

BEAUJOLAIS SOMETIMES SUFFERS in comparison to its northern neighbor Burgundy, its Gamay grape variety being the poor relation of aristocratic Pinot Noir. The wines of Clos de la Roilette in Fleurie are different, however, retaining the brightness, freshness, and supple drinkability that Beaujolais, and Fleurie, is known for, but adding greater depth to the flavor somehow: black currant, cherry, a hint of something mineral. It ages well, too, particularly in fine vintages such as 2009 and 2010.

Drink it with: *Coq au vin, fish in red-wine sauce, duck breast, a plate of* jambon, *steak… Beaujolais isn't known as versatile for nothing.*

BUDGET CHOICE

If a wine can be unpretentious—and it gets personified with all kinds of other adjectives, so I don't see why not—then this sappy, happily cherry-berry fruity red is that wine. Light in tannin, fresh in acidity, and with a just-ripe cherry succulence, it's one to chill and drink with fish.

Château de Pizay Beaujolais, France
12% ABV $ R

A BRIDGE BETWEEN STYLES

Here is another wine that adds depth and texture to Beaujolais's trademark joie de vivre, this time from the Moulin-à-Vent zone, which is known for producing wines with more power and guts. In location and style, it's a bridge between the perfume of Burgundy and the more muscular styles of the Rhône.

Louis Jadot Château des Jacques Clos de Rochegrès Moulin-à-Vent, Beaujolais, France
13% ABV $$$ R

AN AUSTRALIAN NOVELTY

Tarrango is not a grape with much pedigree: It was developed in Australia in the 1960s, a crossing of Portugal's Touriga Nacional and the table grape Sultana. The only example I've tried (and enjoyed) is this bouncy, cranberryish, almost tannin-free red, Australia's answer to Beaujolais.

Brown Brothers Tarrango, Victoria, Australia
12.5% ABV $ R

OREGON NOUVEAU

Many winemakers in Oregon and California have been inspired by Burgundy and Pinot Noir; rather fewer by Beaujolais or Gamay. But when the wine is as pretty, fragrant, elegant, and accomplished as this biodynamic example, you wish that more American vintners would give it a go.

Brick House Gamay Noir, Willamette Valley, Oregon, USA
12.5% ABV $$ R

AU REVOIR, BEAUJOLAIS NOUVEAU?

Sales of Beaujolais boomed in the 1970s and 1980s on the back of a marketing wheeze that turned the annual release of the just-fermented new wines known as "nouveau" in December into a race among producers to release the first bottle, and for consumers to buy them, on the third Thursday of November. Beaujolais Nouveau Day still exists and is celebrated as far afield as Japan, but growers have lost heart, preferring to shift the focus from the lesser-quality nouveau wines toward more serious bottlings.

Firing Up the Grill

WHETHER IT'S A SOUTH AFRICAN *BRAAI*, an Argentinian *asado*, or a Texan hog roast, the food of the grill or barbecue is characterized by powerful flavors. There's the smoke, of course, or perhaps that should be smokes, given the varied effects of the different fuels that might be used, from straight charcoal to mesquite wood chips to lavender, rosemary, and grape vines. Then there are the marinades—sweet and sticky or spicy with garlic, ginger, and chili—and the meat itself, particularly the steaks, hamburgers, and sausages that are the most common grill fodder. Finally, there are the accompanying salads and sauces: green leaves dressed with vinegary dressing, coleslaw, spicy tomato salsas, ketchup, mustard, barbecue sauce. This is the kind of food that will engulf leaner or more subtle styles, so you'll be looking for robust wines. Big reds with the requisite tannin to work as a kind of sponge for the fat of the meat, but with enough generous fruit to marry with the sweeter accompaniments: these will be wines from warmer climates—such as California, Australia, South America, parts of South Africa, and Southern Europe—where the grapes can ease their way to ripeness. And if you're going for white meats or fish, or have red wine-phobic guests, you could dial down the tannin with a powerful, darker rosé.

> *"Wine . . .*
>
> *the intellectual*
>
> *part of the meal."*
>
> ALEXANDRE DUMAS

BRAZIN OLD VINE ZINFANDEL

FROM California, USA
STYLE Powerful Red
GRAPE VARIETY
Zinfandel
PRICE $$
ABV 14.5%

AN ALL-AMERICAN WINE for an all-American food tradition, Brazin's Zinfandel is an unapologetically big, broad-shouldered beast, where the emphasis is very much on the very concentrated blueberry, blackberry, and dark plum fruit, the product of vines aged between 20 and 80 years. There's kola bean and coffee here, too, and a seasoning of spicy oak, but what makes it work is that it is neither too sweet nor too jammy. The fruit is fresh rather than raisined, as can be the case with this variety when the grapes are left too long on the vine.

Drink it with: *All that fruit acts as a juicy counterpoint to slow-cooked American barbecue classics like pulled pork or ribs, with the sweet-acrid tang of mesquite smoke.*

FOR THE *BRAAI*

Southern Africans call the barbecue the *braai*, and it is likely to include *boerewors* sausages and marinated kabobs featuring chicken or lamb (*soasties*), alongside such exotic meats as springbok, kudu (a type of antelope), or ostrich. Boekenhoutskloof's spicy, peppery, and subtly smoky Cape red seems to have been expressly designed to wash it all down.

Boekenhoutskloof Porcupine Ridge Syrah, South Africa
14% ABV $ R

FOR THE *ASADO*

Beef, in a variety of cuts, is the heart of the Argentinian *asado*, though other meats—such as lamb from Patagonia, as well as chicken, fish, and plump *morcilla* sausages—will also get a look-in. It's hard to see beyond the country's vinous specialty, Malbec, as an accompaniment, and this, the cheapest of Catena's many forthright but fragrant wines based on the grape, is reliably good.

Catena Malbec, Mendoza, Argentina
14.5% ABV $ R

A REFRESHING ROSADO

If you're having a barbecue that takes in fish, chicken, and red meat but you want a single wine to go with the lot, a robust but refreshing rosé will be your best bet. It's also preferable on a very hot day, when big red wines can be a little overwhelming. Marqués de Cáceres's version is clean, crisp, dry, and punchy, with candied-strawberry fruit.

Marqués de Cáceres Rosé, Rioja, Spain
13% ABV $ Ro

STICK ANOTHER SHRIMP ON THE BARBIE

Another country where the barbecue assumes the level of cultural icon is Australia. Given that most Australians live within striking distance of a beach, it's not surprising that a common feature of Aussie barbies is seafood and fish. This cool, incisive, low-alcohol dry white, made from Italian variety Vermentino, is the ideal foil for smoky shrimp and crayfish.

Mitolo Jester Vermentino, McLaren Vale, Australia
10% ABV $$ W

We're Pregnant!

THE WORDS MAY COME as a surprise or a shock. They may mark the beginning of a journey you'd been planning and dreaming about for years, or they may emerge like a bolt from the deep sky blue of the tester kit. But whatever the circumstances, the fateful words "We're pregnant!" are among the most important many of us will ever hear or utter. There is wonder—and astonishment, even. What was understood as an abstract idea just a moment before, the miracle of life, is in a moment transformed into a fact of life. We have nine months, you think, before everything changes—nine months to morph from somebody's child to somebody's parent; nine months to turn that disaster of a spare bedroom into a nursery, or to find an apartment with a disaster of a spare room to turn into something resembling a nursery. The urge to celebrate may be tempered by the knowledge that this is just the start; also, as a mother-to-be, you may feel unwilling or unable to drink alcohol. But celebrate we must, even if the wine is not much stronger than water, or if we have just a sip or two. German Riesling would be ideal.

*"Now my belly
is as noble
as my heart."*

GABRIELA MISTRAL

DÖNNHOFF RIESLING KABINETT

FROM Nahe, Germany
STYLE Off-Dry White
GRAPE VARIETY
Riesling
PRICE $$
ABV 10%

GERMANY IS AT THE NORTHERN FRINGES of wine production, and the grape varieties that thrive are those that are able to reach full flavor ripeness before accumulating the high sugar of those adapted to warmer climes. Less sugar means less alcohol in the finished wine—all the more so if, as in this case, the winemaker chooses not to ferment it all into alcohol. Here the subtle sweet touch acts as a cushion against the dashing blade of acidity in an exhilarating example of the Riesling grape variety.

Drink it with: *This wine's delicate but not insipid feel calls for similar food: grilled river trout or, once your pregnancy is over, sushi.*

A DRY NINE MONTHS

German wine, particularly from the esteemed Mosel Valley, has become synonymous with the light, off-dry style of Riesling, but it's become increasingly fashionable to make dry, or *trocken*, styles. Paulinshof has been at the vanguard, and this spicy, mineral wine is lean, lithe, and full of energy.

Paulinshof Urstuck Riesling Trocken, Mosel, Germany
11% ABV $$ W

MONEY'S-NO-OBJECT CHOICE

This particularly fine producer operates in a particularly fine vineyard (Wehlener Sonnenuhr) to make a thrilling off-dry wine that sums up the Mosel: graceful, nimble in the way it feels in the mouth, but carrying a surprising amount of peach and apple fruit flavor and spice on its slender frame.

Joh Jos Prüm Wehlener Sonnenuhr Riesling Spätlese, Mosel, Germany
7.5% ABV $$$ W

A LIGHT AUSTRALIAN CLASSIC

Something of an anomaly in warm-climate Australia, where alcohol levels tend to be high, Hunter Valley Semillon is a unique style of bone-dry white that is low in alcohol but very high in flavor, particularly as it ages, when it takes on toasty, lime-marmalade and lanolin characters.

Tyrrell's Vat 1 Hunter Valley Semillon, New South Wales, Australia
10.5% ABV $$$ W

A CARIBBEAN ALTERNATIVE

Why is the only strong liquor in this book in the section about pregnancy? Because it makes for a brilliant cheat for those who don't want to risk high alcohol. Like Worcestershire or Tabasco sauce, it's so powerful that just a drop in a glass of tonic water is enough to make a dry, sippable tipple.

Angostura Bitters, Trinidad
45.6% ABV $ Spirit

WINE AND PREGNANCY

Should you drink wine during pregnancy? Stark warnings on bottles suggest not at all, but official medical advice is rather less proscriptive, suggesting one to two units of alcohol (a small, ¾ cup [175 ml] glass of 12.5 percent ABV wine) per week as a safe level of consumption in the second and third trimesters. Different cultures have different views, however—hence the arch phrase, "I see you're having a French pregnancy," used by a sommelier when my expectant wife enjoyed a rare glass.

39

The Organic Guest

WHEN YOU'RE CONFRONTED by a row of bottles in the sterile strip-lit aisle of a supermarket, wine's connection with the land—the fact that it's an agricultural rather than an industrial product—seems a distant, rather theoretical idea. You get much the same feeling if you visit some of the larger wineries, which, with their rows of silo-like stainless-steel tanks, feel more like factories than the homely, pastoral idylls they depict on their labels. However, as even the most hardened cynic of a winemaker will tell you, a wine is only ever as good as the fruit from which it is made. No wonder, then, that many prefer to see themselves as farmers rather than artisans, spending more time in their vineyards than they do in their cellars. And no surprise, either, that like millions of other farmers around the world, many of them have been alarmed by the effects, which they've seen firsthand, of excessive chemicals on both land and man, and have switched to organic or biodynamic methods. Most will tell you they've made better wines since doing so, which is not to say that all organic or biodynamic wines are great or even good. They're not. What is incontestable, however, is that an increasing proportion of the world's good and great wines are now made from organic or biodynamic grapes.

"Let us give Nature a chance; she knows her business better than we do."

MICHEL DE MONTAIGNE

WEINGUT WITTMANN RIESLING QBA

FROM Rheinhessen, Germany
STYLE Dry White
GRAPE VARIETY Riesling
PRICE $$
ABV 11%

GIVEN BIODYNAMIC PRACTICES ORIGINATED in the Teutonic world, it's not surprising that German and Austrian farmers were among the earliest adopters. Indeed, a recent survey of organic agriculture suggests Germany accounts for some 47 percent of the world's biodynamically farmed acreage. The country's wine growers contribute their fair share to that statistic, and the wines of Phillip Wittmann, including this electrifying, crystalline dry Riesling, offer a very persuasive argument in favor of biodynamic winemaking.

Drink it with: *Trout (ideally wild, from a river near a biodynamic farm!), with a salad of spicy wild leaves.*

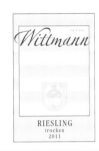

FOR THE ORGANIC BEEF

A kitchen-sink blend led by Syrah and Carmenère, Chilean producer Emiliana's Coyam benefits from the expertise of the country's leading exponent of biodynamic wine-production principles, Álvaro Espinoza. It's a layered and savory red of no little power, with notes of peppery spice and perfumed black fruit.

Emiliana Coyam, Colchagua Valley, Chile
14% ABV $$ R

MONEY'S-NO-OBJECT CHOICE

Better known by its initials, DRC, Burgundy's legendary Domaine de la Romanée-Conti produces tiny quantities of wine each year from its collection of top grand cru vineyards. They are treasured for their remarkable perfume and clarity, their elegance and longevity. And they are produced biodynamically.

Domaine de la Romanée-Conti, La Tâche Grand Cru, Burgundy, France
13.5% ABV $$$$ R

BIODYNAMIC CHAMPAGNE

Champagne Fleury claims to be the first biodynamic producer in Champagne, though several other small growers have now adopted the philosophy. A blanc de noirs (using black Pinot Noir grapes to make a white wine), this is focused and dry, with a red-currant-jam-on-toast character.

Champagne Fleury Blanc de Noirs, Champagne, France
12.5% ABV $$$ SpW

FOR THE BIODYNAMIC TRUE BELIEVER

A tireless evangelist for biodynamics (he can and does talk for hours on the subject, delighting in provoking audiences around the world with his more *outré* ideas), Nicolas Joly is first and foremost a winemaker, and this is a magnificent, ageworthy demonstration of dry Loire Chenin Blanc.

Clos de la Coulée de Serrant Savennières, Loire, France
12.5% ABV $$$$ W

WHAT DOES BIODYNAMIC MEAN?

Inspired by Austrian Rudolf Steiner (1861–1925), biodynamics is a form of organic farming that also follows the astral and lunar calendar. Biodynamic farmers are best known for unconventional practices such as burying cow horns to harness cosmic forces, which have led to criticism that they're dabbling in pseudo-science. But while they may not say it their labels, many of the world's top estates have adopted the system, the improvement in their wines and vines providing all the justification they need.

Promotion

40

You know all about Rudyard Kipling's twin impostors. You know that you should keep your cool and not be too proud about what's happened, just as you shouldn't let the bad days get you down. But after all the hard work and extra hours you've put in; after all the willingness, sheer determination, and (if you say so yourself) skill and aptitude you've shown—well, there's nothing for it but a "Yessss!" as you strike a Usain Bolt–style victory pose. A promotion is one of life's most satisfying achievements. It's not really about the extra something in the paycheck, though you can't deny it will make life a little easier each month. It's more the pride you feel that someone has recognized your achievements. And no, you don't need the words and opinions of others to get you motivated, but knowing that you're appreciated really does add an extra bounce to your step, making it that little bit easier to carry on doing your best. You are officially on the up, and to mark the occasion you might want to choose something from a region on a similar trajectory, one of the future stars of the wine world—the names to watch.

"If you can meet with Triumph and Disaster, And treat those two impostors just the same . . ."

FROM "If" by
Rudyard Kipling

DESCENDIENTES DE J PALACIOS PETALOS BIERZO

FROM Bierzo, Spain
STYLE Red
GRAPE VARIETY
Mencía
PRICE $$
ABV 14%

UNTIL VERY RECENTLY, Spanish wine was largely known beyond its borders for two regions: Rioja and Jerez (the home of Sherry). But just as Spanish chefs began to outstrip their French counterparts with their modernist cuisine, so a new wave of producers transformed Spain's vinous backwaters. The latest name to capture the attention is Bierzo in Galicia, home to the Mencía grape variety, which produces sturdy wines, high in acidity and tannin, but topped, in the best examples (such as this aptly named one), with a charming floral, violet character.

Drink it with: *A Galician* cocido, *a stew of pork, chorizo, steak, and chickpeas, with potatoes and green vegetables.*

A NEW WAVE FROM THE CAPE

Largely unknown a decade ago, this is from what is now South Africa's trendiest region, thanks to the work of very skilled young producers, of whom Adi Badenhorst is a leading light. Baked-apple richness and a teasing brightness of acidity make this Chenin Blanc very special for the money.

A. A. Badenhorst Secateurs Chenin Blanc, Swartland, South Africa
13% ABV $$ W

NEW ZEALAND'S RISING SOUTHERN STAR

The first commercial wines from one of the world's most southerly wine-producing regions, Central Otago, were released in 1987. Now it rivals Burgundy for fine Pinot Noir. Effortlessly seamless and silky, with subtle herbal notes.

Felton Road, Block 5 Pinot Noir, Central Otago, New Zealand
13.5% ABV $$$ R

MAKING NEW FROM OLD

A previously unfashionable variety, Carignan has been making a comeback and nowhere more thrillingly than in Chile's Maule region, where rediscovered old vines make rugged, powerful, but, in this case, meaty-savory and super-bright reds.

Louis-Antoine Luyt Trequillemu Carignan Empedrado, Maule, Chile
14% ABV $$ R

SICILY'S EXPLOSIVE STAR

That Etna is still an active volcano gives an added dimension to its description as one of Europe's most exciting wine regions. Made from the local Nerello Mascalese variety, this is a fluent, elegant, refreshing red.

Graci Passopisciaro, Etna Rosso, Sicily, Italy
13.5% ABV $$ R

OTHER REGIONS ON THE UP

Wine is as much a subject of the whims of fashion as any other sphere of human activity, and wine lovers are always on the lookout for the next big thing. Names in the ascendance while this book was written include Portugal (in particular the Douro, Dão, and Minho regions), the former Yugoslavian countries of Slovenia and Croatia, Etna in Sicily, cool Australian spots such as Tasmania and Victoria's Yarra Valley, and the lesser-spotted parts of southwest France, such as Irouléguy, Jurançon, and Madiran.

Baby Shower

41

THIS EVENT IS NAMED, OF COURSE, for the presents with which the mother is "showered" by her friends, family, and co-workers. Historically speaking, however, the real purpose of a baby shower was to give the mother-to-be an induction into the rites of motherhood. Female relatives and friends would gather to share their collective wisdom, handed down through the generations, on birth, child rearing, the behavior of children and fathers, and the very meaning of life as a mother. There may also have been some attempt—perhaps with a pocket watch swinging on its chain over the expectant mother's belly—to guess the gender of the child. Some elements of this intragenerational exchange still remain, but these days, if you are hosting a baby shower, the event is usually a lighthearted celebration. In any gathering of this kind, the wine is never going to take center stage (and the mother-to-be is unlikely to want to partake). You want something that will play to the crowd, providing an unobtrusive backdrop to the canapés, gifts, and wise (and not-so-wise) words. You will also be buying a fair few bottles, and you don't want to break the bank. Something like the inexpensive whites of Gascony in southwest France will do just fine—country wines that are unpretentious and unassuming, like the counsel of a favorite aunt.

"What gift has providence bestowed on man that is so dear to him as his children?"

MARCUS TULLIUS CICERO

DOMAINE TARIQUET CLASSIC CÔTES DE GASCOGNE

FROM Gascony, France
STYLE Crisp Dry White
GRAPE VARIETY Blend
PRICE $
ABV 12%

IF YOU'VE EVER BEEN WON over by the pungent, verdant tang of the dry white wines made from Sauvignon Blanc in the Loire or New Zealand, then the lesser-known Côtes de Gascogne in the Armagnac-producing region of southwest France is also well worth getting to know. When they're well made, such as this example, these light whites' mix of grapefruit, lemon, and subtle grassy-herbal flavors offers pithy, uncomplicated refreshment at bargain prices.

Drink it with: *At a baby shower—or at any party—the lowish alcohol and refreshing tang mean this will slip down fine on its own as an apéritif, but the lemony tang works as a cleansing complement to seafood, too.*

FOR THE FAIRY CAKES

From its vibrant but not livid pink color, to its wild strawberry flavors, this gently off-dry French rosé is the very definition of pretty, with just enough sugar to pair with cupcakes, but not so much to put off those used to dry wines.

Famille Bougrier Rosé d'Anjou, Loire Valley, France
12% ABV $ Ro

FOR THE WINTER BABY

For most of us, red wine makes more sense than white when the mercury falls. This raspberry-and-brambly-jam-flavored red has an easy, soft juiciness that works well with or without food.

Bodegas Borsao Garnacha, Campo de Borja, Spain
14% ABV $ R

THE GLAMOUR CHOICE

Cheerfully, charmingly frothy, with a sherbety mousse and squeaky-clean pear and lemon flavors, this northern Italian sparkler is the wine to buy if you want to inject a little gloss and glamour into proceedings.

Bisol Jeio Prosecco di Valdobbiadene, Veneto, Italy
11.5% ABV $$ SpW

THE BABY-SHOWER GIFT

A lusciously sweet special bottle for the mother to open when she's good and ready or to drink with the child on his or her 21st birthday: This historic South African wine tastes good whatever its age.

Klein Constantia Vin de Constance, Constantia, South Africa
12.5% ABV $$$$ SW

At a Chinese Restaurant

IN THE WEST WE TEND TO VIEW CHINESE CUISINE as a single entity. Indeed, for the vast majority of Americans and Europeans, "Chinese food" begins and ends with the handful of dishes offered by our neighborhood takeout joint: the chow mein, the barbecued ribs, the egg foo yung. But this is just one side of China's diverse culinary scene—a sanitized, Westernized (albeit, in the right mood, comforting and delicious) take on the cuisine of the southern Canton province. Most Chinese-food aficionados would break things down to at least three further distinct regional styles, each with its own subregional variations: the heartier fare of Mongolia and the north, the fiery spice of central Szechuan, the sweeter styles of the east. As diverse as these cuisines are, however, what they tend to share, at least in a restaurant or formal context, is a style of presentation. Where European meals will feature a succession of dishes to be eaten in sequence, in China a variety of dishes—and therefore flavors and textures—will be served all at once. Finding sufficiently versatile wines to match this kind of banquet is a challenge. But for the curious, at least, it can be a rewarding one.

> *"The way you cut your meat reflects the way you live."*
>
> CONFUCIUS

D'ARENBERG THE HERMIT CRAB MARSANNE/VIOGNIER

FROM McLaren Vale, Australia
STYLE Full-Bodied White
GRAPE VARIETY Blend
PRICE $$
ABV 13%

THE DYNAMIC FOOD SCENE in modern multicultural Australia has a strong Asian influence, so it's not surprising that many of the country's wines work so well with Chinese food. This full-bodied dry white, for example, made by one of Australia's oldest producers, has a leap-out-of-the-glass aromatic intensity—white flowers, acacia, white peaches, and apricots—and a ripe-fruit weightiness and juiciness in the mouth that mean it can cope with the variously fatty and spicy elements of a variety of Chinese dishes.

Drink it with: *This is a good choice for Westernized Chinese staples such as chicken chow mein or crispy aromatic fried duck.*

FOR GINGER SPICE

As well as litchis and roses, like many wines made from Gewürztraminer, this limpid, pristine example from an excellent cooperative producer in the variety's north Italian birthplace also has a note of ginger, complementing the many Chinese dishes that feature this spice.

Cantina Tramin Gewürztraminer, Alto Adige, Italy
13.5% ABV $$ W

FOR SEAFOOD DIM SUM

Whether steamed, baked, or fried, bite-size dim sum dumplings often have a seafood filling and a certain delicacy of texture, both of which provide an excuse, if you needed one, to break open a bottle of this richly fruited but incisive Champagne from an unfailingly consistent producer.

Champagne Charles Heidsieck Brut Réserve, Champagne, France
12% ABV $$$ SpW

STEAMED WITH SOY

The umami-savory saltiness of soy sauce has its closest vinous counterpart in the dry fortified wines of Jerez in southern Spain. This Amontillado style is very dry and nutty, but its intense hit of brothy, saline flavor is perfect to both match and pep up soy-based marinades.

Hidalgo Amontillado Seco Napoleon Sherry, Spain
17.5% ABV $$ F

FOR SZECHUAN SPICE

Created in Germany in the 19th century but now almost exclusively found in South Africa, Bukettraube makes intensely aromatic wines similar in character to Gewürztraminer and Muscat. This example has the fragrance and subtle sweetness to balance the heat of Szechuan pepper.

Cederberg Cellars Bukettraube, Cederberg, South Africa
13.5% ABV $$ W

ON THE LIST AT HAKKASAN

The Hakkasan group of top-end Chinese restaurants began its life with a Michelin-starred venue in London but now has outlets across the USA and the Middle East. Its take on Chinese food is modern but mindful of tradition in signature dishes such as Peking duck with caviar and grilled Wagyu beef with king soy sauce, and its choice of wines is no less innovative, with a range of fine Sherries, German Pinot Noir, and Spanish Malvasia and Mencía some of the unconventional by-the-glass choices.

First Night in Your New Home

You can just about cope with the chaos for now. You've fashioned an impromptu dining room from a deck chair, a piano stool, and a box of vinyl LPs still sealed from the last time you moved. You've ordered some takeout. And you have a special bottle of wine you bought, on the day the sale was confirmed, for this very night. All you need is to find it. Boxes, boxes everywhere, but not a drop to drink. Or, for that matter, something to drink it from. Next time (though right now you fervently hope there won't be a next time), you'll remember to label the boxes a little more clearly than just "kitchen" and "other stuff." For now, you admit defeat. You're never going to find that bottle. Best just call it quits and try the only shop open around here at this time of night. It doesn't, to put it mildly, have a great selection, just the typical corner-store parade of jaded old bottles of unknown provenance and stacks of the usual familiar brands. Some of those brands deserve their reputation as industrial products—vinous Coca-Cola. Others can't be dismissed quite so snobbishly: They have pulled off the very difficult trick of making drinkable wines of character in huge quantities. The wine you choose might not be as special as the bottle you had in mind. But you're surprised, as you drink it from a plastic mug, how good it tastes tonight.

"Though home is a name, a word, it is a strong one; stronger than magician ever spoke, or spirit ever answered to, in strongest conjuration."

FROM Martin Chuzzlewit
BY Charles Dickens

TORRES SANGRE DE TORO

FROM Penedès, Spain
STYLE Smooth Red
GRAPE VARIETY
Garnacha/Cariñena
PRICE $
ABV 13.5%

A TOP-SELLING WINE since its creation in the 1950s, the Torres family's Catalan "bull's blood"—with its familiar, slightly kitsch bull mascot dangling from the cap—is now sold in more than 140 countries and is a reliable staple of the world's corner stores. A robust, brambly blend of Garnacha and Cariñena (known elsewhere as Carignan), there's a smoothness of texture here and a ripeness of fruit that doesn't quite tip into jammy, as well as a certain savory dimension that works well with food.

Drink it with: *Meat- or cheese-based takeouts such as pizza topped with pepperoni, pasta with salami, or even a hot dog.*

THE GOOD SIDE OF CORPORATE

Château Ste Michelle, the owner of the Columbia Crest brand, is Washington State's largest producer by some margin. Lucky, then, that it generally does a good job. With its plum, dark cherry and black currant, this trusty Merlot, for example, is reliably rich and warming.

Columbia Crest Merlot, Columbia Valley, Washington State, USA
14% ABV $$ R

BIG-BRAND AUSTRALIA

The wines of Australian giant Jacob's Creek have always been a model of restraint compared to some of the labels that shot to world fame at the same time in the 1980s and 1990s. The basic Chardonnay is good; the deftly oaked reserve, a step up in concentration and layered texture.

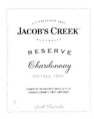

Jacob's Creek Reserve Chardonnay, South Australia
13.5% ABV $$ W

A FAMILIAR FIZZ

A familiar sight behind bars and on supermarket shelves, Lanson's bread-and-butter brut is a Champagne of consistent quality that is specifically made to emphasize fresh, crisp green-apple flavors and lemon-citrus acidity, serving as an exhilarating pick-me-up to toast your new home.

Lanson Black Label Brut Champagne NV, France
12% ABV $$$ W

BIG-BRAND CHILE

Large producers, many of them efficient rather than stylish, dominate the Chilean wine business. However, Errázuriz's flair and ambition, particularly evident in its top wines Seña and Don Maximiano, carry over into its cheaper wines, such as this chunky cassis-scented red.

Errázuriz Cabernet Sauvignon, Aconcagua, Chile
14% ABV $ R

ARTISAN VERSUS INDUSTRIAL

The world's most interesting wines tend to come from smaller producers—something to do with the owners' close attachment to the land. But just as not all small producers are good, so there are large producers capable of great things. Respected wines such as Grange, Dom Pérignon, and Château d'Yquem are all made by large corporations. Many winemakers, too, believe it takes more skill to make large quantities of good, affordable wine than tiny amounts at high prices. The best are capable of both.

44 Done Deal

It would be wrong to call it a more innocent time, not when a worship of hucksterism and hedonism was what passed for a moral code. But those pre-Crash, boom-era years of the 2000s were certainly less inhibited when it came to ostentatious displays of wealth. When historians come to write about the decade, the 2000s will be represented by tales of bankers blowing bonuses on outrageous restaurant wine orders. One particular incident serves as a kind of microcosm of the era: the group of English bankers, celebrating a deal in Gordon Ramsay's upscale Pétrus restaurant in London's Belgravia by blowing some £44,000 on their drinks bill, including several bottles of wine from the legendary Bordeaux château from which the restaurant took its name. The wine bill was so big that Ramsay gave the group their meals free (a mere £400). That the bankers were eventually fired for trying to put the bill through expenses doesn't detract from its allegorical force: That they had the chutzpah to do it so publicly was so very noughties. In today's more austere climate, bonuses may be no less remarkable in some cases, but the recipients are more discreet about showing them off. For these more circumspect Masters of the Universe, and for lesser mortals with smaller deals to celebrate, there is, in any case, no need to push out the private yacht. You can find equivalents for the noughties' bankers' habitual choices—top Bordeaux, cult Napa Cab, prestige cuvée Champagne—at much more reasonable prices. These are special-occasion wines that, unlike a dodgy credit default swap, won't break the bank.

"Take care of the luxuries and the necessities will take care of themselves."

Dorothy Parker

CHÂTEAU SOCIANDO-MALLET

FROM Haut-Médoc, Bordeaux, France
STYLE Powerful Red
GRAPE VARIETY Blend
PRICE $$$$
ABV 14%

THE VERY TOP WINES OF BORDEAUX are a magnet for the moneyed and the ostentatious across the world, with prices in the hundreds and even (for rare older vintages) thousands of dollars. But if you look beyond the estates ranked as cru classé (classed growth), you can find similar quality and character at considerably more realistic prices. Château Sociando-Mallet officially has a more humble cru bourgeois ranking, but it consistently makes red wines that belie its status, with a bottle price around the $50 mark.

Drink it with: *Look for a bottle with at least a decade's age, when the tannins and oak have softened and a tender rack of lamb beckons.*

SMALL-BUSINESS BUDGET

The second wine of a much-admired estate, Château Grand-Puy-Lacoste, ranked in the lowest (fifth-class) rung of the cru classés in the Médoc region of Bordeaux, punches far above its weight. This is a classically elegant but structured claret, with pencil lead, cassis, and cedar.

Lacoste-Borie, Pauillac, Bordeaux, France
13% ABV $$$ R

NOT PÉTRUS

Okay, so it's not cheap, but it's a wine from the same appellation as status symbol Pétrus at a fraction of the price. It is, in fact, the second wine of the peerless Vieux Château Certan, clocking in at around half the price but with the same combination of silky elegance and red-fruited purity.

La Gravette de Certan, Pomerol, France
13.5% ABV $$$$ R

PRESTIGE WITHOUT BLING

Champagne Philipponnat's top single-vineyard cuvée Clos des Goisses is a remarkable wine that has never quite attracted the blinged-up following of Cristal and Dom Pérignon. The houses's toasty basic brut is also excellent, however, and at a price that won't upset the team in accounts.

Champagne Philipponnat Royale Réserve Brut, Champagne, France
12% ABV $$$ SpW

A CULTURED CAB

This velvet-smooth and generously black-fruited Cabernet is from the Margaret River region, which has quickly established itself as one of the world's top producers of the variety. Even so, it has not attained the stratospheric pricing and waiting lists of Napa Valley or Bordeaux.

Leeuwin Estate Art Series Cabernet Sauvignon, Margaret River, Western Australia
14.5% ABV $$$ R

THE WINE SPECULATOR

A striking feature of the wine market recently has been the rise of wine as an investment. The market is heavily concentrated on Bordeaux, where some wines have a track record of improving in flavor and rising in price. Where once these wines were bought by wine lovers, they are now seen as a more lucrative alternative to stocks and shares by companies and individuals who have no intention of drinking them, instead pushing up prices and taking the top wines out of the reach of all but the most affluent.

Birth of a Child

You didn't expect this. Everyone told you that your life would change forever, and you'd kind of listened and nodded politely, thinking they meant the practicalities of life: the diaper-changing, the lack of sleep, the compromised social life. And you'd thought, "I can handle that. It just takes a little bit of adjustment and a bit of planning, that's all." But you hadn't bargained on this feeling, which is … What, exactly? Well, elation begins to describe it, but awe, too, and relief that the birth is over; but most of all, a love so fierce and all encompassing that it's almost frightening. Now you know what they meant. Now you know that your life really has changed forever. The future of this little snuffling creature, with its strangely wise and ancient face, is entirely in your hands. And even as you want those first precious moments to last, you can't wait for that future to unfold. What drink can possibly measure up to these feelings—so pure, so unmediated, so elevated and true? Perhaps only good Champagne, the tried-and-tested drink of celebration and a wine so direct, so pure, so joyful, and so full of life.

"Birth is the sudden opening of a window, through which you look out upon a stupendous prospect. For what has happened? A miracle. You have exchanged nothing for the possibility of everything."

William Macneile Dixon

CHAMPAGNE DELAMOTTE BRUT NV

FROM Champagne, France
STYLE Sparkling White
GRAPE VARIETY Blend
PRICE $$$
ABV 12%

OWNED BY THE SAME PEOPLE as the cult brand Salon, Delamotte may be the greatest Champagne house you've never heard of—a small producer making a range of fabulous fizz that is always very fairly priced. This luminous blend, made from two of the Champagne region's traditional trio of grape varieties, Chardonnay and Pinot Noir (the third is Pinot Meunier), is exquisitely balanced between brioche-like richness and incisive freshness.

Drink it with: *This is not the time to be thinking of food matching, but a smoked salmon and cream-cheese bagel may be just the thing.*

BUDGET CHOICE

Not true Champagne—it comes from the hills of the Languedoc in southwest France—this top-notch French sparkling wine is made using the same methods. (The fizz comes from a second fermentation in the bottle.) It's dry, tangy, fresh, and alert, with crisp apple flavors.

Antech Brut Nature Blanquette de Limoux NV, Limoux, Languedoc, France
13% ABV $ SpW

MONEY'S-NO-OBJECT CHOICE

Most Champagnes are made from a blend of grapes grown in different vintages; however, the very best tend to come from grapes produced in a single year. Look for the 2002 of this remarkable 100 percent Chardonnay for a masterclass in golden, seamless purity.

Champagne Ruinart Dom Ruinart Blanc de Blancs Vintage Champagne, France
12.5% ABV $$$$$ SpW

A NEW WORLD FOR A NEW LIFE

Top Champagne producer Louis Roederer also makes fine sparkling wines using the same grapes and methods at its operation in the Anderson Valley, California. This one has a sunny *tarte tatin*-like fruitiness but is poised, elegant, and fresh, too.

Louis Roederer Quartet NV, Anderson Valley, California
12% ABV $$$ SpW

AUTHENTICALLY CHINESE

This collaboration between specialists in two Spanish classics—the fortified wine Sherry and sparkling Cava—brings together the flavors of both. A drop of Fino Sherry brings a distinctive nutty edge to the rich orchard fruit in a full-bodied, full-flavored fizz.

Colet Navazos Extra Brut Cava, Penedès, Spain
13% ABV $$$ SpW

WHEN IS CHAMPAGNE NOT CHAMPAGNE?

Champagne winemakers believe that only sparkling wine made there should be labeled as such and have waged a global legal battle to ensure that sparkling-wine producers outside their region in northeast France cannot "borrow" the name for their own products. The campaign has been largely successful, with only a few countries—among them Russia and the USA—declining to outlaw the use of the Champagne name on its domestic producers' wines. So next time you have a bottle of American "Champagne," enjoy it, by all means, but remember that, strictly speaking, it's not the real thing.

At a Thai Restaurant

THAI FOOD IS NOT THE EASIEST MATCH FOR WINE. There's so much going on in a Thai meal—so many elements and ingredients with which most wines don't normally agree: the heat of chili, the acidic tang of lime, the sweetness of palm sugar, the richness of coconut, the aromatic complexity of Thai basil, cilantro, lemongrass, ginger, kaffir lime leaves, galangal, and the umami salty-savory flavors of nam pla fish sauce. Each of these would prove tough to match on its own, let alone combined together in the same meal or dish. The wines that do work with Thai food are necessarily, then, quite a specific subset. You need wines with a little sugar, both to act as a cushion for the chili and to cancel out the sweetness in the food. You need decent acidity to cope with the lime. And you need a robustly aromatic character to mingle with all those herbs. Alsace and Germany provide the model for this kind of aromatic off-dry white, but you can find plenty of candidates in a similar style made from grape varieties such as Pinot Gris, Riesling, or Gewürztraminer across central Europe and, increasingly, the world.

"Simultaneously the whole party moved toward the water, super–ready from the long, forced inaction, passing from the heat to the cool with the gourmandise of a tingling curry eaten with chilled white wine."

FROM TENDER IS THE NIGHT
BY F. SCOTT FITZGERALD

DOMAINE JOSMEYER GEWURZTRAMINER LES FOLASTRIES

FROM Alsace, France
STYLE Aromatic White
GRAPE VARIETY
Gewurztraminer
PRICE $$$
ABV 13.5%

THERE'S A REFINEMENT to the wines of Domaine Josmeyer, a family-owned estate of several generations' standing, that sets them apart from many of their peers in Alsace. Their wines have a winning combination of purity, gilded acidity, and aromatic complexity, even when dealing with a grape variety, Gewurztraminer, that has a tendency to run to fat and overwhelming perfume. This wine is no lightweight, but the rose-floral, musky perfume and gingery spice are restrained, clear, and entirely beguiling.

Drink it with: *The aromatic allusions and texture of this wine are perfectly in tune with the range of flavors in Thai cuisine, whether coconut-creamy* tom yam *soup or steamed river fish with ginger and galangal.*

FOR A THAI SALAD

Though delicate in texture and low in alcohol, this off-dry Riesling has a surprising power of tropical fruit flavor that would complement the tropical fruit often used in Thai salads. Its acidity absorbs the lime; its sugar is a foil for the chili, ginger, and other spices.

Schloss Schönborn Hattenheimer Pfaffenberg Riesling Spätlese, Rheingau, Germany
8% ABV $$ W

FOR SPICY PORK

Pork is a common ingredient in Thai cookery, whether in spiced meatballs or shredded in stir-fries, salads, and rice dishes. This rich, full-bodied, just off-dry white has the balance of density and acidity to cut through the fat of the pork, while its aromas echo Thai spices.

Marisco The King's Thorn Pinot Gris, Marlborough, New Zealand
13.5% ABV $$ W

THE BEER SUBSTITUTE

If your Thai-meal beverage is usually beer, it's worth considering a sparkling wine, which offers similar frothy refreshment and, in the case of this blend of Riesling and Grüner Veltliner, a kind of pretty, green aromatic quality similar to Thai herbs.

Schloss Gobelsburg Sekt Brut Reserve, Kamptal, Austria
12% ABV $$$ SpW

IF IT HAS TO BE DRY

A blend of five white grape varieties, this wine is intensely aromatic, with floral and tropical fruit the key flavors. Its palate is densely packed and rich, and though it isn't sweet, it does have a certain robust viscosity to stand up to the spice assault.

Conundrum White Wine, California, USA
14% ABV $$$ W

THAI WINE

Thai wine emerged only in the 1960s, but it is being taken increasingly seriously. The tropical climate means vines can yield more than one crop each year, though better producers focus on a single harvest. Siam Winery is the standout producer; its Monsoon Valley red blend of Shiraz and the local variety Pokdum is well worth seeking out.

The Asthmatic Guest

ALL ALCOHOLIC BEVERAGES can act as triggers for the symptoms of asthma, and wine is most certainly not an exception. According to a spokesperson at the British charity Asthma UK, research suggests that the effect is more likely a consequence of additives and other naturally occurring elements found in wine than the alcohol itself, with the most likely triggers in wine being sulfites, or sulfur dioxide. Though a small amount of SO_2 occurs in all wine as a result of the fermentation process, winemaking choices mean some wines contain more than others. Most winemakers use SO_2 as a preservative in varying amounts, both during the winemaking process and prior to bottling. Many also use it as a way of keeping the winery clean. In recent years, however, a number of winemakers have sought to reduce drastically their reliance on SO_2 or even to work without it entirely (when French producers may use the term *sans soufre ajouté*). This is a risky business that requires great skill and care on the part of the winemakers if they are not to end up with wines that re-ferment in the bottle, oxidize (go brown and Sherry-like) prematurely, or are dominated by off-putting barnyard flavors (from bacterial spoilage). But for self-styled "natural winemakers," it's a risk worth taking—part of a philosophy that owes as much to aesthetics as concerns about health, and driven by a desire to make wine with as few additives as possible. Usually working organically or biodynamically, and eschewing cultivated yeasts in favor of those occurring naturally on the grape skins and in the winery, the best of these natural producers make wines that have a thrilling purity and vitality. And while they won't entirely remove the risk of triggering asthma symptoms, a number of sufferers now won't drink anything else.

"To make natural wine, you must be a natural person."

JOSKO GRAVNER,
ITALIAN WINEMAKER

DOMAINE MARCEL LAPIERRE MORGON

FROM Beaujolais, France
STYLE Elegant Red
GRAPE VARIETY Gamay
PRICE $$
ABV 12.5%

IF BEAUJOLAIS IS THE SPIRITUAL HOME of the natural-wine movement, then the late Marcel Lapierre was one of its earliest prophets in the 1970s and 1980s. Inspired by the ideas of chemist and winemaker Jules Chauvet, and perturbed by the unthinking use of pesticides and herbicides, Lapierre set out to make wine as it used to be made, with minimal additions in the vineyard and winery. Now made by Lapierre's son Matthieu, the red wines that inspired a movement remain superb: so lucid, limpid, and refreshing.

Drink it with: *The kind of thing you'd find in one of Paris's many informal natural wine bars—a plate of* saucisson *and terrine.*

NATURAL LOIRE

The wines of Thierry Germain, one of the Loire's foremost natural producers, are often compared to top-flight Chardonnay from Burgundy—a compliment to their mix of complexity, richness, and clarity. But they have the distinctive appley character that is clearly Chenin Blanc.

Domaine des Roches Neuves l'Insolite Saumur Blanc, Loire, France
12.5% ABV $$ W

VINO NATURALE

After France, Italy has perhaps the largest concentration of natural-wine makers, and many of the most intriguing are working in the ever-improving scene in Sicily. Cos's minimal-SO₂ Frappato brings out that grape's wonderful strawberry and cherry aromatics.

Azienda Agricola Cos Frappato IGT Sicilia, Sicily, Italy
12.5% ABV $$ R

A NATURAL BRAND

Former rugby player Gérard Bertrand is now a major player in the Languedoc-Roussillon wine scene, generally making commercial wines at a cut above the usual. This is his spin on natural wine—a chunky, affordable red that has been made with minimal SO₂.

Gérard Bertrand Naturae Syrah, Languedoc, France
14.5% ABV $ R

THE SOUTH AMERICAN NATURAL

Made from the unfashionable Cinsault variety, using the ultimate accessory for the tradition-minded natural winemaker—the clay amphorae, or *viejas tinajas* (old jars) from which it takes its name—this is a supple, spicy red that works well a little chilled.

De Martino Viejas Tinajas, Itata Valley, Chile
13% ABV $ R

NATURALLY VAGUE

One of the criticisms of the natural-wine movement from the more conventional side of the trade is its lack of regulation. Organic and biodynamic production is officially audited by a variety of independent bodies, but anyone can lay claim to being a "natural" producer—there are no set rules. Regulation seems a way off, too, because each natural-wine maker has a slightly different interpretation of what it means, and because regulation runs against the informal, countercultural spirit of the movement.

A Picnic

Most of us, I suspect, have similar fantasies of what constitutes the perfect picnic. It would, in the author's mind's eye at least, be an early summer's afternoon, when the weather is shirt-sleeves warm rather than bikini broiling, the grass still green, the wild flowers in first bloom. There would be water nearby, but nothing too dramatic, just a stream or a lazily flowing river to provide a view and a place to leave your bottles cooling, attached to the hamper by a length of string. Seating would be provided by a frayed old favorite picnic blanket, cushioned by long grass, large enough for several friends. The food in the hamper is almost incidental, certainly simple and traditional: sandwiches, pies (savory and sweet), maybe a length of salami and a slab of hard cheese and pâté, hard-boiled eggs, a few salad leaves, a bag of tomatoes—robust food for the most part (the exception being the strawberries picked on the way) that can survive the journey to this remote spot without requiring heavy containers or losing its charm in a sweaty wrapper. Finally, the wine, which, unless you're in a Champagne mood, should be humble rather than grand, refreshing, with enough alcohol to promote a snooze beneath a sun hat, but not so much to make a chore of the return journey away from paradise and back to civilization.

> *"There are few things so pleasant as a picnic eaten in perfect comfort."*
>
> Elliott Templeton in
> The Razor's Edge by
> W. Somerset Maugham

CAVE DE SAUMUR RÉSERVE DES VIGNERONS SAUMUR ROUGE

FROM Loire, France
STYLE Light Red
GRAPE VARIETY
Cabernet Franc
PRICE $
ABV 12.5%

RED WINES made from the Cabernet Franc variety in the cool climate of the Loire Valley often have a leafy freshness and a sappy succulence that recall black currants and red currants that are only just ripe. If you're used to the more opulent reds of warmer climates such as Australia or California—where the fruit character is sweeter, riper, sometimes verging on the jammy—this leaner approach can take a bit of getting used to. Chilled down on a warm day, however, they make complete sense: perfumed, refreshing, energetic.

Drink it with: *This has the freshness to wash down a spread including meaty fish like salmon (though not smoked), a pork pie, salami, cold ham, cheese—the usual picnic fare.*

PINK PICNIC

So long as you have a portable cooler—or better yet, some string and that gently flowing stream—to keep the bottle chilled, a crisp, clean, delicately scented Provençal rosé like this one fits just right with a picnic, working well with a variety of foods and on its own.

Domaine Sainte Lucie Made in Provence Côtes de Provence Rosé, France
12.5% ABV $$ Ro

CHAMPAGNE IN THE PARK

The idea of the picnic has had a powerful hold over the British imagination since the Victorians popularized the activity. For a posh picnic, Champagne is a must, and Pol Roger, as well as being top-flight fizz, has long had close links to the upper crust in the UK.

Champagne Pol Roger Brut NV, Champagne, France
12.5% ABV $$$ SpW

THE PURPOSE-BUILT RIESLING

Most picnics are a daytime thing, when we just don't want to drink anything too high in alcohol. This light, off-dry Riesling, conveniently sealed with a screwcap, has been designed for the purpose and has a racy, fruit-salad quality that will match strawberries, too.

Two Paddocks Picnic Riesling, Central Otago, New Zealand
10% ABV $$ W

A HEARTY EVENING-PICNIC RED

A smooth, cheerfully fruity, robust, and affordable red, this is the one to stash away for later in the day, when you've enjoyed the picnic so much that the evening has begun to draw in, you're pulling on the sweaters, and you need a wine with a little warmth.

St. Hallet Gamekeeper's Reserve, Barossa Valley, Australia
14.5% ABV $ R

CORKS AND SCREW CAPS

In many ways, the screw cap is the perfect seal for a wine bottle, particularly at a picnic. It's easy to open and close without the need for gadgets; it's long since lost its association with the cheaper end of the market; and it avoids the risk of the bacteria responsible for the moldy flavor in "corked" wine (trichloroanisole, or TCA). So why do many winemakers stick to cork? The romance of the pull and pop is one reason. Another is that they are not convinced that wines age as gracefully under a screw cap.

49

Baptism

WINE HAS ALWAYS HAD AN INTIMATE relationship with Christianity. When worshippers sip Communion wine in the celebration of the Eucharist, they are, depending on their faith, either literally or metaphorically taking the blood of Christ into their bodies. Over the centuries, the relationship has taken on other, more prosaic forms, too. In the medieval period, for example, monasteries played a defining role in wine's development in Europe, planting vineyards and refining production techniques—from the monks of Cluny in Burgundy, France, to the Carthusians, whose influence extended as far as Priorat in northeast Spain. Much the same can be said of the Americas, where monastic orders—from the Jesuits of Peru, to the Franciscans of California—had a profound influence on the spread of the vine. The link persists today, both in the handful of European wine estates still controlled by monks and in the many classic wine regions whose vineyards were first planted by them. Choosing a wine that makes this historical link explicit seems like an appropriate way of marking an event as spiritually significant as a baptism.

"Eat thy bread with joy, and drink thy wine with a merry heart."

ECCLESIASTES 9:7

BOUCHARD PÈRE & FILS BEAUNE VIGNE DE L'ENFANT JÉSUS

FROM Burgundy, France
STYLE Elegant Red
GRAPE VARIETY
Pinot Noir
PRICE $$$$
ABV 13%

ALL GREAT WINES HAVE A STORY TO TELL, but this red Burgundy has an especially compelling one. In pre-revolutionary 18th-century France, the vineyard that produces the grapes for this wine was owned by the Carmelite order of nuns. A member of that order, Marguerite du Saint-Sacrement, the founder of the Domestiques de la Famille du Saint Enfant Jésus ("Maids of the Family of the Infant Jesus"), is said to have predicted the 1638 birth of Louis XIV, the Sun King, even though his mother, Queen Anne of Austria, was thought to be, in the dreadful parlance of the time, barren. When the king was born, the Carmelites renamed the vineyard in the nun's honor—a title it still has today. The wine is no longer produced by Carmelites: The vineyard has been in the hands of local merchants Bouchard Père & Fils since the Revolution. But the wine's grace, charm, and satin-like sheen still inspire a secular devotion in fans of Pinot Noir around the world.

Drink it with: *With its delicate hints of undergrowth and spices, this would grace a sophisticated baptism lunch with mushroom-based sauces or risotto, or roast duck.*

BUDGET CHOICE

Established by Carthusian monks in the 15th century, La Perla del Priorat is one of many producers with a religious connection in the wild, rocky Catalan region. It makes a typically chewy, dense red with flavors of wild herbs, licorice, and dried fruit.

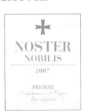

La Perla del Priorat Noster Nobilis, Priorat, Spain
14.5% ABV $ R

BORN WITH A SILVER SPOON

Named for the 17th-century monk who played a major role in the development of sparkling wine in Champagne (if not, as is often thought, inventing it), this top wine from Moët & Chandon is blisteringly, thrillingly pure, precise, and long in the finish.

Champagne Dom Pérignon Champagne, France
12.5% ABV $$$$$ SpW

FOR AN ATHEIST NAMING CEREMONY

Bonny Doon's founder Randall Grahm has a reputation for iconoclasm, regularly attacking the received wisdom of California wine and experimenting with the unusual—in this case, with the Carignan variety in a pepper-spicy, sinewy red inspired by southern France.

Bonny Doon Vineyard Contra, Central Coast, California
13.5% ABV $$ R

FOR LAYING DOWN FOR YOUR BABY

The very smart Taylor's Vintage Ports are rich yet elegant and classy fortified red wines produced in Portugal's Douro Valley. They are built to age for decades, taking on ever more complexity as your child—hard to believe now—moves toward adulthood.

Taylor's Vintage Port, Douro, Portugal
20% ABV $$$$ F

50

30th Birthday

THERE WAS A TIME WHEN A 30TH BIRTHDAY was not such a landmark occasion. Today, in a world where we tend to settle down later and the terms "kidult" and "middle youth" have entered the vernacular, it has taken on more significance. For many of us as we approach the landmark, a 30th birthday looms as the symbolic end of our extended youth—a time when we feel we should get serious about life. Like a belated coming of age, 30 is the new 21. It's also, perhaps, the birthday with the greatest potential for excess. At 30, particularly if you don't have children, responsibility has yet to bite its hardest, you still have the energy and appetite to see the night through to the dawn, and your income level is more likely to match up to your bacchanalian ambitions than it was when you were in your early 20s. So, a 30th birthday feels like an opportunity for one last blast of youthful hedonism, and few wines match that mood better than the Cabernet Sauvignons of California, with their luxurious layers of fruit, fathomless depth of flavor, and smoothness of texture. Many of them age well, too—and what better centerpiece for your celebrations than a wine from your birth year?

> *"The only time you really live fully is from 30 to 60. The young are slaves to dreams; the old servants of regrets. Only the middle-aged have all their five senses in the keeping of their wits."*
>
> HERVEY ALLEN

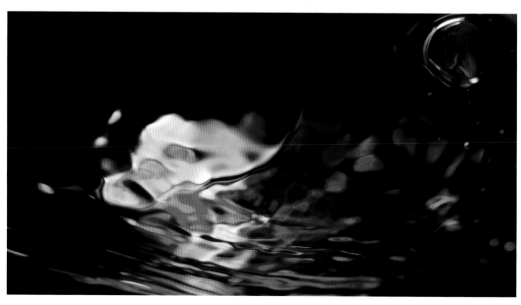

JOSEPH PHELPS NAPA VALLEY CABERNET SAUVIGNON

FROM Napa Valley, California, USA
STYLE Powerful Red
GRAPE VARIETY Cabernet Sauvignon
PRICE $$$$
ABV 14.5%

THIS IS FROM A SELF-MADE BUSINESS—literally, since the eponymous founder himself, formerly in the construction industry, built the winery and planted the vineyards in Spring Valley just outside Santa Helena in the Napa Valley in the early 1970s. In the years since, Joseph Phelps has become one of North America's most respected producers, and this Cabernet Sauvignon from Phelps's vineyards in some of Napa's best spots is very much a special-occasion wine. You could lose yourself in all that rich black fruit, chocolate, subtle black coffee, and olives, so smoothly presented with the finest of tannins.

Drink it with: *There is a reason that the wine lists of the world's best steak houses are filled with California Cabernets: All that power and density make even more sense when lined up alongside a perfectly charred and bloody T-bone.*

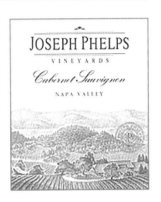

BUDGET CHOICE

The late Robert Mondavi was a pioneer of quality California wine, and though his company was sold before his death at the age of 94 in 2008, his name lives on in one of the state's most reliable, widely available reds, with its abundant cassis and subtle vanilla flavors.

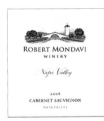

Robert Mondavi Cabernet Sauvignon, Napa Valley, California
14% ABV $$ R

MONEY'S-NO-OBJECT CHOICE

One of the USA's greatest wines, made by the very thoughtful and highly gifted philosopher-cum-winemaker Paul Draper from a blend of Cabernet Sauvignon and Merlot, this is an exceptionally elegant red wine that ages beautifully.

Ridge Monte Bello, Santa Cruz Mountains, California, USA
13.5% ABV $$$$$ R

THE LATIN AMERICAN CHOICE

There's always something disarmingly floral, like violets, about the best Malbecs, which makes for an elegant counterpoint to the sumptuous dark plum and cherry fruit and chocolate in this dark, dense, delicious red.

Mendel Malbec, Mendoza, Argentina
14% ABV $$ R

A HEDONISTIC WHITE

South Africa has made a specialty of white blends (wines made using two or more grape varieties) with a hedonistic richness of fruit. Few are better made than Mullineux's, and with its ripe peach and baked-apple flavors, it's intense but elegant.

Mullineux Estate White, Swartland, South Africa
13.5% ABV $$$ W

Welcoming the In-Laws

IN YOUR CALMER MOMENTS, you know you have a lot to thank your in-laws for. Without them, of course, your beloved wouldn't exist, and wherever you stand on nature versus nurture, they must have done something right. But no matter how much you may have grown to like them over the years, you still feel a little prickle of anxiety whenever they come to visit; you've never quite got over the feeling that you're 15 again, plucking up the courage to knock on the front door before a first date. Sometimes you feel like you're just too dull for their bright and gifted child. Other times you can't stop feeling that everything you do and say is being scrutinized for clues about your personality, for hidden meanings about your intentions and morals. You're feeling it now as you plan which wine to serve them, anticipating the way your paranoid mind will parse the most innocuous-seeming comment. It hasn't even occurred to you that they might actually like and respect you even more if you'd just relax, quit worrying, stop trying to impress, and pour the wine.

"Happiness is having a large, loving, caring, close-knit family in another city."

GEORGE BURNS

MILLTON TE ARAI CHENIN BLANC

FROM Gisbourne, New Zealand
STYLE Off-Dry White
GRAPE VARIETY Chenin Blanc
PRICE $$
ABV 13%

IT SOUNDS LIKE a bit of a backhanded compliment to say a wine will appeal to everyone. Doesn't that mean it's lacking in the kind of full-on personality that necessarily divides opinion? Well, that's not the case with a wine that, in my experience, goes down well with whomever you serve it to; there's lots of character, but it has the ability to appeal to lots of different tastes. It's generously fruited with honeyed baked apple and pear, but that fruit is cleanly presented with crisp acidity. It's made with oak, but that lends texture rather than woody flavor. It's full-bodied enough to appeal to red-wine fans, but crisp and refreshing enough for white-wine drinkers. And while there's a cushion of sugar for those who struggle with bone-dry wines, it's not so noticeable that it will put off dry-wine fans. It's made from biodynamically grown grapes, too. Who could possibly find fault?

Drink it with: *As versatile in its uses as in its appeal, this wine works with everything—from mild Asian dishes to roast poultry and pork or nutty, tangy hard cheeses.*

A CANNY FIZZ

Portugal may not be the first thought for people looking for sparkling wine, but Luis Pato has mastered the art (as well as making some of the country's best still wines), and this well-priced example would surely score points with the in-laws for imagination. Made from the local Fernão Pires (or Maria Gomes) variety, it has a peach-blossom-in-the-breeze levity and charm.

Luis Pato Maria Gomes Espumante Bruto, Bairrada, Portugal
12.5% ABV $$ SpW

A COMPROMISE RED

From Cousiño Macul, one of Chile's oldest wineries, this stalwart Cabernet offers the perfect middle-ground red, appealing both to those who like their wines with the savory flavors, refreshment, and structure associated with the Old World, and to those who like the more exuberant bright black fruit that tends to be described as New World.

Cousiño Macul Antiguas Reservas, Maipo Valley, Chile
13.5% ABV $ R

FOR SWEET-TALKING A LOAN

Alois Kracher was a master of sweet-wine making in Austria, and his work is now continued by his son Gerhard in a bewildering range of different bottles of which this is one of the more affordable. It tastes of apricot and peaches in syrup but without feeling at all cloying or overbearing.

Kracher Cuvée Auslese, Neusiedlersee, Burgenland, Austria
12% ABV $$ SW

FOR PAYING BACK A LOAN

Smart without being crazy expensive like some of its peers in Bordeaux; enjoyable in its youth but with many years ahead of it; lots of fruit (particularly in ripe vintages such as 2009 or 2010) without being a facile fruit-bomb … Everything about this classy claret is on-message as a thank-you gift to your in-laws.

Château Poujeaux, Moulis, Bordeaux, France
14% ABV $$$ R

52

At a Japanese Restaurant

SUSHI, JAPAN'S GREAT GIFT to the culinary world, is a tricky match for wine. The problem is not the raw fish, which on its own works well with any number of delicate white wines. It's what goes with it that makes life difficult for the epicurious. Combined, the fiery heat of the wasabi paste, the sweet spice of the ginger, the acidity of the vinegar-soaked rice, and the intense salty-savoriness of the soy sauce have the capacity to overwhelm even the most powerful wines. Reading through the many blogs and articles devoted to the subject, however, it's clear that a consensus is beginning to emerge: White wines made from Riesling and sparkling wine from Champagne, both of them high in acidity, tend to be recommended most frequently, and can be delicious partners, provided you go easy on that dipping sauce. But sushi is far from being the whole story in a complex food culture where an understanding of texture, harmony, and the "fifth taste element," umami (which might best be described as savoriness) are all paramount. While Japanese food may have spent the first few millennia of its existence evolving in a separate tradition from grape wine, its recent global popularity has thrown the two together, leading to combinations that suggest that, of all the Asian cuisines, Japan's is perhaps the most suited to wine's subtle variations.

"Winter chrysanthemum— heating sweet wine in front of the window."

MATSUO BASHO

GRACE KOSHU KAYAGATAKE

FROM Katsunuma, Japan
STYLE Delicate Dry White
GRAPE VARIETY
Koshu
PRICE $$$
ABV 12%

THE GRAPEVINE HAS BEEN AROUND in Japan since the 8th century AD, but the first commercial wines were not produced until the late 19th century. The industry remains a niche concern, but it is capable of producing wines of some elegance and charm from the native Koshu grape. Few of the wines make it outside Japan, but this example, from a pioneer of quality Japanese wine founded in the 1920s in Katsunuma in Yamanashi prefecture, about 70 miles west of Tokyo, is worth hunting down. Subtly scented with pear and white flowers, it's a delicately insinuating dry white.

Drink it with: *The wine has a bright cleansing effect on the mouth when eating sashimi and sushi with little or no dipping sauce, particularly the lighter fish or seafood such as shrimp, white tuna, or the explosive salmon roe ikura.*

HIGH-SOCIETY SUSHI

The way Champagne is made lends it a certain yeasty quality that has a kinship with soy. Like Riesling, it also has a quicksilver acidity to act as a foil to fish, without being so overpoweringly rich that it overwhelms subtle flavors. It's small wonder that so many sommeliers suggest that elegant Champagnes such as this are the best match for Japanese cuisine.

Champagne Gimonnet Premier Cru Brut, Champagne, France
12% ABV $$$ SpW

A PAN-PACIFIC MATCH

The cutting blade of acidity in good Riesling is an ideal foil for cutting through the sweet oiliness of any fish dish. It's a quality that is evident in this deft Kiwi example, which also has the delicacy of texture and a subtle sweetness to work with a platter of different styles of sushi.

Mt. Beautiful Cheviot Hills Riesling, Canterbury, New Zealand
10.5% ABV $$ W

IN THE MISO SOUP

A bowl of miso soup, with its deep savory flavors, is a good tool for explaining the quality of umami. The appeal of Sherry is rather similar, particularly in drier styles such as this Fino, with its yeast-and-iodine tang. The two match very well in a like-with-like style, although the citrussy crispness of Sanchez Romate's bottling would also pair well with sushi.

Sanchez Romate Fino Sherry, Jerez, Spain
15% ABV $ F

AUTHENTICALLY JAPANESE

In terms of production, sake, which is brewed from rice, has more in common with beer than with wine. When it comes to flavor and texture, however, the opposite is true. This crisp, tangy dry *honjozo*, the lightest of the classic sake styles, fits snugly with Japanese cuisine and is the perfect starter sake for the habitual wine drinker.

Akashi-Tai Honjozo Sake, Japan
11% ABV $ W

53

At a Ski Resort

JUST AS THE APPEAL OF GOLF for many players is all about the 19th hole, so much of the joy of ski can be found in the *après*. The chalet, with its wooden interior and its obligatory open fire, is the paradigm, the Platonic form of cozy—and making your way there after a day spent zooming around off-piste or waddling, shamefaced, to the ski lift, provides a very tangible reward. Fiery schnapps and fondue complete the (admittedly rather clichéd) picture, but wine might get a look-in, too—warming red wines, of course (literally, if you simmer a pot of spiced *Glühwein*). You might want to consider something that matches your surroundings: a mountain wine produced from grapes grown at high altitude. How high? The highest vineyards are in the Andes, with the upper Calchaquí Valley in Argentina's northwestern Salta province laying claim to being the highest of all, at more than 10,170 feet (3,100 m). But vineyards cling to the slopes high up in the Alps and Pyrenees and on Mount Etna, too, and there are less dramatic, but still considerable, elevations in northern California and Australia. Why do winemakers climb these mountains? One reason is to find cooler temperatures that help bring freshness to wine; another is to expose the grapes to more ultraviolet light, which is thought to bring greater complexity. But it's also—at least in part—simply because they're there.

"Bacchus loves the hills."

ROMAN PROVERB

BODEGA COLOMÉ ESTATE MALBEC

FROM Calchaquí Valley, Argentina
STYLE Powerful Red
GRAPE VARIETY Malbec
PRICE $$
ABV 14%

ARGENTINA HAS A CONCENTRATION of high-altitude vines, but Swiss millionaire Donald Hess, who also has vineyards in California, has planted some of the most vertiginous vineyards in the world at his Bodega Colomé. There is a little Cabernet Sauvignon and Tannat, as well as Malbec, in this brooding red, which is dark in color and flavor, with the chocolate and plum lent aromatic freshness by notes of violet and lavender.

Drink it with: *If you want to go for the full-on retro Robert Redford-in-Downhill Racer vibe, then it has to be a cheese fondue, though a rich meaty stew would work just as well.*

HIGH ALTITUDE, LOW PRICE

Viña Falernia is the standout producer in the rising star northern Chilean region of the Elquí Valley, with some of the vines planted at 6,600 feet (2,000 m) in altitude. The Syrah has a distinctive licorice-and-pepper spice, bold black fruit, and a muscular feel.

Viña Falernia Syrah Elquí Valley, Chile
14% ABV $ R

ALPINE RED

Italy's most northerly wine region, the Alto Adige, rises into the foothills of the Alps toward Austria, producing wines of aromatic delicacy and freshness, as in this ringingly clear red, with its succulent red berries and subtle floral character.

J. Hofstätter Lagrein, Südtirol-Alto Adige, Italy
13% ABV $$ R

PYRENEAN RED

Grape growers in Irouléguy, on the French side of the Basque Country in the Pyrenees, work on vineyards planted on inhospitably steep slopes at an altitude of around 1,300 feet (400 m). This red, from Tannat, is gutsy and inky, with dark-cherry flavors and acidity.

Domaine Arretxea Irouléguy Rouge, France
14% ABV $$ R

ALPINE WHITE

From a region between Switzerland and Italy featuring Europe's highest vineyards, at around 4,750 feet (1,300 m), near some of the Alps' top ski resorts, this is an entirely delightful white that combines Alpine flowers and orchard fruit with a mountain-stream-like coolness and clarity.

Cave du Vin Blanc de Morgex et de la Salle Rayon, Valle d'Aosta, Italy
13% ABV $$$ W

A *GLÜHWEIN* RECIPE

If you think mulled wine is a waste of a good bottle of red, you'd be right: You certainly wouldn't want to make it from Château Lafite. But it is a good way of using a bottle of not-so-good wine. The best recipes are roughly 50/50 cheap red and cheap Port, where the extra sweetness and body seem to bring more depth to the final brew. For a liter of *Glühwein*, add a small handful of cloves, a cinnamon stick, the juice of a couple of oranges, and about 40 ounces (1.1 kg) of sugar. Heat until warm but not boiling.

54 Impressing Your Boss

HAVING THE BOSS ROUND FOR DINNER is never going to be an entirely relaxing experience. Even if you like and get along with your superior, you're always going to be thinking to some extent about what could go wrong: the too-relaxed mood that leads to a faux pas; the too-formal mood that makes the whole evening fall flat; the over- or undercooked meat; the perfectly cooked meat placed before your boss's vegetarian partner. Et cetera. You also have an eye on what you want to communicate with your choice of wine, because, like everything to do with your boss, there's always a subtext. You want to look simultaneously generous, canny, and smart; reliable, polished, and poised. You want to display your independence without giving them the idea you are after their job. Wines that, at their best, convey at least some of these qualities are those known as Super-Tuscans. These are wines made in Tuscany, Italy, that, when they were first produced in the 1960s, challenged the local wine authorities by employing grape varieties and techniques that were outlawed at the time. The slick, stylish results they came up with soon attracted worldwide attention, and today they're an established part of the scene. It's an interesting backstory to discuss with your boss as he sips wines that, in content and presentation, are as polished and poised as you are.

"The best leader is the one who has sense enough to pick good men to do what he wants done, and self-restraint enough to keep from meddling with them while they do it."

THEODORE ROOSEVELT

GAJA CA' MARCANDA PROMIS

FROM Tuscany, Italy
STYLE Dry Red
GRAPE VARIETY Blend
PRICE $$$
ABV 13.5%

ONE OF ITALY'S most renowned winemakers, Angelo Gaja is best known for his work in Piedmont (your boss may well have spotted the name on some very swish restaurant lists), but he also has an estate in Bolgheri on the Tuscan coast, where he makes wines in a similarly lush and sumptuous style. Promis, the lower- (if not low-) priced red from the estate, blends Sangiovese, the traditional grape of Chianti, with Syrah and Merlot for flavors of coffee, dark plum, and mentholated black currant, with a velvety mouthfeel.
Drink it with: *Rich red-meat dishes—beef fillet, rack of lamb, venison—with red-wine sauce.*

BUDGET CHOICE

Most Super-Tuscans are expensive—producers think of them, rather self-consciously, as their top wines, and they price them accordingly. Carpineto's "baby Super-Tuscan" is made for a wider audience, blending 70 percent Sangiovese with Cabernet Sauvignon in a juicy and savory red full of cherry and plum.

Carpineto Dogajolo Rosso, Tuscany, Italy
13% ABV $ R

THE SUSPICIOUSLY EXPENSIVE CHOICE

How far do you want to go to impress your boss? She may be a little embarrassed (and wonder if she's paying you too much) if you present this, arguably Italy's most famous wine. Then again, she may enjoy herself too much to care, since the reputation of this much-imitated Bordeaux-style blend is entirely justified.

Tenuta San Guido Sassicaia, Tuscany, Italy
14% ABV $$$$$ R

THE SLICK TRADITIONAL TUSCAN

Not a Super-Tuscan—it conforms to the regulations of the Chianti Classico region and is labeled accordingly—but a biodynamically produced 95 percent Sangiovese of exceptional harmony and length, with pure cherry fruit, a suggestion of oregano and Asian spice, and seamless, silky texture.

Querciabella Chianti Classico, Italy
13.5% ABV $$ R

VICTORIAN CLASSICO

Like Nebbiolo—its northwest Italian rival for the title of Italy's most esteemed red grape variety —Sangiovese has not been too successful away from home. But this part-Italian-owned Australian estate has proved it can work abroad in a powerful, structured, but fragrant take on Tuscany.

Greenstone Vineyards Sangiovese, Heathcote, Victoria, Australia
13.5% ABV $$$$$ R

INDIGENOUS VERSUS INTERNATIONAL

The success of the Super-Tuscans from the 1960s onward spawned a great number of imitators across Italy, with many growers abandoning traditional grape varieties in favor of "international" varieties such as Cabernet Sauvignon, Merlot, Syrah, and Chardonnay. Recently, however, there has been a return to those indigenous varieties across Europe as growers look to differentiate themselves and their regions, and drinkers have tired of wines that, some argue, taste like they could come from anywhere.

55

Sunday Brunch with Friends

IF AN ITEM OF FOOD IS NAMED FOR A PORTMANTEAU WORD, it's usually a reliable signal that it's worth ignoring. Most of these combinations—frappuccino, crossandwich—are just plain silly. But brunch is different: It's a useful word that gives a name to something enjoyable that didn't previously have one. (The more mellifluous and traditional "elevenses" comes close but really refers more to a snack than a meal.) There is something inherently relaxing about brunch, in part because it's very much a weekend thing, something we'd rarely have during the working week. It's a lazy, unhurried meal, a chance to really enjoy the breakfast foods you're normally in too much of a rush to prepare. Eggs (in any and every which way), smoked salmon, bacon, sausages, pancakes loaded with maple syrup, French toast, waffles, fresh fruit salad To drink? Freshly squeezed juice and coffee. But wine? Well, why not? While some brunch foods (eggs) may offer a challenge to pair (thanks to the combination of slippery texture and simultaneously deep but subtle flavor), others (bacon) work beautifully with spicy reds. Besides, you have nothing pressing to do today. Just the papers to read and the company of your friends to enjoy.

"My only regret in life is that I didn't drink more Champagne."

JOHN MAYNARD KEYNES

CHAMPAGNE TARLANT ZERO BRUT NATURE

FROM Champagne, France
STYLE Sparkling White
GRAPE VARIETY Blend
PRICE $$$
ABV 12%

THE CLASSIC BRUNCH TIPPLE is a mimosa—the blend of sparkling wine and orange juice that allows you to drink alcohol while simultaneously believing you're making a healthy start to the day. You could, if you really wanted to, add some orange juice to this Champagne, though frankly you'd be better off using something a little less expensive; you'd lose the delicate flavors of the Champagne, and a slightly sweet Prosecco in any case does the job better for around $10. And besides, why kid yourself? Especially when the wine has the bracing wake-me-up qualities of this very dry Champagne, which is made without the addition of the *liqueur de dosage* with which most Champagnes are sweetened before they are bottled for sale. Sometimes, in some Champagnes, zero *dosage* translates into zero pleasure— they're just too dry and forbiddingly acidic. Here, it results in clarity rather than austerity, with orange and lemon citrus flavors and just a hint of Danish-pastry richness.

Drink it with: *Champagne always works well with smoked salmon, even—perhaps especially, given that your palate is at its most receptive during the morning—at brunch.*

FOR THE EGGS

Eggs are a tricky thing to match with wine. Deep but subtle in flavor, and unctuous in texture, they need something with a little richness, but they don't respond well to oak or tannin. Full-flavored unoaked white wines fit that bill—and this soft, golden melon-and-peach-scented Tuscan white is a prime example.

Poggio al Tesoro Solosole Vermentino, Bolgheri, Italy
13% ABV $$ W

FOR THE BACON

The Syrah grape variety often has a certain smoky-bacon or bacon-fat character that sits well with the meat itself. You can taste it in this particularly supple and savory red made by rising-star winemaker Eric Texier in the lesser-known Brézème appellation in France's southern Rhône.

Eric Texier Brézème, Côtes du Rhône, France
13.5% ABV $$ R

IN LIEU OF ORANGE JUICE

We're conditioned to expect orange flavors at brunch, and the Falanghina variety, when grown on the volcanic soils of its native Campania in southern Italy, provides them, producing a rich but zesty and aromatic white wine that is alive with the tang and pleasingly bitter bite of blood orange (juice and zest).

Vesevo Beneventano Falanghina, Campania, Italy
13% ABV $$ W

FOR THE PANCAKES AND MAPLE SYRUP

Caramelized apples, peaches, and yellow plums combine with the cut and bite of fresh apples and a waxy and unctuous texture in this robustly structured sweet wine from the Loire—a wine with the backbone and sweetness to partner with the intensity of maple syrup.

Château Gaudrelle Vouvray Moelleux, France
12% ABV $ SW

56

Fall

THOUGH THEY MOST CERTAINLY ARE NOT IDLE the rest of the year, in the fall—when the grapes are harvested, crushed, and fermented—winemakers survive on pure adrenaline. It is, in many ways, a stressful time. Judgments have to be made that will affect a whole year's labor: From late summer onward, vintners will always have one eye on the weather as they taste the grapes and decide if they are to wait for that little bit more sugar, that extra degree of ripeness, or to preserve the acidity, balancing that against the threat of rain that may spoil the whole crop if the grapes are left on the vine. Long days with very little sleep will follow in the weeks after the decision to harvest, as the grapes come into the winery and are sent to different tanks to begin the journey from juice to wine. For the rest of us, too, this season marks a return to more frenzied activity after the languor of the summer. You feel the change in the tingle and snap in the air. This is the time to put away the light, fresh wines you've been enjoying, in favor of something richer, though not yet the powerful wines that will warm us in winter. Wines made from the Syrah grape variety in France's northern Rhône Valley, with their subtle smoke like bonfires, their hedgerow berries and black pepper, their herbs and earth, best evoke the scents and flavors of this transitional time: wines of "mellow fruitfulness."

*"Season of mists
and mellow fruitfulness!
Close bosom-friend
of the maturing sun;
Conspiring with him
how to load and bless
With fruit the vines
that round the
thatch-eaves run."*

FROM *"ODE TO AUTUMN"*
BY *JOHN KEATS*

YANN CHAVE CROZES-HERMITAGE

FROM Rhône Valley, France
STYLE Spicy Red
GRAPE VARIETY Syrah
PRICE $$
ABV 13.5%

IN THE OFFICIAL HIERARCHY of the northern Rhône Valley, Crozes Hermitage is considered some way behind more prestigious and much smaller appellations such as Hermitage, Côte-Rôtie, and Cornas. Perhaps as a consequence, winemakers tend to be rather less ambitious, but that is not always the case. Among those who make wines that really sing in Crozes Hermitage is Yann Chave, and this red offers a remarkably pure expression of the Syrah grape variety from this part of the world—and at a remarkably good price. Expect a sinuous texture, black fruit of great clarity, and that distinctive note of cracked black pepper.

Drink it with: *Lyon is the gastronomic center of the Rhône Valley—of all France, in many people's opinion—and among its many culinary contributions to the world are its fine pork-and-tripe sausages* (andouillettes)*, a food for which this wine, it almost feels, was invented.*

BUDGET CHOICE

Domaine Alain Voge is based in the prestigious appellation of Cornas, but the estate also makes a more affordable and very characterful 100 percent Syrah under the generic Côtes du Rhône label, with the grapes all coming from the northern part of the valley. It's full of succulent black fruit with subtle smoke.

Domaine Alain Voge Les Peyrouses Côtes du Rhône Syrah, France
13.5% ABV $ R

A SAVORY CLASSIC

Small vineyards on steep slopes characterize the small northern Rhône appellation of Côte-Rôtie (which translates as "Roasted Slope"). And the wines, made in small quantities, are highly sought after, marrying, in this instance, meat, smoke and ethereal fruit. You can cellar them for years, too.

Domaine Jamet Côte-Rôtie, Rhône, France
14% ABV $$$$ R

AN AUTUMNAL WHITE

The Viognier grape variety originates in the Rhône Valley, where it makes fabulously opulent (and expensive) whites in Condrieu. From a nearby vineyard, this is an affordable autumnal alternative: heady ripe apricot and honeysuckle but dry and sprightly on the palate.

Domaine Ogier Viognier de Rosine, Vin de Pays des Collines Rhodaniennes, Rhône, France
12.5% ABV $$ W

AN AMERICAN FALL

Founded by Master Sommelier Greg Harrington, Washington's Gramercy Cellars makes some of the best Syrah in the Americas, in a style that owes a lot to the northern Rhône. Earth, smoke, and spice add the grit to the sleek and seamless black fruit.

Gramercy Cellars Walla Walla Valley Syrah, Washington State, USA
14% ABV $$$ R

57

At a French Restaurant

THE GREATEST CUISINE IN THE WORLD? It's a crazy question, of course—cooking, despite the best efforts of TV executives, is not a competition. But of all the world's great culinary traditions, it is that of France, the originator of the very idea of the restaurant, that has been the most influential, the one that chefs most frequently cite as an inspiration. As with food, so with wine: The classic French wine styles remain the benchmarks and muses for many of the world's winemakers, the grape varieties used to make them now planted in vineyards almsot everywhere wine is made. The two facts are not unrelated: France's wines have developed hand in hand with its food, and part of what makes them so admired is their ability to work well at the table— indeed, many are gawky and awkward, too tannic or acidic, without a gastronomic partner to bring them to life. If that partner hails from the same region (duck for the powerful reds of southwest France, say, or Chavignol goat's cheese for the crisp, grassy whites of Sancerre), so much the better. After all, as any good chef will tell you, "What grows together, goes together."

> *"A day without wine is like a meal without sunshine."*
>
> JEAN ANTHELME BRILLAT-SAVARIN

DOMAINE DU CROS LO SANG DEL PAIS MARCILLAC

FROM SW France
STYLE Dry Red
GRAPE VARIETY
Fer Servadou
PRICE $
ABV 12.5%

LO SANG DEL PAIS translates as "the blood of the country" in the local dialect of this corner of southwest France near the town of Rodez in the Aveyron, and there is an appropriately ferrous, bloody character to this light, succulent red, as well as bright raspberry and blackberry fruit. It's the kind of thing that responds well to a half hour or so in the fridge, emphasizing its refreshing qualities.

Drink it with: *This is what you'd call a bistro wine— unpretentious, served in a* pichet *or carafe, and working with a variety of dishes, its acidity cutting through the* confit de canard *(duck leg) popular in the region, or with a plate of* saucisson *and* terrine.

L'APÉRITIF

Consider French sparkling wine, and the first thing you think of is Champagne. But as we've seen elsewhere in these pages, there's much more besides. Domaine Pfister's Alsatian take on fizz is beautifully done. Mixing Chardonnay (as in Champagne) with the local Pinot Blanc, it's creamily rich and long.

Domaine Pfister Crémant d'Alsace, France
12% ABV $$ SpW

LES FRUITS DE MER

Petit Chablis is the poor relation of the Chablis region, its wines often considerably less vibrant and concentrated than "the real thing." But Domaine Moreau-Naudet is a very skilled producer (it also makes Chablis proper), and this crisp, steely, dry white is an affordable foil for oysters or *coquilles St-Jacques* (scallops).

Domaine Moreau-Naudet Petit Chablis, France
12.5% ABV $$ W

LES PLATS PRINCIPAUX

Domaine Gauby is a trailblazing producer that has helped put the hitherto ignored Agly Valley in the wild hills of Roussillon on the wine map. The rich but nervy white version of this wine would be a fine match for a fish or white-meat main; the herb-inflected red is the choice for French bistro classics such as coq au vin, Toulouse sausage, and *steak frites*.

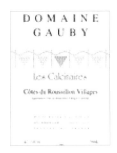

Domaine Gauby Les Calcinaires Rouge Côtes de Roussillon Villages, France
13.5% ABV $$ R

LES DESSERTS

Jurançon's position in the foothills of the Pyrenees, where the grapes are cooled by mountain breezes, helps give its wines their incisive snap of acidity. The grape varieties—Petit and Gros Manseng—bring the tang and sweetness of a tropical fruit salad. The result: an intense sweet wine for *tarte tatin, clafoutis*, or crème brûlée.

Domaine Bellegarde Jurançon Moelleux, France
13% ABV $$ SW

58

A Boys' Night at Home

So, you've lined up the snacks, the TV is tuned to the ball game, and the dining table has been transformed into a card table. One by one, the boys arrive with their six-packs of beer and their banter, and you each adopt your persona. You may be in a neat and cozy suburban house, but between you you're going to conjure up the feel of the Italian restaurant backroom, the Vegas hotel suite, the beat-up old bar by the docks. It's as if the evening has been directed by Martin Scorsese or Francis Ford Coppola, soundtracked by Tom Waits, and you're a bunch of made men. Tough, terse, self-contained, you communicate via the arcane language of poker: all gut-shot straights, under the guns, and flops. Most of you gave up smoking years ago or never took it up in the first place, but a night like this needs a smoke-filled room, and so each of you puffs on a fat cigar. In your glass, you feel there should be bourbon or golden rum, but you gave up hard liquor with the smokes when you got married, and in any case you need a clear head in the morning—you're going to the office, not carrying out a hit. Instead, you've found wines that fit the Montecristo's sweetly acrid flavors: robust reds scented by tobacco, cedar, and chocolate to sip until you fuhgeddaboudit.

"When men drink, then they are rich and successful and win lawsuits and are happy and help their friends. Quickly, bring me a beaker of wine, so that I may wet my mind and say something clever."

Aristophanes

MONTES ALPHA CABERNET SAUVIGNON

FROM Colchagua Valley, Chile
STYLE Powerful Red
GRAPE VARIETY Cabernet Sauvignon
PRICE $$$
ABV 14.5%

AURELIO MONTES IS A KEY FIGURE—an alpha male—in the evolution of Chilean wine from small local concern to major international business, acting as a consultant winemaker and ambassador for Chilean wine worldwide, as well as developing his own labels in Chile, California, and Argentina. This massively concentrated red embodies the Montes approach. With its layers of ripe black-currant-pastille fruit, mocha coffee, and toasty-smoky oak, it's not for the fainthearted or lovers of elegant wine, but its power and muscle mean it does cope very well with a Romeo y Julieta.

Drink it with: *A boys' night in generally involves takeout of some description, but this would work better with a beefy burger than a pizza or Chinese food.*

PLAYING FOR PENNIES

Another alpha male, the outspoken André Van Rensburg, is the key figure at this historic Vergelegen estate. His best wines are rated near the top of South Africa's pecking order, but this more affordable Bordeaux-inspired red blend has an impressive underlying power, a smoothness of texture, an abundance of dark fruit, and a mocha-coffee character.

Vergelegen Cabernet/ Merlot, Stellenbosch, South Africa
14% ABV $ R

AN OFFER YOU CAN'T REFUSE

A super-Valpolicella, made, like its Tuscan equivalents, in a modern style and with a dollop of the "international" grape variety Syrah alongside the indigenous Corvina, this sumptuous red from a single-vineyard has a core of cherries, sweet tobacco, and almonds, as well as some dusky, toasty oak.

Allegrini La Grola, Veneto, Italy
13.5% ABV $$$ R

ONE FOR THE ROAD

Port and cigars may feel a little Victorian, the preserve of the florid of face and the gout-ridden, but it's a combination that works very well when the Port in question has the mix of cigar box, dried plum, and soft sweetness of this dense but mellow blend of two vintages.

Churchill's Crusted Port, Douro, Portugal
20% ABV $$ F

A SMOKIN' WHITE

Not, perhaps, a wine for drinking with a cigar—maybe more a warm-up white before you get to the serious stuff—but this Sauvignon Blanc does have a subtle smoky touch, as suggested by the name, and in part thanks to the short time it spends aging in oak barrels, which also lend a bit of cream and weight to the tropical fruit.

Ferrari-Carano Fumé Blanc, Sonoma County, California, USA
14% ABV $ W

59

Neighborhood Block Party

THE SINGLE BIGGEST consideration when you're planning wine for a large-scale party is price. Nobody is going to expect you to uncork your collection of the finest wines of Bordeaux; nobody will be demanding Champagne. The bar is set low, in other words, and your guests, knowing that you've had to buy a lot of bottles, will be happy if the wine passes the minimum test of being pleasantly drinkable. It is possible, however, to emerge from scouring the lowest end of the market with a little better than that. You can find cheap party wines that are cheerful rather than merely bearable, if you know where to look. The most reliable sources of value reds tend to be found in southern Europe: the Languedoc-Roussillon in France, Puglia and Sicily in Italy, and many of the lesser-known regions of Spain and Portugal. Chile (for red and white) also stacks up well on the quality-to-price ratio, as do many whites from South Africa and southwest France, as well as (though it's rather more hit-and-miss) the Spanish sparkling wine Cava. And versatile rosés from all over the world are rarely expensive.

"Wine maketh merry: but money answereth all things."

ECCLESIASTES *10:19*

LES JAMELLES SYRAH

FROM Languedoc, France
STYLE Rich, Fruity Red
GRAPE VARIETY
Syrah
PRICE $
ABV 13.5%

APPROPRIATELY ENOUGH FOR a party that has as one of its aims the idea of fostering cooperation in the neighborhood, the Les Jamelles brand is the result of a very worthwhile collaboration between a pair of Burgundian winemakers and local growers in the Languedoc region of southern France. It's one of those ubiquitous brands that generally does a good job—and sometimes slightly more than that—at accessible prices. In recent vintages, the Mourvèdre has been particularly tasty, but it's normally much harder to find than this Syrah, which is a typically bright, black-fruited spicy red, suitable for all large party occasions.

Drink it with: *Soft in tannin, and forward in fruit, it works fine solo out of a plastic or paper cup, or for mopping up savory buffet snacks.*

CHEAP, CHEERFUL CHILEAN

The Pedro Ximénez grape variety, most famous for the darkest and sweetest fortified wines of Andalusia, is also widely planted in Chile's northerly Elquí Valley, where it is used to make the national grape spirit pisco. Viña Falernia, however, uses it to create a crisp, floral, and elegant dry white perfect for parties.

**Viña Falernia
Pedro Ximénez,
Elquí Valley, Chile**
13% ABV $ W

A PORTUGUESE STEAL

Brigando is Portuguese for thief (or brigand), and the price of this boldly fruity red makes it a steal. Australia meets Portugal in a blend of Shiraz with the local Touriga Nacional and Tinta Roriz that is hearty and robust without being too tannic and tough to sip all on its own.

**DFJ Vinhos Brigando
Shiraz, Lisbon, Portugal**
12% ABV $ R

CELEBRATE WITH BUBBLES

Codorníu is the elder of the two giants of Cava production (the other being Freixenet), and it puts out a large number of bottles each year. Not every bottle is a world conqueror, but this tangy fizz, with its subtle flavors of apples and nuts, is much improved in recent times and is certainly keenly priced.

**Codorníu Original
Brut Cava, Spain**
12% ABV $ SpW

CUT-PRICE CAPE CLASSIC

Such good value for a crowd-pleasing Cape white blend, largely made using Viognier, which gives the wine its fragrant peach-and-blossom lift. Marc Kent is the talented winemaker behind it, and the succulent red and rosé partners made under the same Wolftrap label are equally good value.

**Boekenhoutskloof
The Wolftrap White,
South Africa**
13% ABV $ W

60

The Liberal Guest

WHEN THE GENTLE PURR OF the Prius on your drive signals the arrival of your liberal guest, it's time to uncork some wines that live up to their avowedly high ethical standards—those that are labeled with the Fair Trade logo. In contrast to coffee and chocolate produced under the banner, there was a time when to drink Fair Trade–certified wine was to put your ethics far ahead of your tastebuds. The movement, which ensures a fair price and fair treatment for all the workers concerned in an accredited wine's production in countries where that is sadly not always the case, as well as funding projects for grape-growing communities, began in earnest a little over a decade ago. Unfortunately, the first bottles to emerge were decidedly sub-par plonk costing a dollar or two more than more conventionally sourced equivalents. The scene has developed, and while much of the produce still leaves a lot to be desired, in the trio of countries where the movement has taken hold—Argentina, Chile, and South Africa—a number of good to very good bottles are now being made in the Fair Trade movement, at prices that feel as "fair" to the buyer as to the seller.

"To dine, drink Champagne, raise a racket, and make speeches about the people's consciousness, the people's conscience, freedom and so forth while servants in tails are scurrying around your table, just like serfs . . . this is the same as lying to the holy spirit."

ANTON CHEKHOV

CITRUSDAL SIX HATS CHENIN BLANC

FROM Western Cape, South Africa
STYLE Tangy Dry White
GRAPE VARIETY Chenin Blanc
PRICE $
ABV 12.5%

THE LEGACY OF SOUTH AFRICA'S shameful political past can still be seen throughout the country, and the winelands are no exception. White ownership remains the norm, and the farmworkers, largely black, often live in conditions of extreme poverty. But the industry is taking steps to improve the situation, and winemaker and farmer Charles Back has been among those who have led the way—both in his own business, Fairview, and in the Fair Trade projects he has helped set up, owned and run by people from previously disadvantaged communities. This very clean, crisp dry white from the Citrusdal project, with its tangy green and custard-apple fruit, is classic South African Chenin Blanc at a very fair price, and with a proportion of the profits going directly to the poverty-stricken local communities.

Drink it with: *The braai, or barbecue, is a South African specialty, and this white would be very happy alongside some barbecued chicken left to steep in a sweet marinade of honey, soy sauce, and paprika.*

THE CHILEAN FAIR TRADE CHOICE

A portion of the profits from Spanish multinational Torres's Chilean brand Santa Digna is used to fund social projects for local grape growers. This vibrant berry-scented sparkling wine made from the unheralded País variety is a highlight in the range.

Torres Santa Digna Sparkling Rosé, Curicó, Chile
12% ABV $$ SpRo

THE ARGENTINIAN FAIR TRADE CHOICE

This is a robust, sumptuous red made by a family business using grapes bought from the Fair Trade–certified Viña de la Solidaridad ("Vineyard of Solidarity"), a group of 19 small farmers whose very name pushes some left-wing buttons.

Soluna Premium Organic Malbec, Mendoza, Argentina
14% ABV $$ R

COOPERATIVE CHOICE

The nearest equivalents to Fair Trade production in Europe are the continent's many cooperatives—groups of growers who collectively own their business. Not all of them are as focused on quality as they might be, but Plaimont in Gascony, France, most certainly is, in this distinctively tangy pineapple-and-mango-flavored white.

Producteurs Plaimont Les Bastions Blanc, Saint-Mont, France
13% ABV $ W

THE ACTIVIST'S CHOICE

The late Bartolo Mascarello was known for his communitarian politics as much as for his very fine wines. (One of his wines was famously labeled with a message campaigning against right-wing Italian prime minister Silvio Berlusconi.) His daughter now carries on his work with this fluent red full of succulent black cherry.

Bartolo Mascarello Dolcetto d'Alba, Piedmont, Italy
13% ABV $$ R

61

40th Birthday

THERE ARE TIMES NOW—as you stand breathless in the gym surrounded by people young enough to be your children, or when the phrase "age inappropriate" emerges, unbidden, as you survey yourself sucking in your gut in the pitiless changing-room mirror—when Benjamin Franklin's famous quote feels like cold comfort.

Never mind judgment or wisdom, you think; *I want my youth back*. Lately, as the big day approaches, you've started reading biographies and magazine profiles of talented, successful individuals, paying undue attention to the age at which they wrote that bestselling novel or started that multibillion-dollar business. Thank the stars for Steve Jobs, who was 41 when his triumphant second act at Apple began, or for Raymond Chandler, 51 when *The Big Sleep* was published. Many wines, too, only come into their own with maturity. In Rioja, in northwest Spain, they understand this

> *"At 20 years of age the will reigns; at 30 the wit; and at 40 the judgment."*
>
> BENJAMIN FRANKLIN

well. A wine labeled "gran reserva" may only be released after a minimum of two years in barrel and three in bottle; many producers will wait much longer. The best, whenever they arrive, have a settled mellow character, though still with a sprightly spring in their step. Like you, they are ready now but still have time on their side.

LA RIOJA ALTA VIÑA ARDANZA RIOJA RESERVA

FROM Rioja, Spain
STYLE Dry Red
GRAPE VARIETY Blend
PRICE $$$
ABV 13.5%

ONE OF THE RIOJA REGION'S oldest producers, La Rioja Alta has stayed true to traditional methods. The company's atmospheric bodega in the wine town of Haro has row upon row of American barrels and dusty, cobwebbed bottles. The wines, too, have a wonderful old-fashioned feel. Where many Riojas today favor big, dark fruit and density, La Rioja Alta's have a leathery, meaty character alongside soft strawberry and subtle coconut and tobacco: complex, mellow, suave, savory.

Drink it with: *The soft flavors and texture, and the subtle savory seam that runs through this Rioja, have an affinity with a perfectly roasted, pink-centered, melt-in-the-mouth piece of lamb.*

BUDGET CHOICE

Another fine old Rioja bodega, making great wines at every price point—in this instance, in the crianza style, with less time spent aging in wood and bottle, and more immediately fruity flavor (strawberry and blackberry), with a dusting of coconut.

CVNE Crianza, Rioja, Spain
13.5% ABV $ R

MONEY'S-NO-OBJECT CHOICE

A stately wine from a stately bodega and sourced from a beautiful property up in the hills of La Rioja Alta, this wine has a complexity of spice box, vanilla, and red and black fruit that deepens and turns more savory the longer it ages.

Marqués de Murrieta Castillo Ygay Gran Reserva Especial, Rioja, Spain
13.5% ABV $$$$$ R

THE AUSTRALIAN PRETENDER

Unlike other classic European grape varieties, Rioja's Tempranillo is not widely planted outside Spain and Portugal. But this beauty, which also features the Portuguese Touriga Nacional, has a punchy, vibrant, violet-edged fruitiness and velvety tannins.

SC Pannell Tempranillo/ Touriga Nacional, McLaren Vale, Australia
14% ABV $$ R

THE WISE WHITE

The whites of Rioja are less well known than the reds, but in the right hands they provide an attractive alternative to oak-aged Chardonnay. Here, the oak aging lends a nuts-and-vanilla backdrop to the peach and white-flower fruit.

Bodegas Muga Rioja Blanco, Spain
13% ABV $$ W

FRENCH AND AMERICAN OAK

The two main sources of wooden barrels in winemaking are France and the USA. In Rioja, winemakers have traditionally used American oak, which lends "sweeter" characters, such as coconut and vanilla. Recently, however, many modern producers have switched to more expensive French barrels, which have a toastier, spicier impact.

62

Moving On

VERY FEW PEOPLE EXPECT to have a job for life anymore. The very idea of staying with one organization from graduation to retirement, of a 40-year career of incremental progress punctuated by the occasional switch of desk or floor, feels, for better or worse, like something from another age. In today's flexible (some might prefer "brutal") labor market, we've barely got our feet under the desk before we're plotting our next career move (or having it plotted for us); we prefer to run the risk of looking disloyal rather than complacent or lacking in drive. The wine world is rather less tumultuous than most industries. Many producers have been owned and run by the same family for generations or, in some instances, centuries. But it doesn't exist in a vacuum, and over the past few decades, winemakers have been subject to the same challenges and opportunities of globalization as any other professionals. Most winemakers now consider it a vital part of their training to spend their formative years working vintages all over the world, before beginning their careers in earnest. And many wine producers have broadened their horizons by setting up new ventures overseas. To mark an occasion that is much more frequent than it once was, then, it must be a bottle from one of these vintners—the kind who prefer not to sit still.

> *"What you are to do without me I cannot imagine."*
>
> ELIZA DOOLITTLE IN PYGMALION
> BY GEORGE BERNARD SHAW

CHATEAU STE. MICHELLE EROICA RIESLING

FROM Washington State, USA
STYLE Aromatic White
GRAPE VARIETY Riesling
PRICE $$$
ABV 11%

ERNIE LOOSEN IS ONE of Germany's best winemakers. He is also one of the world's most restless. He has operations in both the Mosel Valley (Dr. Loosen, owned by his family for 200 years) and the Pfalz in his native land, and since 1999 he has also been helping produce one of North America's finest Rieslings in Washington State. To do so, he teamed up with Chateau Ste. Michelle, the largest producer in the region. The result is a piercingly pure dry white with vibrant stone fruit underscored with lime and minerals.

Drink it with: *This wine, with its bright streak of lime, has great affinity for fish in a Thai marinade of lime and lemongrass.*

BUDGET CHOICE

José Manuel Ortega gave up a lucrative job in investment banking to pursue a dream of making wine. He now has interests in Chile, his native Spain, and Argentina, where he produces this fragrant, floral white from the local speciality grape, Torrontés.

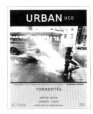

O Fournier Urban Uco Torrontés, Mendoza, Argentina
13% ABV $ W

MONEY'S-NO-OBJECT CHOICE

Aubert de Villaine is the proprietor of the great Burgundy estate Domaine de la Romanée-Conti (DRC). He also makes similarly refined red wines (from, in this instance, Merlot and Cabernet Sauvignon) in the Napa Valley, with his American wife's cousins, owners of Hyde Vineyards.

HdV Belle Cousine, Hyde de Villaine, Carneros, California, USA
14.5% ABV $$$$ R

AN AUSSIE IN PORTUGAL

One of a wave of Australian winemakers that brought a new approach to European winemaking in the 1980s and 1990s, David Baverstock has stayed in Portugal's sunny Alentejo, applying his skills to luscious, full-flavoured wines such as this red made from Portugal's most favored indigenous red grape variety, Touriga Nacional.

Esporão TN, Touriga Nacional, Alentejo, Portugal
14% ABV $$ R

A FRENCHMAN IN OZ

Having greatly expanded his family's holdings and profile in the Rhône Valley, Michel Chapoutier took his organic-minded philosophy to Australia, where he produces expressive, spicy red wines from the Rhône variety Syrah (known as Shiraz in Australia).

Domaine Terlato & Chapoutier lieu dit Malakoff Pyrenees Shiraz, Victoria, Australia
14.5% ABV $$$ R

At an Organic Restaurant

YOU'VE WALKED PAST THIS PLACE a few times now, but you've always thought it wasn't the place for you. It's not that you have anything against organic practices. Quite the opposite: You respect anyone who is prepared to take the long-term view and choose hard work over short-term profit and quick chemical fixes, and you're quite happy buying organic fruit and vegetables at the grocery store. But something about this venture rubbed you up the wrong way. Something about the way it was using its organic status to position itself in the market made you suspicious of its motives and intentions. The prices, too, bring out the skeptic in you. Maybe organic food is more expensive to produce, but is it really *that* much more? The place has a whiff of the hemp hair shirt about it: all politics and no pleasure. The wines are probably organic, too, and you've never been convinced by that idea. However, one day, you stop at the window and find yourself looking at the wine list. You notice the name of one of your favorite producers, one you had no idea was organic. Then you spot another, and another. Maybe there's something in this. Maybe you'll stop by after all . . .

"Let food be thy medicine and medicine be thy food."

HIPPOCRATES

MATETIC CORRALILLO SYRAH

FROM San Antonio, Chile
STYLE Powerful, Spicy Red
GRAPE VARIETY
Syrah
PRICE $$
ABV 14.5%

CHILEAN WINEMAKERS like to point out that their country is effectively sealed off from the rest of the winemaking world by a *cordon sanitaire* formed by the Pacific Ocean, the Andes Mountains, the Antarctic, and the Atacama Desert, leaving its vineyards relatively free from pests and disease and, therefore, well suited to organic production. Top producer Matetic, in the up-and-coming coastal San Antonio district, has taken this a stage further, farming with biodynamic principles that take into account the phases of the moon and other outré ideas (see "Organic Guest"). Whether it's the result of the biodynamic methods or just good winemaking is a matter of debate, but the result has been wines of the highest quality, particularly when using the Syrah grape variety in a number of different bottlings. This, the least expensive, shows off the estate's trademark mix of power, depth, and clarity, all freshly milled black pepper, inky ripe blackberries, and svelte, smooth texture.

Drink it with: *A rare hunk of organically reared steak.*

FOR ORGANIC SALAD

An estate best known for its sweet wines from Sauternes, Château Guiraud has recently switched to organic production after being acquired by a consortium that includes a pair of Bordeaux's leading producers. This classic dry white blend of Semillon and Sauvignon Blanc has a honeyed grapefruit zip.

Le G de Château Guiraud Bordeaux Blanc, France
13.5% ABV $$ W

FOR ORGANIC PASTA

On the site of a former monastery, Badia a Coltibuono is a historic Tuscan estate, but the owners have the true believer's passion of the recent convert when it comes to organic production. This pure, limpid, cherry-scented and herb-inflected red is all the better for it.

Badia a Coltibuono Chianti Classico, Tuscany, Italy
14% ABV $$ R

FOR ORGANIC STEAK

Michel Chapoutier is an engaging and provocative presence in French wine and one of its foremost exponents of biodynamic and organic methods. He presides over a prolific vinous empire, with projects in France and Australia, but the Rhône is his home. This meaty, spicy 100 percent Syrah from the north of the region is one of his best cuvées.

Chapoutier Les Meysonniers, Crozes-Hermitage, Rhône Valley, France
13.5% ABV $$ R

FOR ORGANIC ASIAN

A small family-owned estate run by a husband-and-wife winemaking team, Te Whare Ra has a natural approach that involves biodynamic and organic practices and leads to wines of grace and clarity. This dry Riesling uses 30-year-old vines for an explosive mouthful of lime zest and juice and a feel that is as cool as a steel blade.

Te Whare Ra D Riesling, Marlborough, New Zealand
12.5% ABV $$ W

64

The Wine Geek

"An old wine-bibber having been smashed in a railway collision, some wine was poured on his lips to revive him. 'Pauillac, 1873,' he murmured and died."

FROM THE DEVIL'S DICTIONARY BY AMBROSE BIERCE

THE WINE GEEK is the most difficult guest of all. It's not so much that their obsession with wine makes them rude or dull, but rather that they are almost impossible to please. They pride themselves on being fussy, on having taste so discriminating that practically nothing satisfies them, and, as with any obsessive, they can't switch out of their hypercritical mode—like a cineaste placed in front of a rom-com, they are temperamentally incapable of enjoying a "commercial" wine. How to deal with a guest like this? Go obscure. It barely matters if they actually like it: For a wine geek, "liking" is only a small part of wine's appeal; it's the sense of exploration and discovery that gets them going. So head off the beaten track to one of the many emerging wine-producing nations and regions in Europe. Try central, eastern, or southeastern Europe (Slovenia, Croatia, Georgia, Greece) or the lesser-spotted areas of France (names such as Jura, Marcillac, Fenouillèdes), Spain (Bierzo, Manchuela, Ribeiro), or Italy (Etna, Aglianico del Vulture, Valle d'Aosta).

MORIC BLAUFRÄNKISCH

FROM Burgenland, Austria
STYLE Spicy Elegant Red
GRAPE VARIETY
Blaufränkisch
PRICE $$
ABV 13%

AUSTRIAN WINE FELL into the doldrums internationally in the 1980s, after a scandal in which dangerous chemicals were found in a handful of producers' wines. But like an aging singer/songwriter making a triumphant comeback with stronger, wiser material later in life, in the past decade Austria has become one of the names to drop for the average wine geek. The whites, made from Grüner Veltliner and Riesling, were the first to find favor. Latterly the reds, particularly from local Blaufränkisch and Zweigelt, have begun to attract plaudits. When they are as good as those made by cult producer Moric, you can understand why. Fragrant, silky, and elegant like Pinot Noir, with a subtle peppery spice, this is a wine that anyone can love.

Drink it with: *The Austrian classic dish of breaded veal, the Wiener schnitzel, will appeal to the wine geek in three ways: Its flavors are not so strong that they'll intrude on the wine; it's a local dish for a local wine, an association that the wine geek treasures; and as a 1970s cookbook staple, it has a perverse retro-ironic appeal.*

THE OBSCURE SPANIARD

The wine geek has moved on from the better-known Spanish regions such as Rioja and Ribera del Duero, to emerging hotspots such as Manchuela, where growers are making beautiful wines from the hitherto unheralded Bobal grape variety. This is a juicy, light red to serve cool.

Bodegas y Viñedos Ponce Clos Lojen, Manchuela, Spain
13.5% ABV $$ R

THE GEEKY JACKPOT

For the layman, this French rarity is a complex, thoroughly delicious wine: nutty, curry-spicy, with dried and fresh orange citrus. For the wine geek, it hits the jackpot: historic yet obscure, and made in an unusual way (it ages, like Fino Sherry, beneath a layer of yeast). They could talk about it for hours.

Berthet-Bondet Château-Chalon Vin Jaune, Jura, France
13.5% ABV $$$$$ W

THE ORANGE WINE

You've heard of red, white, and rosé . . . But orange wine? Made from the juice of white grapes that spend a much longer time in contact with their skins than usual, these are wine-geek catnip, and when made well, like this one from Slovenia, they are intensely flavored, spicy, and tannic like a red.

Kabaj Rebula, Goriška Brda, Slovenia
13.5% ABV $$$ W

AGED IN AMPHORAE

Several producers in the ex-Soviet republic of Georgia are reviving the tradition of making wine in clay amphorae. This collaboration between Swedes, Americans, and Georgians is a fine example: pure red and black currants and a hint of cherry skin and nuts.

Pheasant's Tears Saperavi, Kakheti, Georgia
12.5% ABV $$ R

65

At Your Neighborhood Bar

FOR THE MOST PART, WINE IS LOW ON your local bartender's list of priorities. Beer and spirits are what pay the bills, and getting to grips with wine and all its complications is a headache they'd rather outsource. There are exceptions, of course, and not just if you're lucky enough to live near to a dedicated wine bar. You can find wine-loving bartenders in unexpected places, and they often put fine-dining restaurants to shame with their knowledge, range, and enthusiasm. Some may even have installed the latest wine fridges, enabling them to keep opened bottles of wine for weeks—an innovation that has transformed the selection of wines offered by the glass, since fastidious bar owners no longer need to worry about opening a wine when they're likely to sell only a single glass. However generous or mean the range on offer, the wine you're looking for in a bar is very different from your choice in a restaurant. Without food to soften their harder edges, tannic red wines, highly acidic white wines, and obviously oaky wines of all kinds can seem a little less appealing. Brightness of fruit and softness of texture are the desired effects, but as always with wine, the elusive concept of balance is the key to how well it slips down.

"If we sip the wine, we find dreams coming upon us out of the imminent night."

D. H. LAWRENCE

CONO SUR BICICLETA PINOT NOIR

FROM Central Valley, Chile
STYLE Lively, Fruity Red
GRAPE VARIETY Blend
PRICE $
ABV 13.5%

PINOT NOIR HAS BEEN growing in popularity in Chile in recent years, and Cono Sur, led by its highly regarded winemaker Adolfo Hurtado, was one of the first producers in the country to take it seriously. The company makes some more powerful, age-worthy versions as well, but this widely distributed cheapie is more the kind of thing you'd be likely to find and choose in your local bar. The price is certainly right (it's one of the best-value examples of a grape variety that tends to be expensive), but it also has the abundant berry fruitiness and softness, coupled with just the right amount of freshening acidity, to have by the glass without food.

Drink it with: *Unpretentious bar food such as sausages and fries or nachos and cheese will work just fine, though the wine is surprisingly versatile with food and without.*

THE BAR IN WINTER

A dark-colored wine with lots of guts and concentration, as you might expect from South Australia, this spends a few months in oak barrels, too, but it's not in the least bit heavy. The fruit is bright and brambly, not jammy, and the tannins are soft—an effortlessly drinkable winter warmer.

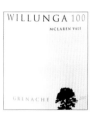

Willunga 100 Grenache, McLaren Vale, Australia
14% ABV $$ R

IN THE BEER GARDEN

There's a rounded texture and generous fruit to the unoaked white wines of Alsace that make them pretty perfect for solo sipping, though this creamy, just-dry Pinot Blanc, with its apple blossom flavors and crisp, faintly mineral finish, is a versatile food wine, too. Try it with fish, white meat, creamy sauces, or cheese.

Domaine Zinck Pinot Blanc Portrait, Alsace, France
13% ABV $$ W

A CHEEKY GLASS OF FIZZ

It's unlikely you'll be looking to blow your budget on Champagne when you've just popped in for a quick drink in your local, but a glass of fizz needn't be prohibitive. Italian Prosecco and Spanish Cava are both considerably cheaper, or you may find that your bar stocks a sparkling wine from Burgundy that offers similar apple and toasty flavors to Champagne at much lower prices.

Cave de Lugny Crémant de Bourgogne, Burgundy, France
12% ABV $$ SpW

BY-THE-GLASS ROSÉ

A punchy dry or off-dry rosé makes an excellent by-the-glass choice because it has some of the character and flavors of red wine with none of the astringency. This robust southern French selection, from a great-value region where the Rhône meets the Languedoc, has plenty of succulent redcurrant, as well as a sprinkling of pepper.

Château Guiot Rosé, Costières de Nîmes, France
13% ABV $ Ro

Splitting Up

IF, AS TOLSTOY SAID OF FAMILIES, all happy marriages are alike, but every unhappy marriage is unhappy in its own way, it follows that the end of every relationship has its own unique character. Still, breakups do tend to fall into categories. Some couples manage to find time for a final, rueful glass or two to mark a truce and the acceptance of bygones. The wine for this kind of breakup—quiet, dignified, bittersweet—is very different from the one demanded by the more spectacular, raging, reconciliation-is-impossible, if-I-ever-see-you-again-it-will-be-too-soon split. In this case, each party is looking to erase the past, to make an assertion of independence, and to mark the beginning of something new, something better. They may even convene their friends and family for that most postmodern of celebrations, the breakup party. And it may just have to be Champagne on ice when the longed-for divorce is finalized.

"He taught me housekeeping. When I divorce, I keep the house."

ZSA ZSA GABOR

PIEROPAN SOAVE CLASSICO LA ROCCA

FROM Veneto, Italy
STYLE Dry White
GRAPE VARIETY
Garganega
PRICE $$
ABV 12%

A CERTAIN LIMPID COOLNESS is the main feature of this graceful white wine from a single vineyard in the Soave region of northeast Italy. You wouldn't call it insipid, but it is calm and composed—gently persuasive rather than confrontational in its presentation of its pear, melon, honeyed-almond, and tarragon-like herb flavors. This is a drink for forgiving and, rather than forgetting, remembering, a little wistfully perhaps, the good times rather than the bad, and for toasting a better future for both of you as you go your separate ways.

Drink it with: *Whether ruing a bad romance or celebrating newfound freedom, treat yourself to a dish from the city that has played host to so many luxurious meals and where this wine features on so many restaurant lists, Venice—something like sepe al nero, cuttlefish cooked in its own ink.*

AFTER THE EXPENSIVE DIVORCE

You may be in the mood to drink away the blues, wash away the bitterness, and will yourself into the future, but between them, your ex and your lawyers have left you with next to nothing to spend. Thankfully, unlike you-know-who, Torres's evergreen crisp dry white has never let you down—and though it may cleanse your palate, it won't clean you out.

**Torres Viña Sol,
Penedès, Spain**
12.5% ABV $ W

THE RUEFUL RED

The conciliatory red alternative to the Soave is this no less restrained and harmonious red, also from the northeast of Italy. With its light red berries and haunting floral fragrance, it is soft, lithe, and pure—a reminder of more innocent times and worth spending a little of the money you saved by keeping your split out of the courts.

**Monte dei Ragni
Valpolicella Classico
Superiore, Veneto, Italy**
13.5% ABV $$$ R

I'VE ALREADY FORGOTTEN YOU

The battle is officially over: You never have to see *them* again. Your closest friends are here, and, sweetly, they've even brought along a little eye candy. Are you ready for all that? Well, this sensual white wine may persuade you to stick a toe back in love's dangerous waters. Its heady, almost erotic perfume of honeysuckle and apricots awakens sensations you thought had died with your past relationship.

**Domaine Cuilleron,
La Petite Côte,
Condrieu, Rhône, France**
13% ABV $$$$$ W

THE BITTER END

Some of us don't want to forget, much less forgive. We want to dwell on the pain a little first, if only to fix in our minds how bad this feels, so we never repeat the mistake again. We chase the truth of catharsis, not the trite chimera of closure, and the (delicious) seam of bitterness and tar that runs through this otherwise pretty red wine chimes precisely with a mire-wallowing and score-settling mood.

**Endrizzi Serpaia
Morellino di Scansano,
Tuscany, Italy**
12.5% ABV $ R

67

A Girls' Night at Home

FOR A GIRLS-ONLY OCCASION, the wines that feel most appropriate are those that have been made by women winemakers. There was a time when that would not have left you all that much to choose from. Indeed, for much of European history, women weren't even permitted to enter the winery at a certain time of the month, the fear being that their very presence would spoil the wine. Even when this stubbornly persistent superstition had all but died out, finding women in positions of power in the wine world was unusual (Champagne's two very famous widows, 19th-century Mme. Clicquot Ponsardin—the Veuve Clicquot—and 20th-century Mme. Bollinger, being two notable exceptions). Things have slowly changed, however, and while there are still not as many women in prominent winemaking jobs as there are men, and while some countries still lag behind, the mere fact that a wine was made by a woman is no longer newsworthy. In fact, if you were feeling particularly ill disposed toward the opposite sex, you could quite easily drink only wine made by women, a different bottle each day, for the rest of your life. *Salut!* Or maybe, *Touché!*

> *"There's nothing a man can do that I can't do better and in heels."*
>
> GINGER ROGERS

CASA MARÍN CARTAGENA PINOT NOIR

FROM Chile
STYLE Elegant Red
GRAPE VARIETY Pinot Noir
PRICE $$
ABV 14%

MARÍA LUZ MARÍN'S STORY is an inspiring one. She spent many years working as a winemaker in what was a male-dominated Chilean winemaking scene, always with one eye on creating her own venture, where she would be free to make the wines she wanted. When the time came to strike out on her own, she chose a region—the San Antonio Valley, toward the Pacific coast to the west of Santiago—that was still *terra incognita* as far as wine was concerned. But in the decade or so since, she has proved that its cooler climate and soils were ideally suited to making elegant, vibrant whites and lighter reds. She developed the Cartagena brand as a way of offering more affordable wines, but as this Pinot shows, they still carry the distinctive Marín stamp: graceful, elegant, red-fruited, supple, and subtly mineral.

Drink it with: *This works fine on its own, since the tannins are supple and soft, but is also excellent with white meat, duck, and meaty fish such as salmon.*

BUDGET CHOICE

Victoria Pariente—who named her bodega in Rueda, northwest Spain, for her father—is a great believer in the potential of the region's local grape variety, Verdejo. In Pariente's hands, it makes for a crisp Sauvignon Blanc-like aromatic white that mixes tropical fruit and wild herbs.

Bodegas José Pariente Verdejo, Rueda, Spain
13% ABV $ W

MONEY'S-NO-OBJECT CHOICE

One of the most highly regarded domaines in one of the most highly regarded wine regions in the world, Domaine Leflaive is owned and run by the visionary Anne-Claude Leflaive. This is a truly great white wine for a very special occasion: rich yet pure, harmonious, and vital Chardonnay.

Domaine Leflaive Chevalier-Montrachet Grand Cru, Burgundy, France
13% ABV $$$$$ W

DON'T CALL ME SHEILA

Vanya Cullen has made her family estate in Western Australia one of Australia's most respected since taking over the winemaking in the late 1980s, becoming the first woman to earn the title of Qantas Winemaker of the Year. Marked by its intense, pure black fruit and fine tannins, this is typical of her style.

Cullen Margaret River Red, Western Australia
12.5% ABV $$ R

A KIWI PIONEER

Jane Hunter is no longer in charge of day-to-day winemaking at her eponymous winery, but this pioneer of Marlborough Sauvignon Blanc still runs the show as managing director. This wine remains a fine example of the region's style: punchy, pungent gooseberry, passion fruit, and elderflower in a bright, crisp package.

Hunter's Sauvignon Blanc, Marlborough, New Zealand
13% ABV $ W

68

Thanksgiving

WE THINK OF THANKSGIVING as a quintessentially North American holiday, and it's true that the turkey, pumpkin pie, and big-game football are not celebrated in the same way anywhere else in the world. Still, the roots of Thanksgiving can be found in the wider European tradition of the harvest festival. The occasion that was widely thought to be the original Thanksgiving celebration—a feast organized by Puritan settlers in Plymouth, Massachusetts, in 1621—was conceived as a way of giving thanks for a particularly bountiful harvest, a custom brought over from England. Even today, you don't have to go too far during fall in Europe to come across some form of celebration to mark the harvest, with wine regions providing some of the most lively and entertaining *fêtes de vendanges* (France) or *fiestas de la vendimia* (Spain). As you consider the wine for this occasion, then, it's to this tradition that you are harking back, a tradition where wine is the symbol not just of gratitude but of our connection to the land. For a suitably North American act of homage, the wine that works best as a match for the rather varied fare on offer—echoing the acidity of the cranberry sauce, cutting through the fat of the turkey without overpowering it; providing a freshening counterpoint to the starch of the sweet potatoes—is a fine domestic Pinot Noir.

"Our rural ancestors,
with little blest,
Patient of labour when
the end was rest,
Indulg'd the day that
hous'd their annual grain,
With feasts, and
off'rings, and a
thankful strain."

FROM *"IMITATIONS*
OF HORACE"
BY *ALEXANDER POPE*

BERGSTRÖM CUMBERLAND RESERVE PINOT NOIR

FROM Willamette Valley, Oregon, USA
STYLE Elegant Red
GRAPE VARIETY Pinot Noir
PRICE $$$
ABV 12%

PRODUCED BY AN AMERICAN FAMILY (with a little Swedish thrown in), this wine is very much a pan-generational collaboration, with the vineyards planted by Mom and Pop Bergström and now worked by winemaker son Josh along with his brothers and sisters. Perfect for an American family occasion, it's a gorgeous expression of Willamette Valley Pinot Noir, lithe and fluent in texture, and laced with bright red fruit and what winemakers in the grape variety's home in Burgundy (a region this wine nods toward stylistically) would evocatively refer to as *sous-bois* (or undergrowth).

Drink it with: *Their racy acidity, fragrant perfume, and silky-smooth tannins mean the lighter reds made from Pinot Noir are always a popular choice for Thanksgiving turkey, cutting through the richer meat and standing up to some of the sweeter accompaniments, without in any way overwhelming the lighter cuts.*

THANKSGIVING ON A LOWER BUDGET

Once touting itself as a virtual winery, owning neither a winery nor vineyards, Firesteed now has the former but still gets its fruit from local growers in Oregon and, for its other wine, Italy. Look past the marketing, however, and you have a plump, fleshy, turkey-ready modern Pinot at a very decent price.

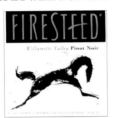

Firesteed Pinot Noir, Willamette Valley, Oregon, USA
14% ABV $$ R

THANKSGIVING TREAT

Sandhi is a relatively new collaboration between some big names on the California wine scene (including the man behind the cult Cab Screaming Eagle), but it's already made a name for itself with some of the country's most delicate and elegant Pinot Noirs in Santa Barbara.

Sandhi Evening Land Tempest Pinot Noir, Santa Barbara, California, USA
13.5% ABV $$$$ R

A THANKSGIVING TOAST

Taittinger is one of Champagne's most respected houses, and its Comtes de Champagne is one of the region's greatest wines. But if you're looking to stick to an American theme, the company also has a presence in California, where it produces this cool, elegant fizz with its appropriately autumnal orchard fruit.

Domaine Carneros by Taittinger, Brut Vintage, California, USA
12% ABV $$$ SpW

FOR THE PUMPKIN PIE

For that traditional American Thanksgiving classic, pumpkin pie, this is a modern American classic sweet wine, made from Orange Muscat grapes that have been fortified with spirit but that retain their brightly aromatic fruit character, with mandarin and peach leaping out from the glass.

Quady Essensia Orange Muscat, Central Valley, California, USA
15% ABV $$ SW

Hosting Colleagues at Home

THE SUCCESS OF ANY ORGANIZATION—public or private, large or small—depends on the chemistry of the group. The idea is, of course, that weaknesses are counterbalanced by strengths, with the mercurial creative matched by the stolidly industrious, and the impetuous whiz kids offset by the wise old diplomats. Bringing the different parts together is the purpose of this evening, and so you may want to choose wines that embody the notion of the whole being greater than the sum of its parts. These are examples of the art of blending, a skill that is important in all wines, but that is particularly evident when winemakers bring together two or more grape varieties. In the classic red wines of Bordeaux, for example, plump Merlot puts flesh on the strong bones of Cabernet Sauvignon; in the traditional southern Rhône blend, Syrah's spice and perfume meets Grenache's sweet fruit and Mourvèdre's gutsy power. There are classic white combinations, too, such as Bordeaux's much-imitated recipe, where zesty, aromatic Sauvignon Blanc is given weight and body by Sémillon, or the mix of the white juice of red grapes Pinot Noir and Pinot Meunier with Chardonnay in Champagne. As with the right mix of colleagues, the blended wine is an inexact chemistry that, in the right place, at the right time, can feel more like alchemy.

"From wine what sudden friendship springs!"

FROM "THE SQUIRE AND HIS CUR," BY JOHN GAY

ALVARO CASTRO AND DIRK NIEPOORT DADO

FROM Portugal
STYLE Rich, Spicy Red
GRAPE VARIETY Blend
PRICE $$$$
ABV 14%

A WINE THAT TAKES the principles of blending to extremes, this delicious curio from Portugal is the work of two of the country's best winemakers: Alvaro Castro, the master of the Dão region, and Dirk Niepoort, the talented maverick of the Douro. As the name Dado suggests, the wine uses grapes from the vineyards of both partners—old vineyards, too, which have been planted with a mix of local grape varieties. That means it's a blend of field blends, a way of making wine where all the varieties are harvested and fermented together. This is unusual in modern winemaking, where producers generally prefer to harvest and vinify separately, since each variety ripens at a different time. But in the right vineyards, and with skilled winemakers, it can bring complexity, and that has certainly been the case here for a dense, intensely spicy, and perfumed red that's full of brambly fruit, textured with grippy tannins and lifted with freshening acidity.
Drink it with: *The culinary equivalent of the blended wine is the single-pot stew. In Portugal, that may mean the rich, mildly spicy* chanfana *of goat or lamb, with garlic, paprika, onions, and red wine, with or without peri-peri sauce.*

A BUDGET BORDEAUX BLEND

In St.-Emilion, Merlot tends to be the senior partner in the blend— in this case, with varying proportions of either or both of the Cabernets Sauvignon and Franc, depending on the vintage. Made by one of the region's most respected names, this is generous in fleshy black fruit, texture, and price.

Christian Moueix St.-Emilion, Bordeaux, France
13% ABV $$ R

A CLASSIC RED RHÔNE BLEND

While solo Syrah rules in the northern Rhône Valley, in the south it tends to team up with Grenache and Mourvèdre, sometimes supported by a cast of other minor players. Not here, though, where Grenache plays the lead in a chunky, crunchy production from the Rasteau village.

Domaine des Coteaux des Travers Réserve Rasteau, Rhône, France
13.5% ABV $$ R

A MATES' WHITE BLEND

Although the blend here includes a little Chardonnay, it's very much inspired by the whites of the Rhône, with the other two of the titular amigos being Marsanne and Roussanne (plus a tiny drop of Viognier). The result is a wine that mixes herbs, yellow plum, and more tropical fruit into a seamless, rounded whole.

McHenry Hohnen 3 Amigos White, Western Australia, Australia
13.5% ABV $$ W

A GREAT SOUTH AFRICAN WHITE BLEND

South African winemakers produce some of the world's most arresting white blends, generally featuring old-vine Chenin Blanc as a key component. The innovative Eben Sadie's flagship white adds Grenache Blanc, Clairette, Viognier, and Chardonnay for a nervy, intense, exotic white that's worth clubbing together with colleagues to buy.

Sadie Family Wines Palladius, Swartland, South Africa
14% ABV $$$$ W

70

Election Night

ON ELECTION NIGHT, WE GET TRIBAL. It's like following a sports match but with something more than a trophy or regional pride at stake. Unless you're a psephologist or statistics junkie, however, it can be a long night of charts, graphs, polls, and projections. You also have to get through more hours than is healthy of network TV's political news coverage. To liven up proceedings, you could try a drinking game. You'll need a pair of wines to represent the two political affiliations. And since all tribal politics rely to a degree on broad-brush stereotypes, that's how the wines will be treated. Here's how you play. Every time the left makes a gain, you pour a glass of Burgundy—a region where the wineries are generally owned and run by the vigneron. When the right wins, you switch to Bordeaux, a more corporate world, where the châteaux are more likely to be owned by financiers and luxury-goods corporations. If you're still awake by the time the final result comes in, crack open the Champagne. The brand you choose (grower or *grande marque*) and the reason (to commiserate or celebrate) will likewise very much depend on your political tribe.

> *"Thinking is not to agree or disagree. That's voting."*
>
> ROBERT FROST

THYMIOPOULOS EARTH AND SKY

FROM Naoussa, Macedonia, Greece
STYLE Powerful Red
GRAPE VARIETY Xynomavro
PRICE $$$
ABV 14.5%

BEFORE THE NIGHT begins in earnest, before the exit polls have come in and partisanship takes over, try a bit of neutrality, in spirit if not flavor: a wine from the home of democracy. Greek wine is underrepresented in stores around the world, but it has some fine raw material to work with, grapes you don't find anywhere else such as, in this case, Xynomavro. This version from winemaker Apostolos Thymiopoulos is made from old vines (he also makes a cheaper, lighter style from young vines if you can't find this bottling). It's an explosively aromatic, densely textured wine, with cherry and damson fruit, offering plenty to chew over.

Drink it with: *Lamb souvlaki—strips of lamb marinated in lemon, oregano, mint, and garlic, and served in pita bread with* tzatziki, *a yogurt, cucumber, and mint dressing.*

THE LEFT CHOICE

Since inheriting his small family domaine, Pascal Roblet has worked diligently at improving the quality of his patch of vines in the villages of Pommard and Volnay. This exceptionally pretty, limpid Pinot Noir from the lesser-known village of Monthélie has Roblet's trademark fragrance at a more accessible price.

Domaine Roblet-Monnot Monthélie, Burgundy, France
13% ABV $$$ R

THE RIGHT CHOICE

A powerful argument in favor of corporate investment, Château Belgrave has been much improved since it was acquired by the large merchant house Dourthe. It is officially ranked as one of Bordeaux's crus classés, but it remains affordable, relatively speaking—a classic cedar-and-cassis claret.

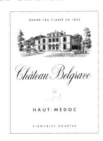

Château Belgrave, Haut-Médoc, Bordeaux, France
13.5% ABV $$$ R

CELEBRATING ON THE LEFT

Bérèche is one of the leading exponents of Champagne's burgeoning selection of farmer fizz, those bottles that are made by growers who would once have sold their grapes to the big houses. Their Non-Vintage offering is biscuity rich but racy and refined.

Champagne Bérèche & Fils Brut Champagne, France
12% ABV $$$ SpW

CELEBRATING ON THE RIGHT

Like so many top Champagne brands, Krug is now owned by the LVMH luxury-goods group, but it has lost none of its charm in the handover. A combination of full-bodied texture, silky mousse, exotic fruit, and electric acidity just about justifies its elevated price.

Champagne Krug Grande Cuvée, Champagne, France
12% ABV $$$$$ SpW

71

Hanukkah

THE LIGHTING OF THE NINE-BRANCHED CANDELABRA, or menorah, may be the centerpiece of the eight-day festival of lights, but as with many holidays food also plays a major role in the festivities. Much of that food will be fried in oil, which has a symbolic as much as a culinary purpose, harking back to the miracle of the oil in the original Hanukkah story, when a single day's supply of oil burned for eight days in the holy temple of Jerusalem after the Maccabees had seized it back from the ancient Syrians. Staples include the potato, onion, and matzo pancakes known as latke, served with apple sauce and sour cream, and the small doughnuts *sufganiot*, dusted with sugar and sometimes filled with jelly. Dairy products, particularly cheese, are also commonly served, inspired by the story of Judith, a Jewish heroine celebrated alongside the Maccabees at Hanukkah, who is said to have softened up a soldier from the persecuting Syrian army with cheese and wine before dealing him a fatal blow with a sword. Finally, there are the items that owe more to Jewish feasting tradition than to Hanukkah per se: the braised or slow-roasted beef brisket, a baked root-vegetable kugel, pretzels . . . And the wine? Strictly observant Jews will seek out kosher bottles (see opposite), which are now produced all over the world. Others may look to the ever-improving wines of the Holy Land. But many will be sourcing only versatile bottles to share with the many dishes on offer at what is often a relaxed family occasion.

"Chanukah is the festival of lights. Instead of one day of presents, we have eight crazy nights."

FROM *"THE CHANUKAH SONG"* BY *ADAM SANDLER*

CHÂTEAU VALANDRAUD KOSHER WINE

FROM St.-Emilion, Bordeaux, France
STYLE Powerful Red
GRAPE VARIETY Blend
PRICE $$$$$
ABV 13.5%

KOSHER WINES HAVEN'T ALWAYS had the highest reputation for quality, their image rather tied up with the icky, sticky, low-quality sacramental red wines put out by the more famous brands in the American market. Part of the problem has been the processes used to make them *mevushal*—that is, sterilized (pasteurized) so that they can be handled by non-observant Jews. Until recently, the wines were boiled, destroying their delicate flavors. But things have moved on a great deal in recent years. Modern kosher wines use a process known as flash pasteurization, which is considerably less damaging. And several serious producers are now producing kosher bottlings. For non-Jewish producers, it's not an easy undertaking, since kosher laws demand that the grapes and wine must be handled only by observant orthodox Jews throughout the process. For this wine, a team of assistant rabbis is enlisted to handle the grapes from a reserved patch of vines, guided by the estate's chief winemaker. I haven't tasted the kosher cuvée, but the owners insist that it compares in quality to the non-kosher bottling, which, on the single occasion I tried it, was a sumptuous, inky, densely rich red.

Drink it with: *At Hanukkah, this is the one to have with the beef brisket or other roasted red meats.*

A VALUE KOSHER CALIFORNIAN

Founded by a Jewish family of Slovakian descent who came to the USA after World War II, Baron Herzog has a range of well-made, well-distributed, and well-priced kosher wines. This off-dry Chenin, with its apple and tropical-fruit tang and subtle sweetness is a good Hanukkah all-rounder.

Baron Herzog Chenin Blanc, Clarksburg, California, USA
14% ABV $ W

A KOSHER ISRAELI WHITE

Israel has a vibrant winemaking scene, where many wines (though not all, by any means) are kosher. They can be hard to find outside the country, but this Burgundian-inspired and kosher barrel-fermented Chardonnay is a worthy upmarket candidate for the Hanukkah holiday table.

Domaine du Castel C Blanc du Castel, Israel
13% ABV $$$ W

LATKE FIZZ

The cleansing crispness and fizz of good Champagne is ideal for washing down plates of fried food such as latke, and it also matches well with another Hanukkah favorite, smoked salmon. It's handy, then, that this popular favorite is available in a kosher bottling.

Champagne Heidsieck & Co. Monopole Brut NV, Champagne, France
12% ABV $$ SpW

FOR THE SUFGANIOT

As light and fluffy as the doughnuts, and with a similar dusting of sweetness, this softly sparkling kosher white from Italy is uninhibited in its floral and fresh-grape aromas and has sufficient acidity to keep it the right side of the sweet-to-sickly continuum.

Bartenura Moscato, Asti, Italy
5.5% ABV $ SpW

72

At a Vegetarian Restaurant

IF THE PROPRIETOR IS WORTH his or her organic sea salt, then the wine list at a vegetarian or vegan restaurant should be as varied as its conventional peers. Certainly, from a food-matching point of view, it would need to be, since vegetarian dishes are no less diverse in their range of flavors than those that involve meat. A dish where the dominant flavor is tomato, for example, works best with a different wine (Chianti seems to do the trick) than a dish based on mushrooms (Pinot Noir). Indeed, this would be the case if there were a piece of animal protein on the plate: Generally, it's the sauce, or whatever provides the strongest flavor in the dish, that will dictate what wine you pair with it. Where a vegetarian restaurant may feel constrained in its choice of wines, however, is in deciding whether those wines should be vegetarian themselves. The concept sounds absurd, but it's an important consideration for strict vegans who wish to avoid all animal substances in their diet. Many wine producers use albumen (egg white), isinglass (fish bladder), or gelatin as a means of clarifying their products before bottling. (Bull's blood, which used to serve the same purpose, has long since fallen from favor.) Most vegetarian, and certainly vegan, restaurants stock only wines that use alternative methods. And if you're drinking at home, the list opposite is 100 percent vegan.

"Animals are
my friends . . .
and I don't
eat my friends."

GEORGE BERNARD SHAW

BONTERRA CHARDONNAY

FROM Mendocino,
California, USA
STYLE Dry White
GRAPE VARIETY
Chardonnay
PRICE $$
ABV 13.5%

THERE HAS ALWAYS BEEN some crossover between the organic and vegetarian movements, so it's no surprise that the USA's largest and most prominent exponent of organic and biodynamic wine growing should also produce wines without animal products. This typically rich, sun-kissed, barrel-aged Chardonnay has an array of tropical fruit and a rich, creamy, almost nutty texture. The ample, hedonistic quality gives the lie to the reactionary idea that anything tagged vegan is necessarily joyless and austere.

Drink it with: *That nutty tang, exotic fruitiness, and weight would work well with a Moroccan couscous dish featuring dried fruit (apricots, dates), cinnamon, cumin, cilantro, and almonds.*

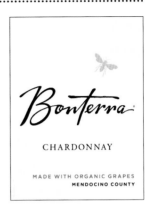

A VEGAN APÉRITIF

A gentle waft of herbs infuses the pear, apple, and citrus fruit in a fizz that does not stint on flavor despite its light and airy texture. Once again, an organic wine—and one that, as well as starting a vegan meal, has a touch of sweetness to serve alongside a fruit sorbet.

La Jara Prosecco Spumante Extra Dry, Veneto, Italy
11% ABV $$ SpW

FOR VEGETARIAN STEWS

From another biodynamic producer, this time in France's southern Rhône Valley, this red blend is beefy in structure and has a hit of bacon in flavor but is still nonetheless suitable for vegans. With its notes of olive, rosemary, and black fruit, it would work well with a rich vegetable, bean, and olive casserole.

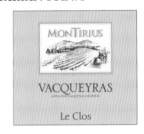

Montirius Le Clos Vacqueyras, Rhône, France
14.5% ABV $$ R

FOR A VIETNAMESE SALAD

Viognier, once a rarity found only in the Rhône Valley, has spread across the winemaking world rapidly in recent decades. Family-owned Yalumba has become something of a specialist in the variety, showcasing its heady honeysuckle-and-apricot perfume to great effect in this vegan-friendly bottle.

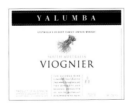

Yalumba Y Series Viognier, Eden Valley, Australia
13% ABV $$ W

FOR MUSHROOM-BASED DISHES

A simple but cheerful Pinot Noir that is mostly about the fresh strawberry and raspberry fruit but has a very faint earthy character and a cranberry acidity that echoes the mushroom flavor while cutting through its slippery texture.

Maison Roche de Bellene Bourgogne Pinot Noir Vieilles Vignes, Burgundy, France
12% ABV $ R

73

The Conservative Guest

"I'M ASSUMING," your Republican guest says more or less the moment he climbs out of his SUV and just before lighting his cigar, "that we won't be having any of that French crap we had the last time?" With a tight smile, you assure him that, no, you won't be. But not because you agree with him that "we do it better than them now anyhow" (not always, anyway). It's just that you really can't face going over the same old dreary discussion about Iraq, Chirac, and treachery yet again, or hearing him make that crack comparing the French to a simian fond of both a certain stinky dairy product and a particular form of military "tactic" in a tone that suggests he thought up the remark himself. No, this time you're better prepared: no French wines—in fact, nothing "Yurpean" at all. You've gone straight for the patriotic mother lode, the vinous equivalent of freedom fries: a choice of wines from across the good old US of A. Well, almost. You couldn't resist throwing in a ringer: a wine that says Washington State on the label but is made by a man with a certain je ne sais quoi.

> *"The business of Progressives is to go on making mistakes. The business of the conservatives is to prevent the mistakes from being corrected."*
>
> G. K. CHESTERTON

JOSEPH SWAN VINEYARDS MANCINI RANCH ZINFANDEL

FROM Russian River Valley, Sonoma, California, USA
STYLE Dry Red
GRAPE VARIETY Zinfandel
PRICE $$$
ABV 13.5%

IN ITS WAY, THE ZINFANDEL GRAPE VARIETY seems to embody all that is good about that cornerstone of the Republican worldview, the American Dream: an immigrant that came to the States and reinvented itself, becoming an all-American success story in the process. Its most familiar incarnation is the big, blueberry juicy-jammy style, but Joseph Swan's version is more about elegance than power, with the tang of plum skin, and Pinot Noir–like silken texture and red-berry fruit.

Drink it with: *Duck—perhaps even one that your gun-loving, hunting-and-fishing guest has killed and brought along for the occasion.*

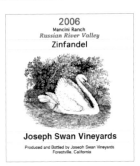

FROM NEW YORK STATE

The Finger Lakes region of New York State is the USA's answer to Germany's Mosel Valley, with the cool climate well suited to the hardy Riesling grape variety, which here has an electrifying steeliness and energy, topped with a floral prettiness of aroma and lime and stone fruit.

Hermann J. Wiemer Dry Riesling Reserve, Finger Lakes, New York State, USA
12% ABV $$ W

FROM VIRGINIA

Wine has been produced in Virginia since the English arrived more than 400 years ago. Famously, Thomas Jefferson also tried and failed to make wine here. Today, it's best known for lushly aromatic Viognier and powerfully fruit-driven Cabernet Franc such as this example, which has the variety's trademark floral perfume and pure, polished black fruit.

Barboursville Vineyards Cabernet Franc Reserve, Virginia, USA
14.5% ABV $$ R

FROM OREGON

Oregon's wine scene has a hippie-alternative feel (biodynamic methods are common here) that may not appeal to your guest. But the unshowy elegance of family-run Bergström's Chardonnay and Pinot Noir crosses the political divide: The satin-sheet soft and honeyed Old Stones is a suave diplomat.

Bergström Old Stones Chardonnay, Willamette Valley, Oregon, USA
12.9% ABV $$$$ W

CÔTES DE L'ETAT DE WASHINGTON

Frenchman Christophe Baron works in a patch of land in Washington State's Walla Walla Valley, where the stony soil resembles the famous *galet* pebbles found in vineyards in Châteauneuf-du-Pape. The Syrah he planted in his Cailloux vineyard yields a wine of spice, meat, olives, tar, and dark fruit, similar in style and quality to the best of the Rhône.

Cayuse Vineyards Cailloux Vineyard Syrah Walla Walla Valley, Washington State, USA
14.5% ABV $$$$$ R

74

50th Birthday

BY THE TIME OUR 50TH BIRTHDAY COMES AROUND, most of us feel comfortable in our skin. We know who we are—we have come to terms with our strengths and weaknesses and have no need to prove anything to the world. This is the prime of life, a time when we can look back on many achievements, even as we are still achieving and dreaming of more. No doubt our tastes have changed over the years: In film, music, and art, we are no longer so easily impressed by the loud or the obvious; we become more irritated by the flashy and the too eager to please, and we may seek out more nuance, shades of gray, subtlety. In wine, then, we may find kinship with the red wines of Burgundy, in eastern France. Made from a fickle grape variety (Pinot Noir) in a part of the world where the weather is not always kind to the vine, red Burgundy is a wine that requires patience, skill, and perseverance on the parts of both the grower and the buyer. But the hunt is worthwhile. It speaks softly, but for those with the willingness to listen, no other wine style offers the grace, poise, and silk-sheet sensuality of great red Burgundy.

"To be yourself in a world that is constantly trying to make you something else is the greatest accomplishment."

RALPH WALDO EMERSON

DOMAINE DU COMTE ARMAND VOLNAY

FROM Burgundy, France
STYLE Elegant Red
GRAPE VARIETY
Pinot Noir
PRICE $$$
ABV 13%

OFFICIALLY, THIS WINE, from the village of Volnay, comes roughly halfway down Burgundy's complex quality hierarchy, which runs from wines made exclusively from the small top-ranked grand cru vineyards at the top, to wines made from grapes throughout the area—labeled simply "Bourgogne"—at the bottom. But there's nothing third-rate here: supple, succulent, and harmonious, with Pinot Noir's ethereal red fruits and subtle earthiness.

Drink it with: *Like all classic European wines, Burgundy has developed with the local food culture, and a classic dish such as* poulet de Bresse *(or the best free-range chicken you can find locally) with wild mushrooms would serve this wine well.*

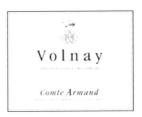

BUDGET CHOICE

Budget red Burgundy is almost an oxymoron: The prices of decent bottles tend to start where other less renowned regions stop. But this delicate, floral, entirely pretty red shows it is possible to find affordable reds in the region.

Domaine Hudelot-Noëllat Bourgogne Rouge, Burgundy, France
13% ABV $$ R

MONEY'S-NO-OBJECT CHOICE

There are grander names in Burgundy than Jean Grivot, but none is making better, more sensual, or more thrilling wine. From a top grand cru site (Richebourg), this will bring out the poet in you: lucid, fluent, serene, ethereal.

Domaine Jean Grivot Richebourg Grand Cru, Burgundy, France
13% ABV $$$$$ R

A SPECIAL SOUTHERN PINOT

Pinot Noir has adapted to New Zealand better than anywhere else in the world outside its Burgundian homeland. Here, it makes slightly plusher, more brightly fruited, but still silkily seductive wines, such as this one from the country's Pinot specialist region, Central Otago.

Rippon Vineyard Mature Vine Pinot Noir, Central Otago, New Zealand
14% ABV $$$ R

SOMETHING A BIT LESS STRONG

Chablis is in the far north of Burgundy, not all that distant from Champagne, and its white wines share the famous fizz's incisive crispness, as well as an invigorating steeliness to sharpen the palate for oysters.

Daniel Dampt Chablis, Burgundy, France
12.5% ABV $$ W

GREAT RED BURGUNDY VINTAGES

Burgundy's climate is cool, and conditions are highly variable from year to year, so each vintage has a markedly different character. Among the more highly regarded vintages for red Burgundy are 2010, 2009, 2005, 2002, 1999, 1996, 1995, 1990, 1989, 1988, 1985, 1978, 1971, 1969, 1964, 1959, 1957, 1952, 1949, 1947, and 1945.

75 The Wine Snob

IN THE MINDS OF SOME PEOPLE, anyone who shows more than a passing interest in wine is, by definition, a wine snob. But let's ignore those killjoys for now and concentrate instead on defining the real wine snob. These are distinct from true wine lovers in that they don't really love wine at all. What they love is demonstrating their superiority (social, financial, or intellectual) through their choice of wine. The wine snob is the person who buys only wines that have been given a score of 95 points or more from a famous wine critic; who dismisses anything outside the traditional classic wine regions of the world; who has absorbed the showy syntax, but not the semantics, of wine talk. For their own good, as much as yours, this snobbery deserves to be challenged, and to do this you could serve "blind" wines from so-called lesser regions that are every bit as good as their more famous peers. If your guest is hung-up on Bordeaux, you could pick one of the many excellent interpretations of the classic Bordeaux blend (Cabernet Sauvignon, Merlot, and a few other varieties) from California, Washington State, Chile, or Tuscany. If they only drink Burgundy, try a Pinot Noir from New Zealand or Oregon, or a new-wave Australian Chardonnay from Victoria or the Adelaide Hills. They won't remain a snob for long.

"It's a naive domestic Burgundy without any breeding, but I think you'll be amused by its presumption."

JAMES THURBER

CHÂTEAU TOUR DES GENDRES LA GLOIRE DE MON PÈRE

FROM Bergerac, France
STYLE Middleweight Red
GRAPE VARIETY Blend
PRICE $$
ABV 13.5%

BORDEAUX IS THE WINE SNOB'S habitual choice. The region's top bottles are status symbols in the manner of a Swiss watch or an haute couture brand. In terms of flavor, if not cachet, however, you can find something very similar from the neighboring southwest French region of Bergerac, where winemakers use the same grape varieties and techniques in much less celebrated sites. With its notes of cigar box and cassis, and its refined texture, this blend is a dead ringer for Bordeaux bottles costing many times the price.

Drink it with: *Classic French meat dishes such as navarin of lamb—a shoulder of lamb cooked slowly with vegetables and wine.*

THE AMERICAN RED BURGUNDY

For the hard-core wine snob, Burgundy outscores Bordeaux, since the prices are just as high but the finest wines are produced in much smaller quantities. However, Oregon has proved itself adept at making wines from the same red grape variety, Pinot Noir, with great purity of fragrant red fruit and a subtle earthiness.

Eyrie Pinot Noir, Oregon, USA
13.5% ABV $$$ R

THE KIWI WHITE BURGUNDY

Strikingly elegant, with a touch of flint (think of the smell of a cigarette lighter being struck) and layers of orchard fruit, vivid acidity, and a long, clear finish. This is such fine Chardonnay that your guest will surely feel he's been served a wine from Burgundy's famous Côte d'Or.

Kumeu River Estate Chardonnay, Auckland, New Zealand
14% ABV $$$ W

THE NOT SANCERRE

The wine snob likes his Sauvignon Blanc to come from the variety's spiritual home, Sancerre and Pouilly-Fumé in France's Loire Valley, but it is now made to a very high standard all over the world and rarely better than in South Africa. From vineyards on the Cape peninsula, this is a rich, rounded, but vital mix of elderflower, tropical and citrus fruit, and minerals.

Cape Point Vineyards Stonehaven Sauvignon Blanc, South Africa
13% ABV $$ W

THE UN-TEUTONIC RIESLING

Another star of the Cape, this is the answer to anyone who claims— as the snob is wont to do —that fine dessert wines can only ever come from the top estates of Germany and Austria. It's gorgeously sweet and peachy, with a squeeze of lime freshness that prevents it from being cloying.

Paul Cluver Noble Late Harvest Riesling, Elgin, South Africa
10.5% ABV $$ SW

76

Renewal of Vows

THERE ARE PERHAPS THREE MAIN REASONS why a couple may want to renew their wedding vows. The first and most idealistic comes from a shared feeling of pride and wonder that the marriage remains as strong today as it did when the couple first got together, and a desire to tell the word about it. The second may be no less romantic in its way, and also involves a stable and loving couple, but is inspired by a long-simmering regret that the wedding itself wasn't quite the festival of romance for which the couple had hoped, so they're doing it again, maybe several years or decades down the line, this time without the malign interference of bad weather, illness, or family. The third and perhaps most compelling reason of all has more in common with the Burton/Taylor style of romantic engagement. It's a last-ditch attempt to bring calm to a tempestuous relationship, a bandage to cover the wounds of an affair or betrayal, a gesture of hope and faith over festering reality. While the motivations may be different, the spirit of the ceremony is the same—it's about taking control of your lives and not letting things drift, about looking to the future rather than to the past—a spirit symbolized in your wine choice of bottles from estates, regions, or countries that have shown, sometimes in the face of the most difficult odds, the same capacity for renewal.

"She sealed his lips with a wanton kiss; 'Though I forgive your breaking your vows to heaven, I expect you to keep your vows to me.'"

FROM THE MONK
BY MATTHEW GREGORY LEWIS

EBNER-EBENAUER GRÜNER VELTLINER

FROM Weinviertal, Austria
STYLE Crisp Dry White
GRAPE VARIETY
Grüner Veltliner
PRICE $$
ABV 13%

THIS SCINTILLATING DRY WHITE is an apt choice for a renewal ceremony in so many ways, not least the fact that it is made by a wife-and-husband team (Marion Ebner and Manfred Ebenauer). It also hails from a country, Austria, that, through the sheer persistence and talent of its best winemakers, has overcome the mother of all PR disasters, after a wine-adulteration scandal hit the news around the world and decimated exports in the 1980s. The style of the wine itself is appropriate, too: There's something of the joy of spring, that season of renewal, about its lively acidity and green herbal aromas, coupled with orchard fruit and subtle white pepper and celery salt.

Drink it with: *Ideal with your shellfish appetizer at the renewal dinner—clam linguine, crab salad, or shrimp.*

A GERMAN RENAISSANCE

German wine is still trying to recover from the damage perpetrated on its image by the oceans of mediocre Liebfraumilch it churned out in the 1970s and '80s. The Rheinhessen was the source of much it, but young winemakers such as Stefan Winter have done much to challenge the sweet-and-watery stereotype of the region with zesty, racy, mineral, dry whites.

Winter Estate Riesling QbA, Rheinhessen, Germany
12% ABV $$ W

A SPARKLING RECOVERY

One of the most familiar names and labels in the wine world, Champagne Mumm's Cordon Rouge had a long period in the doldrums while under the ownership of multinationals Seagram and Allied Domecq, but is now back on graceful, refined form since being acquired by Pernod Ricard in the mid-2000s. One to toast the future.

Champagne GH Mumm Cordon Rouge Brut NV Champagne, France
12.5% ABV $$ SpW

A CHANGE IN THE WEATHER

Just as a change in weather can lift our mood and make us predisposed to look kindly on the world and the people in it, sometimes a good vintage is all it takes to change perceptions of a wine region. The 2009 vintage certainly did that for Beaujolais, reminding drinkers that there was more to the region than Nouveau in charming red-fruited wines like this.

Domaine Jean-Paul Dubost Beaujolais-Villages Tracot, Beaujolais, France
12.5% ABV $$ R

BACK FROM THE DEAD

Few regions have enjoyed quite such a remarkable turnaround in fortunes as Priorat in Catalonia, a largely forgotten and abandoned corner of Spanish wine until the 1980s, when intrepid producers began to attract worldwide attention and crazy prices for craggy, powerful, mineral reds such as this. Perfect for your renewal-meal red meat.

Cellar Pasanau Ceps Nou, Priorat, Spain
14% ABV $$$ R

77

Winter

It might not feel that way in late February, when your body craves light and warmth and its cupboard of vitamin D is bare, but it is possible to romanticize winter. The season, as the Canadian essayist Adam Gopnik says in his book *Winter*, has its own particular beauty and charm—a pared-back austerity and purity that give us space to think and dream. Without winter, Gopnik writes, "we would be playing life with no flats or sharps, on a piano with no black keys." Without winter, too, we would not have the joy of returning to the snug indoors, of throwing off thick coats and boots to slump, ruddy-cheeked, beside a roaring fire, with a book and a warming glass. The perfect winter wine addresses both these sides of winter's allure. Nebbiolo from Piedmont in northwest Italy is a strong wine, its alcohol usually tipping the scales above 14 percent, its tannins sandpaper rough, its flavors tarry; it's a wine to beat away the cold, to make you cozy. But above all this structure and power, the dreaming takes place: in the frosty snap of acidity and the aromas, captured like an essence in some magical northern distillery, of roses and red fruits, of mushrooms and forest floor. With age, the best have an ethereal grace that summons the spirit of Schubert's *Winterreise*, the equivalent, in liquid form, of a view of snowy fields in the pale winter light.

"What good is the warmth of summer, without the cold of winter to give it sweetness?"

John Steinbeck

PRODUTTORI DEL BARBARESCO BARBARESCO

FROM Piedmont, Italy
STYLE Powerful Red
GRAPE VARIETY
Nebbiolo
PRICE $$$
ABV 14%

NEBBIOLO REACHES ITS GREATEST HEIGHTS in the two famous Piedmontese red-wine zones Barbaresco and Barolo. Such great heights, alas, that the wines are highly prized, with prices to match. One producer capable of making Barbaresco with the requisite mix of pretty floral and deeper, tarry flavors at accessible prices is local growers cooperative Produttori del Barbaresco, whose wines also have an accessibility of texture, with refined tannins.

Drink it with: *The local pasta—tajarin, a fresh egg-yolk pasta somewhere between spaghetti and tagliatelle in shape—served with butter and white truffles or a rich meat ragù.*

BUDGET CHOICE

If Barbaresco and Barolo are out of your financial league, then another alternative might be a Nebbiolo from the wider Langhe region. These wines are designed to be drunk younger than their more serious siblings, but in the hands of this top Barolo producer, G. D. Vajra, they are a polished, perfumed delight.

G. D. Vajra Nebbiolo Langhe, Piedmont, Italy
14% ABV $$ R

MONEY'S-NO-OBJECT CHOICE

One of Italy's most celebrated wines, made in a traditional way with nearly four years in Slavonian oak barrels, is a transparent articulation of Nebbiolo's paradoxical allure. Power, depth, acidity, and tannin combine with haunting, delicate, evanescent aromas and flavors.

Giuseppe Mascarello e Figlio Barolo Riserva Monprivato Cà d' Morissio, Piedmont, Italy
14% ABV $$$$$ R

INVERNO BIANCO

Winter calls for richer whites than the rest of the year, if only to match the richer foods we're inclined to eat. Piedmont's Arneis variety has a broadness of texture and orchard fruit that works well with roast birds—here pepped up with a perky underlying mineral acidity.

Cornarea Roero Arneis, Piedmont, Italy
13% ABV $$ W

A BEAKER OF THE DEEP SOUTH

This red is made from the Primitivo variety in Italy's heel and brings the southern sun to a winter's glass: plump with the ripest of dark cherries and plums, but with a twinge of licorice and dark-chocolate bitterness. It's deep, sumptuous, and cozy.

Paolo Leo Primitivo di Manduria, Puglia, Italy
14.5% ABV $$ R

78

On a Cruise

In the age of the low-cost, no-frills airline, where air travel has lost both its wonder and its patina of glamor, the allure of the cruise is easy to understand. It's hard to feel part of the international jet-set when you're stuck in a three-hour line for a full-body search; easy to forget the wonders outside the window when you're wedged in a cattle-class aisle seat. Cruise ships, by contrast, still offer a hint of romance, a sense of being connected to the golden age of the luxury ocean-going liners, the *Queen Mary* or the RMS *Olympic*. On a cruise there is the feeling of the traveling being as important as the arrival, of the normal rules and rhythms of life being suspended, where we have the time and space to think as we gaze toward the distant horizon. There is also, perhaps, a deeper connection to all those travelers who have gone before us, from the movie stars of Hollywood's Golden Age right back to the ancient Greek soldier, the Arabic spice trader, the British wine merchant. Indeed, wine's history has been shaped by maritime trade, with the early success of many of its established names—Bordeaux, Port, Sherry, Madeira—dependent on their proximity to a major port or a trading route. It is these bottles that remind us of this romantic seafaring past—and that add to its contemporary glamor—that are worth stowing on board a cruise ship today.

"Why do we love the sea? It is because it has some potent power to make us think things we like to think."

Robert Henri

TE MATA AWATEA CABERNET MERLOT

FROM Hawkes Bay, New Zealand
STYLE Structured Red
GRAPE VARIETY Blend
PRICE $$$
ABV 13.5%

THIS BEAUTIFULLY BALANCED Bordeaux-inspired red has strong nautical associations. It takes its name from one of the vineyards used to produce it, which is owned by a family with links to the shipping trade who named it for a famous ship, the SS *Awatea* (depicted on the label), which plied the route between New Zealand and Sydney before being converted into a troop carrier during World War II. There's a maritime influence inside the bottle, too: Hawkes Bay's warm climate is moderated considerably by the cool breezes that come off the nearby Pacific Ocean, and that helps give the wine its balance of intense black fruit, fine tannins, and freshening acidity.

Drink it with: *On a Pacific cruise, with a roast shoulder of New Zealand lamb.*

FIRST STOP, BORDEAUX

From the apt if slightly misleadingly named Entre Deux Mers region of Bordeaux (it translates as "Between Two Seas," when really it falls between the Garonne and the Dordogne rivers), this is a rich and tangy blend of Sauvignon Blanc and Semillon to honor Bordeaux's maritime history.

Château Mont-Pérat Blanc, Bordeaux, France
13% ABV $$ W

PORT OUT

Brandy was first added to the red wines of Portugal's Douro Valley to give them extra resilience as they made their way to England on stormy seas. Though producers are still known as shippers today, the addition of spirit is now an entirely stylistic choice, bringing depth and body to this suavely sweet, barrel-matured wine.

Taylor's Ten Year Old Tawny Port, Douro, Portugal
20% ABV $$$ F

STARBOARD HOME

Only fortified wines made in Portugal's Douro Valley can be labeled as Port, but Andrew Quady makes Port-style wines (hence the name) using the same grapes in California to great effect, as in this chocolate-and-dried-fruit-flavored example.

Quady's Batch 88 Starboard, California, USA
20% ABV $$ F

ON A MEDITERRANEAN YACHT

The choice for a sundowner or to accompany lunch on deck as you island-hop around the Med, this sophisticated modern Greek white from Crete, in true mind-broadening style, brings together the local (Vilana) with the well travelled (Sauvignon Blanc) for a zesty but rounded oak-aged white.

Mediterra Anassa White, Crete, Greece
13.5% ABV $$ W

60th Birthday

WE MIGHT EXPECT A 60TH BIRTHDAY to be a sedate, gently nostalgic affair—a time for gathering close friends and family for a smart meal and a few glasses of something classy, or maybe a few quiet days away. But that's not always the case. Stories abound of the rich and powerful using the event as a way of showing off their wealth and status. It might be the $1 million paid by Blackstone founder Steve Schwarzman to have Rod Stewart perform a private concert to see in his seventh decade. Or it might be the similar amounts shelled out by British retail magnate Sir Philip Green to Chris Brown, Robbie Williams, The Beach Boys, and Stevie Wonder to provide the background music, while guests including Kates Hudson and Moss and Naomi Campbell—each of whom had been flown to a sealed-off resort near Cancún, Mexico, on Green's private jets—nibbled on $80 burgers, reportedly decked out in identical T-shirts bearing the legend "PG60," like some gruesome A-list take on the sports team on a pre-season tour. While the rest of us might wince at this sort of conspicuous excess, the more charitable among us might acknowledge that, in their own somewhat crass way, Schwarzman and Green are sending a message that many of us would endorse: You are never too old to party. And if, for your own bash, you don't have the billionaire's ability to buy access to the stars, you can always buy one of their wines instead.

> *"60s is the new 40s.*
> *The only difference is*
> *the level of experience."*
>
> ANONYMOUS

FRANCIS COPPOLA DIAMOND COLLECTION CABERNET

FROM California, USA
STYLE Powerful Red
GRAPE VARIETY
Cabernet Sauvignon
PRICE $$$
ABV 14.5%

OF ALL THE MANY CELEBRITIES who have dabbled in wine, the great director of *Apocalypse Now* and *The Godfather* is the one who has taken the business most seriously—almost at the expense, it seems, of his film work—since he's gone about building a large commercial enterprise in California that includes several different labels. Here he uses fruit sourced across the state to produce a typically sweet-fruited, voluptuous red, with coffee, balsamic, and spicy oak. Hefty in scale, it's a big wine for the big screen.

Drink it with: *Boldly flavored meat dishes such as* daube *of beef cooked with olives and red wine.*

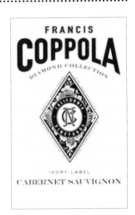

ROCK STAR FOR HIRE

The British rock star Sting persuaded Bruce Springsteen and Lady Gaga, among others, to perform with him at his 60th birthday party. For yours, you could do worse than call in Sting's full-throated and very slick, if slightly expensive, red from his biodynamic estate in Tuscany.

Tenuta il Palagio Sister Moon IGT Toscana, Tuscany, Italy
14% ABV $$$$ R

THE NAME'S BOND

This is not a celebrity wine per se but is one associated with one of the silver screen's most enduring characters, James Bond, who shows his usual fastidious taste in the finer things in life in choosing this rich, rounded Champagne with its flavors of *tarte tatin*.

Champagne Bollinger Special Cuvée Brut NV, Champagne, France
12.5% ABV $$$ SpW

HOLLYWOOD BY WAY OF OTAGO

Like Francis Ford Coppola, New Zealand actor Sam Neill, star of *The Piano* and *Jurassic Park*, was also bitten hard by the wine bug, and he is very much involved in his estate in New Zealand's rugged Pinot Noir-specialist region Central Otago, whence comes this seamless, scented red.

Two Paddocks Pinot Noir, Central Otago, New Zealand
13.5% ABV $$$ R

THE SPORT STAR

Maybe it's that 19th-hole thing, but golfers have a disproportionate representation in the list of celebrity wine proprietors, with names including Greg Norman, Nick Faldo, Arnold Palmer, and the South African Ernie Els, who is involved with this punchy, zesty, tropical-fruity Cape white.

Ernie Els Big Easy White Western Cape, South Africa
13.5% ABV $ W

80

Silver Wedding Anniversary

TWENTY-FIVE YEARS. It just doesn't feel like a quarter of a century, or maybe it's just that a quarter of century doesn't feel like it used to. If, on your wedding day, you'd looked back to the you 25 years before, well, you were just a kid, almost a different person. But looking back to the you that got married . . . You haven't changed all that much, have you? You're the same person, you think the same way, even if the wedding photos clearly show you don't look the same. Einstein was right, and at this rate you'll be celebrating your 50th anniversary thinking today was yesterday. "Enough!" your partner says. "Enough of all this moaning. This isn't a day for gloomy reflections on the meaning of life. Perhaps we shouldn't have bought those watches—all this heavy stuff about time. You should be happy!" And they're right, as usual: You do need to snap out of it; you do have a lot to celebrate. You need to adjust your perspective. Time flies when you're having fun, and for the most part, these 25 years really have been fun. Tonight's party—with a little wine to match the silver theme, a few friends, and family—will be fun, too. As for the next 25 years? You can think about that tomorrow.

"Being with you and not being with you is the only way I have to measure time."

JORGE LUIS BORGES

SILVER OAK CELLARS NAPA VALLEY CABERNET SAUVIGNON

FROM: Napa Valley, California, USA
STYLE
Powerful Red
GRAPE VARIETY
Cabernet Sauvignon
PRICE $$$$
ABV 14.5%

THE SYMBOLISM IS PERFECT, of course: the silver oak representing the strength of your marriage at the close of its 25th year. But this is a classic wine of its type, too, from one of Napa's best producers. Strong, robust like an oak, swathed in velvety tannins, with a dark core of plum, black currant, and blackberry fruit, some savory olive, and a kiss—maybe more of an embrace—of spicy, toasty oak in barrel form. Like your marriage, it ages well, too, and you may even be able to source the appropriate vintage for this anniversary.

Drink it with: *Strong food. Try roasted meat such as shoulder of lamb, belly of pork, or rib of beef.*

BUDGET SILVER

More appropriate symbolism on the label here—*argento* is Italian for silver, as well as a reference to the wine's origins—but this is an excellent party wine: affordable, full of the fragrant plummy fruit characteristic of the Malbec variety, and with a smooth and fleshy feel.

Argento Malbec, Mendoza, Argentina
14% ABV $ R

ORIENTAL SILVER

Reinvigorated in recent decades, and with a history dating back to the ancient world, the Lebanese wine scene now features a number of appealing producers. Massaya, part-owned by the family behind Châteauneuf-du-Pape's Vieux Télégraphe, is among the best, as seen in this spicy, concentrated, Rhône-alike.

Massaya Silver Selection Red, Bekaa Valley, Lebanon
14% ABV $$ R

WHITE SILVER

One of the original success stories in Australian wine's rise to global prominence in the 1980s and 1990s, Wolf Blass remains a source of consistent quality today. This Chardonnay, a blend of fruit from cooler South Australian spots, is creamy and fruit driven without being broad or flabby.

Wolf Blass Silver Label Chardonnay, South Australia
13.5% ABV $$ W

SPARKLING SILVER

Think Italian sparkling wine, and most of us probably bring to mind Prosecco and Lambrusco. But Franciacorta from Lombardy is the country's nearest equivalent to Champagne, using the same methods and grape varieties to make, in this instance, a breezy, biscuity all-Chardonnay fizz. The "25" in the name, incidentally, refers to the months, rather than years, between harvest and release.

Berlucchi Franciacorta Brut 25 Chardonnay, Lombardy, Italy
12.5% ABV $$$ SpW

81

Team-Building Tasting

PSYCHIATRISTS DIVIDE THE WORLD into extroverts and introverts, placing us all on a sliding scale between the two. The modern office might be understood in a similar way, with the distinction between those who enjoy team-building exercises and believe strongly in their positive effects on the working environment, and those who are more skeptical. Put these two personality types together on, say, a military assault course or a self-built white-water raft, and the results may not be quite what the organizers had in mind. Put them together in a comfortable room with a selection of wines, however, and the likelihood of a positive outcome seems far higher. The aim of the exercise isn't just to enjoy a drink together. A spittoon (spit-bucket) should be employed, and a task element will bring a little structure. Using the wines here, you can get to understand the basic differences between five of the most commonly used grape varieties, the first step in wine appreciation. Divide into teams. Compare, contrast, discuss. Then bring in a competitive touch: a blind tasting to see who can identify each variety. When you're done, pour a glass of your favorite and let (constructive) discussion begin.

"There's no 'I' in team."

"Yes, but there are three in his name."

AUTHOR'S EXPERIENCE OF
TEAM-BUILDING DAY

CASILLERO DEL DIABLO CABERNET SAUVIGNON

FROM Central Valley, Chile
STYLE Fruity, Powerful Red
GRAPE VARIETY Cabernet Sauvignon
PRICE $
ABV 14%

THIS IS AN ULTRA-RELIABLE RED from Chile's largest producer that is affordable, easy to find, and, given the extraordinary levels of production, remarkably and consistently good. For a team-building tasting (where you would most likely serve this wine last), it works because it couldn't be made from any other grape variety; it has Cabernet Sauvignon's trademark tannin, power, and black-currant fruit, as well as a subtle hint of mint, without the sweet jammy edge of many mass-market wines.

Drink it with: *Empanadas—these small baked pies filled with minced meat, olives, raisins, and hard-boiled eggs would make a suitably filling South American snack to accompany the discussion.*

LEARN ABOUT RIESLING

The first wine in the comparative tasting—it's the lightest in terms of alcohol and body—is a typical Australian Riesling. Look out for the dashing, almost tart, cleansing character (Riesling is a high-acid grape) and the vivid lime flavor.

Peter Lehmann Riesling, Eden Valley, Australia
12% ABV $$ W

LEARN ABOUT SAUVIGNON BLANC

Another large producer (Brancott is owned by the French multinational Pernod Ricard) and another reliable, affordable wine—one that shows off the classic varietal character of New Zealand Sauvignon Blanc: abundant passion fruit, gooseberry, and capsicum, with crisp citrus.

Brancott Estate Sauvignon Blanc, Marlborough, New Zealand
13.5% ABV $ W

LEARN ABOUT CHARDONNAY

This is a beginner's course in what to expect from the Chardonnay grape variety when it has been carefully aged in oak-barrels: subtle buttered toast, richness of texture, soft banana and melon fruit, but with a squeeze of lemon acidity to keep the mouth fresh.

Sonoma-Cutrer Sonoma Coast Chardonnay, California, USA
13% ABV $$ W

LEARN ABOUT SYRAH

Spicy black pepper, blackberries, licorice, and herbs: The archetypal aromas and flavors of a young wine made from the Syrah grape variety are all on display here, as is a chewy, almost sinewy texture.

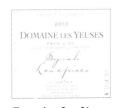

Domaine Les Yeuses Les Epices Syrah, Languedoc, France
13% ABV $ R

TASTING THEMES

Grape varieties always make for an interesting tasting, but they're not the only subject. Try comparing wines made from the same grape variety from different regions; or by different producers within a single region; wines of different vintages; different wines from a single producer . . . The list, and fun, goes on.

82

Pearl Wedding Anniversary

"SHERRY?" YOUR PARTNER EXCLAIMS upon seeing what you've chosen as the special bottle to celebrate this important anniversary. "I know we're getting on a bit, but surely we haven't got to the Sherry stage yet. What else have you got planned, a little ballroom dancing, maybe? Are we going to look at some retirement-home brochures?" It's the reaction you'd expected. After all, the great Andalusian fortified wine has struggled to escape the notion that it's only for the elderly and the stuffy, the sort of thing you'd get served at a particularly dull and lifeless drinks reception in a library, a museum, or, indeed, a retirement home. You know better, though. You haven't merely chosen this bottle because the figure on the label means the wine inside is, on average, the same age as your marriage (though nobody could deny there is a kind of time-traveling magic there). No, there's more to it than that. You've chosen a fine old Sherry because it has a range of aromas and flavors like no other wine, because it goes well with the food you're going to have, and because—and this is what really matters, tonight of all nights—it's romantic: the inspiration of poets since Shakespeare, a liquid equivalent of the sultry passions of flamenco. "Now do you understand, my love?"

"To love or have loved,
that is enough.
Ask nothing further.
There is no other pearl
to be found in the
dark folds of life."

FROM LES MISÉRABLES
BY VICTOR HUGO

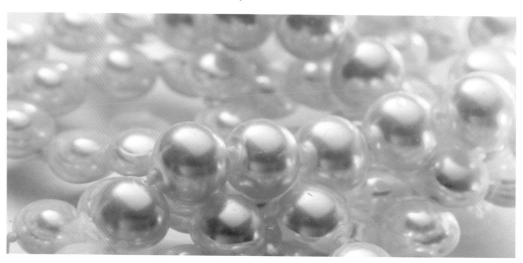

GONZÁLEZ BYASS APÓSTOLES 30 YEAR OLD PALO COR

FROM Jerez, Spain
STYLE Fortified
GRAPE VARIETY
Blend
PRICE $$$
ABV 20%

THERE ARE TWO BRANCHES of Sherry's stylistic family tree. On the one side, you have the Fino and Amontillado styles, where the wine ages under a naturally occurring layer of yeast (known as *flor*) in the barrel, imparting a briny, yeasty tang. On the other is Oloroso, where *flor* does not develop, leading to wines of a nuttier cast. The Palo Cortado style, however, is neither one thing nor the other, starting its life as a Fino and then mysteriously becoming more like an Oloroso. Like all Sherries, Apóstoles is made using a solera system, where the barrels are replenished with new wine whenever wine is removed for bottling. The solera in this instance began in 1862, and the average age of the wine is more than 30 years old. The result is dry and lingering, with an astonishing intensity of raisin, nut, brine, and brothy meatiness.

Drink it with: *You could consume this through the meal, but it's particularly effective with the cheese course.*

BUDGET CHOICE

A more affordable way into the delights of Palo Cortado Sherry from one of the region's most consistent bodegas, this doesn't have the age statement on the label, but it's no stripling, and it has great verve and tang to the toffee, coffee, and subtle nuttiness.

Lustau Solera Reserva Palo Cortado Península Sherry, Spain
19% ABV $$ F

MONEY'S-NO-OBJECT CHOICE

A rare recent newcomer to the Jerez scene, Bodegas Tradición specializes in small-production, prestigious Sherries that marry power and grace. This Palo Cortado, with its toffee, nuts, and citrus character, is based on high-quality barrels bought from a pair of historic Sherry bodegas and aged in Tradición's own cellars.

Bodegas Tradición 30 Year Old VORS Palo Cortado Sherry, Spain
20% ABV $$$$$ F

DINNER BLANCO

If you just can't get your head around Sherry, here's a dry white wine from the opposite end of Spain to Jerez in the remote rural Catalan district of Terra Alta. It sits toward the opposite end of the flavor spectrum, being all about the fresh peachy fruit and subtle touch of herbs.

Herencia Altés Garnatxa Blanca, Terra Alta, Spain
13% ABV $ W

DINNER TINTO

From the unheralded Utiel Requena region around the city of Valencia, and made from the local Bobal grape variety, this is a robust warm-up Spanish red with a romantic message before you get to the Sherry. It ripples with ripe fresh red and black berries and violet perfume.

Bodega Sierra Norte Pasión de Bobal, Utiel Requena, Spain
14% ABV $$ R

83 Making That Big Decision

YOU'VE TRIED ALL THE USUAL TRICKS. You've made a list of pros and cons and gone through each individually. You've flipped a coin, but soon found yourself insisting on a best of three, then five, then seven. You've told yourself to sleep on it and then spent all night sifting the evidence as the sheets grew ever more tangled around you, the sudden clarity you felt at midnight turning to a primal fear of some terrible, hitherto unimaginable consequence just before dawn. Your friends are no help: too optimistic, too pessimistic, not romantic enough, not practical enough. But time is running out, the deadline looming, its shadow lengthening. You've always tried to live by the creed that no one made a sensible decision under the influence. But maybe this time you can make an exception. You pull out a bottle of Amarone, a wine from the Veneto region near the city of Verona in northern Italy that is, unusually, made from black grapes that have been stored in special lofts after harvest and allowed, intentionally, to dry into raisins. The wine is dark, opaque, but vibrant. You take a sip (it's a wine for sipping), and find its intense, bittersweet flavors suit your bipolar mood. Then the clouds begin to part. Yes, that's it, that's what you'll do. No wonder the Italians call a complex, powerful wine such as Amarone a *vino da meditazione.*

> *"It does not take much strength to do things, but it requires a great deal of strength to decide what to do."*
>
> ELBERT HUBBARD

ALLEGRINI AMARONE DELLA VALPOLICELLA CLASSICO

FROM Portugal
STYLE Rich Red
GRAPE VARIETY Blend
PRICE $$$$
ABV 15.5%

A SPECIALTY OF THE VALPOLICELLA REGION in the province of Verona, northeast Italy, Amarone is a hefty, dry (occasionally just off-dry and slightly sweet) red that gets its unique character from a winemaking process in which the black grapes have been dried for three to four months before they are pressed and fermented. In Allegrini's case, the result of using grapes that are almost but not quite raisins is wine as (dry) bittersweet Black Forest gâteau: morello cherries dipped in black chocolate, served with coffee. It's an intense experience that repays the attention of the slow sipper.

Drink it with: *As you ponder your imponderable, try the Amarone with a chunk of salty Parmesan cheese.*

THE POOR MAN'S AMARONE

A modestly priced alternative to the full Amarone experience is to find a bottle from the same region made in the *ripasso* style, where "normal" wine made from unraised grapes is put through a barrel containing the skins of Amarone grapes. A lighter, but still cherry-rich red.

Valpantena Torre del Falasco Valpolicella Ripasso, Veneto, Italy
14% ABV $ R

THE RICH MAN'S AMARONE

The late Giuseppe Quintarelli was widely regarded as the master of Amarone, crafting wines of formidable concentration, complexity, and purity, typically offering meat, aniseed, and spice, as well as a perfumed, floral quality. This tradition is now continued by his family.

Quintarelli Amarone della Valpolicella, Veneto, Italy
16.5% ABV $$$$$ R

ADVICE FROM A GAUCHO

An Italian-Argentinian collaboration in the Andes that aims to recreate the Amarone style (hence the anagrammatic name) using Argentinian specialty Malbec as a base, this has a round and fleshy feel, a touch of sugar, and layers of plum, cherry, and chocolate.

Bodegas Renacer Enamore, Mendoza, Argentina
14.5% ABV $$ R

THE SWEET WHITE ANSWER

In the Soave region of the Veneto, white grapes (this one uses Garganega) are left on straw mats to shrivel until the February after the harvest, concentrating their sugars and flavors for an exquisitely elegant, honeyed sweet wine.

Pieropan Le Colombare Recioto di Soave Classico, Veneto, Italy
13% ABV $$$ SW

GRAPES AND RAISINS

Amarone and Recioto are not the only wines made using dried grapes. The practice is common across Italy and the Mediterranean, with famous styles including the Vin Santo of Tuscany, the *vins de pailles* (straw wines) of the Jura and the northern Rhône in France, and the treacle-like PX of Sherry and Montilla in southern Spain.

70th Birthday

DOES ANYONE ACHIEVE EVERYTHING they want to in life? Perhaps only the truly Zen manage it, and only after a lifetime devoted to erasing all their earthly desires. All the same, by the time of our 70th birthday, it's only natural that we might take stock of what we have done so far and ask ourselves what new experiences and achievements we could yet add to our personal collection. It may be that we come to the conclusion that our grander unfulfilled ambitions now belong to the past rather than to the future; that they were not as important as we'd thought they were; that they were just plain unrealistic in the first place. But if we're not going to be President, and we won't win the Nobel Prize or the World Freestyle Snowboarding Championship, we may yet target that longed-for competence in a musical instrument or foreign language, take that cordon bleu cookery course, or make that trip to Machu Picchu. And then there are the smaller things: You never did listen to the complete Ring Cycle or read *Remembrance of Things Past*, or try a wine from one of the five top estates on Bordeaux's Left Bank. Tonight presents the perfect opportunity to start putting at least one of those things right.

"To be 70 years old is like climbing the Alps. You reach a snow-crowned summit, and see behind you the deep valley stretching miles and miles away, and before you other summits higher and whiter, which you may have strength to climb, or may not. Then you sit down and meditate and wonder which it will be."

HENRY WADSWORTH
LONGFELLOW

CHÂTEAU HAUT-BRION

FROM Pessac-Léognan, Bordeaux, France
STYLE Dry Red
GRAPE VARIETY Blend
PRICE $$$$$
ABV 13%

CAN IT EVER BE WORTH SPENDING hundreds or even thousands of dollars on a bottle of wine? It's a delicate question, and the answer may depend on your politics as much as on your finances. But if you've squared it with your conscience and bank manager, then a 70th birthday celebration would surely be the time to do it, and this historic red wine—the oldest and, at time of writing, the cheapest of the five top Bordeaux châteaux known as first growths—would be a worthy candidate for the splurge.

Drink it with: *A simply seasoned joint of rare roast beef will show off the wine without overwhelming its subtle complexities.*

OLD WORLD ELEGANCE

Elegance is the word that usually attaches itself to Château Lafite, the largest and—since it became a must-have among China's super-rich—the most expensive of the first growths. Cabernet Sauvignon leads the blend in a wine that takes on ever more perfume and silk as it ages, in the best vintages, for decades.

Château Lafite Rothschild, Pauillac, Bordeaux, France
13% ABV $$$$$ R

PLUSH VELVET

Transformed by the ownership of the Greek Mentzelopoulos family since the late 1970s, the grand vin of Château Margaux from the eponymous subregion is not short on power but is characterized by its polished plushness, velvety texture, and alluring aromatic intensity.

Château Margaux, Margaux, Bordeaux, France
13% ABV $$$$$ R

POWER AND REFINEMENT

The French like to use gender terms to differentiate wines, with "feminine" generally equating to perfume and softness, "masculine" to power and firmness of texture. If you buy the distinction, then Latour is the most masculine of the first growths, dark, brooding, and handsome.

Château Latour, Pauillac, Bordeaux, France
13% ABV $$$$$ R

THE UPSTART

The only château to be promoted (in 1973) to the top rank since the Classification was established in 1855, Château Mouton Rothschild is the brashest of the first growths—in the best sense. The wine is luxurious, extravagantly perfumed, and exotic in character.

Château Mouton Rothschild, Pauillac, Bordeaux, France
13% ABV $$$$$ R

THE 1855 CLASSIFICATION

The 1855 Classification of the top red wines from Bordeaux's Médoc region (plus one, Haut-Brion, from Graves) and sweet white wines from Sauternes and Barsac has proved remarkably resilient and still influences the way wines are regarded and sold today. Unlike Burgundy and Champagne, where it is the vineyards that are ranked, in Bordeaux it is châteaux—originally based on reputation and price—that are divided into classed growths (crus classés): first (top) to fifth for reds, first to second for sweet whites.

85 Celebrating Your Retirement

WAS THAT REALLY IT? All those thousands of deadlines that came and went. Not one missed—well, only a few, and who remembers them now? The moments when you thought you were finished, and the moments when you thought you could do no wrong. The colleagues who made life unbearable, and the ones who made it a joy. The meanness of the boss who passed you over for promotion, and the wisdom of the mentors who showed you the ropes. There'll be no more disputes about photocopiers, no more gossip and joking around at the water cooler, no more rude *bzz, bzz, bzz* from the alarm at six in the morning. You've packed away that family photo that sat on the desk all those years, switched off that screensaver for the final time, and had your last sandwich from the deli around the corner from the office. But oh, the things you did, the things you achieved in all those years. Yes, that really was it—but it's a new time now. Look back tonight, look forward tomorrow. Put on the Edith Piaf. Pour another glass of Port. *Non, je ne regrette rien.*

> *"Port is not for the very young, the vain and the active.*
>
> *It is the comfort of age and the companion of the scholar and the philosopher."*
>
> EVELYN WAUGH

FONSECA VINTAGE PORT

FROM Douro Valley, Portugal
STYLE Fortified Sweet Red
GRAPE VARIETY Blend
PRICE $$$$
ABV 21%

WITH ITS LINES OF TERRACED VINEYARDS cut into the steep banks of the Douro river as it wends its way to the city of Porto and the Atlantic Ocean, the Douro Valley, home of Port, is one of the world's most beautiful wine-growing areas. Fonseca is one of the great historic names of the region, and its Vintage Port, the peak of its production made only in exceptional years, is also a thing of beauty, with the deep, dark, explosively perfumed fresh fruit of its early years transformed into soft, mellow dried fruits with age. At that point, it becomes the perfect tipple for late-night reflections on life's vicissitudes.

Drink it with: *A lump of mature hard cheese or a bar of dark, bitter chocolate with a high cocoa content.*

BUDGET CHOICE

Arguably the best example of the cheaper LBV style of Port on the market, this is a wine of great richness, depth, concentration, and power, with a fragrant lift of violets, red and black fruit, and spice.

Warre's Bottle Matured Late Bottled Vintage Port, Douro Valley, Portugal
20% ABV $$ F

MONEY'S-NO-OBJECT CHOICE

Made from grapes produced in a small plot of very old vines in the heart of the Noval estate (or quinta), Nacional is rated by many to be the supreme expression of Vintage Port, combining aromatic delicacy, understated power, and that intangible wow factor of all great wines.

Quinta do Noval Nacional Vintage Port, Douro Valley, Portugal
20% ABV $$$$$ F

A SICILIAN RETIREMENT

Marsala is an unjustly neglected, historic fortified wine style from Sicily that Marco De Bartoli has done much to bring back to world attention. Made from the local Grillo white grape variety, this is sweetly mellow with honey, nuts, and apricots.

Marco De Bartoli Marsala Superiore 10 Anni, Sicily, Italy
18% ABV $$$$ F

SOMETHING A BIT LESS STRONG

The Douro's unfortified red wines have improved rapidly in recent years, and this elegant example from the talented Dirk Niepoort offers some of the briary fruit flavors of great Port, with a Pinot Noir-like silkiness and considerably less alcohol.

Niepoort Charme, Douro Valley, Portugal
13.5% ABV $$$$ R

GREAT PORT VINTAGES

Vintage Port is only made in years that producers declare to be the best. The best will mature in bottle for decades—provided they are kept away from light at a consistent, cool temperature. Here are some of the great postwar vintages: 2009, 2007, 2005, 2003, 2000, 1994, 1970, 1966, 1963.

86

Christmas Eve

FOR THE NEAR-HYSTERICAL CHILDREN, high on candy canes and making frantic laps around the living room, their attention spans now so wafer-thin that even the *Spongebob Squarepants Christmas Special* can't keep them quiet for more than 30 seconds, Christmas Eve is all about tomorrow, when the real fun starts. As an adult, you may feel rather differently, knowing, deep down, that the excitement is its own reward—that the anticipation of pleasure can equal, perhaps even exceed, its fulfillment. Well, you would make these wise assessments if it weren't for the racket downstairs and all the things that still need to be done. At least, as you settle down to wrap the presents, you know you've finished the shopping . . . But does this thing need batteries? And at least you have everything prepared for tomorrow's dinner . . . But the turkey's still in the freezer! Quite soon, you find yourself wishing for the next day as fervently as the kids. Then later, steeling yourself for a night wrestling with wrapping paper and boxes full of expensive plastic imports, you tune in to carols on the radio, pour yourself a glass of Santa's Sherry, and at last give in to the feeling of anticipation that, even at this age, despite all the work and stress, you still haven't outgrown. Merry Christmas!

"Christmas is the season for kindling the fire of hospitality in the hall, the genial flame of charity in the heart."

WASHINGTON IRVING

EL MAESTRO SIERRA OLOROSO SHERRY

FROM Jerez, Spain
STYLE Fortified White
GRAPE VARIETY
Palomino
PRICE $$
ABV 19%

ITS TRADITIONAL CHRISTMAS ROLE may be in helping spin out the Santa fantasy, but there are plenty of other reasons to have a bottle or two of Sherry to hand at this time of year. This superbly rich wine is made in the Oloroso style, which means it hasn't developed the layer of yeast in the barrel that gives Fino or Amontillado its distinctive yeasty flavor. Aged for an average of 15 years, it is instead propelled by a dried-orange citrus tang, as well as nuts and spice and a very long finish.

Drink it with: *You may have told the children that all those bags of salty snacks were for tomorrow—but they're in bed now, if not quite asleep. One bag won't go amiss, and the salt mingles so well with the Sherry. Perhaps a slice of the stollen cake, too?*

BUDGET CHOICE

Fino is a lighter style of Sherry, fortified to 15 percent ABV and aged under the layer of *flor* yeast that gives it its distinctive salt-and-yeast feel. Valdespino's Inocente is elegant and crisp as much as it is savory, and there's lemon and even a touch of something floral amid the iodine, making it work with seafood as well as nibbles.

**Valdespino Inocente
Fino Sherry, Spain**
15% ABV $ F

FOR REALLY TREATING SANTA

Amontillado is a style of Sherry that begins its life in barrel under a layer of *flor* yeast but continues its maturation once the layer has died. It yields, in this instance, an intensely deep, dry style—a kind of savory dark caramel with a salty, yeasty power.

**Lustau Almacenista
Cuevas Jurado
Manzanilla Amontillado
Sherry, Spain**
18.5% ABV $$ F

CHRISTMAS EVE DINNER WHITE

This delightful rich dry white made from the Chenin Blanc grape variety in France's Loire Valley would grace the table for Christmas dinner itself. But if your guests have already arrived, or you're more organized than this author, why wait to sample its baked-apple charms?

**Domaine Huet
Le Haut-Lieu Sec,
Vouvray, France**
13% ABV $$ W

CHRISTMAS EVE DINNER RED

Port, of course, is the other festive fortified wine of choice, but most of us leave it for the post-Christmas dinner cheese. By way of a preview, however, we could uncork a bottle of this dry table wine from the same region and grape varieties, and with the same range of dark fruit flavors from a producer that also makes very good Port.

**Quinta do Crasto Tinto,
Douro, Portugal**
14% ABV $ R

87

Ruby Wedding Anniversary

"I DON'T KNOW WHAT I'D DO WITHOUT YOU." It's one of life's throwaway lines; a pleasantry, really—something people use without thinking. You say it yourself all the time, to your partner, as the next level up from a plain "thank you." It's only today—when all the well-wishing cards, the flowers, and your partner's typically inspired gift have prompted you out of your usual daze and got you thinking about the past 40 years—that you realize you mean it sincerely. What *would* you do without them? It's impossible to imagine. There is an inventory—of gestures, sounds, and phrases; of thoughts, feelings, and scents—that is hidden, taken for granted in the rituals of your day-to-day lives together, an inventory that you notice only in its absence, when you and your partner are apart for too long. Over the years, the separate strands of your lives have looped and wrapped around each other to such an extent that they'd be impossible to disentangle now. Your marriage, in this respect, resembles the Port you're sipping to mark the occasion, which, not coincidentally, shares the same age. You can still sense the youthful fruit as it was when it was harvested 40 years ago. You can imagine the resinous smell of the new barrel. Fond memories. But the wine is better now. Smoothed and seasoned by the passage of time, it has long since exceeded the sum of its parts.

"Up, up, fair bride, and call
Thy stars from out their
several boxes, take
Thy rubies, pearls, and
diamonds forth, and make
Thyself a constellation of
them all."

FROM *"AN EPITHALAMIUM"*
BY *JOHN DONNE*

QUINTA DO NOVAL 40 YEAR OLD TAWNY PORT

FROM Portugal
STYLE Fortified
Sweet Red
GRAPE VARIETY
Blend
PRICE $$$$
ABV 21%

DECADES OF PEACEFUL REST in wooden barrels have brought a mellow maturity to this fortified wine that echoes your marriage. "Complex" is certainly a much-overused word when it comes to wine, but this one genuinely deserves the epithet: toffee, caramel, nuts, spice, and a suggestion of the black fruit that would have been in abundance when it was first introduced to barrel all those years ago.

Drink it with: *There is toffee sweetness enough here to match with a caramel or fruit dessert, but it is perhaps at its happiest alone or with something very simple like a plate of salted almonds, allowing its complexities to unfold unimpeded.*

A GENUINE RUBY

Dirk Niepoort—who makes not only Port but also some of the Douro's finest unfortified wines—produces a particularly expressive example of Ruby, a style that shows Port at is most youthful and vibrant and is designed for drinking rather than for cellaring.

Niepoort Ruby Port, Douro, Portugal
20% ABV $ F

MONEY'S-NO-OBJECT CHOICE

Unlike Vintage Ports, which are designed to age in bottle, Tawny Ports are bottled ready to drink, and Sandeman's is another magnificent example of the effects of long wood aging. There's a honeyed delicacy, white and dark chocolate, and nuts, as well as dried dates and figs.

Sandeman 40 Year Old Tawny Port, Portugal
21% ABV $$$$$ F

A RUBY-DINNER BRANCO

The traditional production pecking order in Portugal's Douro Valley had Port at the top, followed by red wines, and finishing with whites. Times have changed, however, with wines such as Wine & Soul's textured, herb-flecked, sensitively oaked blend showing the region's potential for fine white wine.

Wine & Soul Guru Branco, Douro, Portugal
13% ABV $$$ W

A RUBY-DINNER TINTO

In just a couple of decades, the Douro has established itself as one of Europe's top red wine-producing regions, and Poeira has emerged as one of the front-running estates in less than half that time. Its eponymous top wine is worth the extra cash, but this is a wonderful red blend in its own right, a darkly fruited, gutsy, but fragrant gem.

Pó de Poeira Tinto, Douro, Portugal
14.5% ABV $$ R

88

End of the Evening

IT'S LAST CALL AT THE BAR, and everyone's feeling a little sentimental. This is when the Frank Sinatra LPs come out: maybe *In the Wee Small Hours*—something slow and heartfelt while you're thinking about life's bigger questions and emotions. In Frank's day, the martinis would have long been put away by now, replaced by tumblers of Scotch or bourbon, neat or on the rocks. But there are wines that fit the same kind of vibe, wines that suit the sad-soul swoon of a slowly spiraling saxophone or the smoky catch in the world-weary crooner's voice. These will be strong wines, for sure—literally fortified; wines for sipping, like single Islay malt or small-batch Kentucky, similar in color and just as intense in flavor. But unlike hard liquor, these wines are not so strong that their effects will trail you home as the night segues into dawn, then accompany you, like a sneering black dog, through the entire next day. You make a note to yourself, some hard-won wisdom that could only come from too many sessions in these wee small hours: 20 percent versus 50 percent proof. It doesn't sound much, but it makes all the difference in the cold light of tomorrow.

> *"What is better than*
> *to sit at the end of the day*
> *and drink wine with friends,*
> *or substitutes for friends?"*
>
> JAMES JOYCE

EQUIPO NAVAZOS LA BOTA DE AMONTILLADO

FROM Sanlúcar de Barrameda, Spain
STYLE Fortified
GRAPE VARIETY Palomino
PRICE $$$
ABV 18.5%

LIKE WHISKY, COGNAC, and other late-night staples, Sherry gets its color, and much of its flavor, from the interaction with the wooden casks in which it is aged. Like all Sherries, this one has been resting in a solera system, where wines of multiple vintages are blended together, with a little new wine added to replace the wine drawn off for bottling; the average age of the wine in this Sherry is 18 years old. It makes for a wine of layered, nutty intensity—savory, with a hint of salted caramel.

Drink it with: *To recreate the experience of the tapas bars of Andalusia, try serving this Sherry with a bowl of salted almonds, some olives, and a plate of Serrano ham.*

THE BOURBON ALTERNATIVE

Vin Santo is not a fortified wine but is the product of a process that involves first drying usually white (but sometimes red) grapes until the winter, then pressing them and putting the juice (or must) into wooden barrels. The result is an elegantly sweet wine, with spice and honeyed apricots.

Badia a Coltibuono Vin Santo del Chianti Classico, Tuscany, Italy
16% ABV $$$ SW

THE SCOTCH ALTERNATIVE

The Portuguese island of Madeira in the North Atlantic makes remarkable, indestructible wines that can age for centuries. This dry style from the esteemed Barbeito, with its dried fruit and nuts and subtle salty tang, has a sensory kinship to the great Scottish spirit.

Barbeito 10 Year Old Sercial, Madeira, Portugal
19% ABV $$$ F

THE COGNAC ALTERNATIVE

Fine fortified wines have been made in Rivesaltes in the Roussillon—in southwest France, near the border with Spain—since the 14th century. This darker example has a toffeed sweetness, with notes of walnuts and a dried-fruit zestiness.

Domaine Sarda-Malet Le Serrat Rivesaltes Ambré, Roussillon, France
16% ABV $$ F

LATE-NIGHT LIGHTER

Like some styles of Sherry (Fino, Manzanilla), this unfortified white wine from eastern France is aged under a layer of *flor* yeast, which gives it a distinctive savory undertow reminiscent of English breakfast staple Marmite, along with the tang of fresh apples.

Stéphane Tissot Arbois Savagnin, Jura, France
13% ABV $$$ W

OXYGEN AND WINE

The interaction with oxygen is what causes a wine to develop its complex aromas and change in color as it ages in barrels before bottling, as well as in bottles afterward. Some winemakers deliberately allow more oxygen to come into contact with wine, to bring nutty and dried-fruit flavors. Other styles, however—such as crisp, aromatic whites—are made with as little contact as possible to preserve fruity and floral notes. If your $10 Pinot Grigio from the latest vintage is brown, it's a problem; if your 30-year-old Sherry is a similar color, all is as it should be.

89

Making Amends

AT THE TIME, YOU WERE CONVINCED you were in the right; and who, listening to you, could possibly have disagreed? Your argument—as it made its way from clause to elegant clause, from thesis to antithesis to triumphant synthesis—rose to Martin Luther King Jr.–like heights of oratorical flair, and without noticing, you'd closed your eyes as if hypnotized by the resonance of your voice, the musical clarity of your ideas. You could have gone on all night. You almost wished you'd recorded the whole thing. Opening your eyes again, in readiness for the inevitable open-armed apology of your opponent—your partner—you realize they're no longer there. Calling after them, you go to the kitchen and find a note, more eloquent in its way than anything in your fine monologue: "Nothing you can say can make this right." You've really blown it this time, and you're going to need more than just flowers and chocolates to fix it. A bottle of wine may help—one that not only says sorry but, in its settled, mellow, character, somehow conveys the maturity and sincerity of your apology. Wines that draw on the time-honored wisdom of traditional winemaking methods, and that have had sufficient time in the bottle for their tannin and acidity to soften, calm down, and present their true face to the world.

"A bottle of good wine, like a good act, shines ever in the retrospect."

ROBERT LOUIS STEVENSON

BODEGAS MUGA PRADO ENEA GRAN RESERVA

FROM Rioja, Spain
STYLE Elegant Red
GRAPE VARIETY
Blend
PRICE $$$
ABV 13%

THERE IS A SENSE OF COMPOSURE about the best traditional Riojas. Partly that's to do with the way they're made: There's no hurry here, no rushing in; it's released only when it's ready, after a mere six years of aging in barrel and bottle, though it could cellar for a while longer yet. The wine, logically enough, feels mature, grown-up, too, with a smooth and stately character and flavors of vanilla, coconut, spice, leather, and red fruit intertwined on the palate. It has a calming but not soporific effect. There's plenty to think about as you drink, but something about its character means you'll do so in reflective rather than combative fashion.

Drink it with: *In Mexican author Laura Esquivel's best-selling novel-cum-cookbook* Like Water for Chocolate, *the main character remembers a peasant expression about how tamales, a corn-based dough boiled in leaves, will never rise if they're made around people who are arguing. Stuffed with meat or cheese, the comforting dish fits snugly with this Rioja, and once you've explained the meaning, its symbolism will surely be appreciated.*

BYGONES ON A BUDGET

Inspired more by the traditional winemaking of Rioja in Spain than California, as is the case with many of its peers, Bodegas Weinert is resolutely traditional in approach, releasing its wines only after long aging in large oak barrels —a process that gives this suave red blend a leathery, meaty, complexity.

Weinert Carrascal Tinto, Mendoza, Argentina
14% ABV $ R

WHEN AN APOLOGY IS PRICELESS

There is the wisdom of the ages in this most classical of Tuscan red wines from Biondi-Santi, a producer of historic pedigree. There is also elegance and subtlety, as well as power and depth. This is a wine with the authority, if you will, to mediate even the most rancorous of disputes.

Biondi-Santi Brunello di Montalcino, Tuscany, Italy
14% ABV $$$$$ R

WINE AS FORGIVENESS GIFT

It's seldom a good idea to judge a wine by its label, but for this purpose the impact of an attractive-looking package is as important as the contents. Thankfully, this wine is as stylish and finely drawn as the label's bush vine, a ripe, fleshy, but focused red from the Danish maker of cult wine Pingus.

Peter Sisseck Psi, Ribera del Duero, Spain
13.5% ABV $$$ R

WHEN IT'S TOO LATE TO MAKE AMENDS

A wine to offer consolation rather than simply drown sorrows, this hearty red, a collaboration between two winemaking friends— José Maria Soares Franco and João Portugal Ramos —offers a warming bear-hug of forest fruit and smooth tannins.

Duorum Tons de Duorum Tinto, Douro, Portugal
14% ABV $ R

Christmas Morning

SIR WINSTON CHURCHILL, who famously enjoyed a glass or two of Champagne as he went through his morning correspondence, may have begged to differ, but for most of us, opening a bottle before lunch is just a step too far down the path toward dissolution and decadence. If there were an exception to this general rule of early-hours abstinence, however, it would have to be Christmas Day, a time when the normal routine is suspended in a spirit of celebration, tolerance, and goodwill to all. No matter how you and your family structure the day—presents first thing in the morning or late in the evening; the big feast for lunch or dinner; a visit to the church or a walk in the park; games by the fireside or a boozy nap slumped in an armchair in front of a movie—the fun starts as soon as you wake. And whether you're spending the morning in the kitchen or under the tree, a glass or two of something special (and ideally light, given the other drinks that will follow later in the day) will only add to the joyous mood.

"'Twas Christmas broach'd
the mightiest ale;
'twas Christmas told the merriest tale;
a Christmas gambol oft could cheer
the poor man's heart
through half the year."

SIR WALTER SCOTT

ELIO PERRONE MOSCATO D'ASTI

FROM Piedmont, Italy
STYLE Sparkling Sweet White
GRAPE VARIETY Muscat
PRICE $
ABV 5.5%

A FORMER COLLEAGUE OF MINE used to call Moscato d'Asti "happy juice," and when you taste examples as well made as this, you can understand why. It's a summer wine in many respects, perfect for picnics and pool-side sipping, thanks to its combination of sweet, fresh Muscat grapes, buoyant acidity, and gentle spritz. But those very same qualities fit so well with the uninhibited childish glee of Christmas morning, and that low alcohol means you won't get carried away and peak too soon.

Drink it with: *A Christmas breakfast of fruit and pancakes. Or you could save some for later as a refreshing accompaniment for lighter, creamy styles of cow's or sheep's cheese.*

BUDGET CHOICE

An Australian take on a distinctly Italian style, this sweet Moscato was made in the relative cool of Victoria by one of Australia's grooviest, most experimental wineries. It has a pretty pink color, gentle spritz, and an invigorating pink-grapefruit flavor and acidity.

Innocent Bystander Pink Moscato, Victoria, Australia
6% ABV $ Ro

IF ONLY CHAMPAGNE WILL DO

Sometimes it's worth looking beyond the established big houses of Champagne, to the smaller producers making wines from their own vines. Larmandier-Bernier's 100 percent Chardonnay is dry, alert, citrussy, and a touch mineral: a fine way to wake up.

Larmandier-Bernier Blanc de Blancs Extra Brut Champagne NV, France
12% ABV $$$$ SpW

A LIGHT, AFFORDABLE FIZZ

From the Veneto region, on the opposite side of northern Italy to Asti, this Prosecco has a vivacious sherbetty mousse and crisp, apple and pear flavors, making for a lighter, less penetrating fizz than classic Champagne. Mixed with orange juice, it makes a great Mimosa, too.

La Marca Prosecco di Conegliano Valdobbiadene Extra Dry NV, Veneto, Italy
11.5% ABV $$ W

LOW ALCOHOL WITHOUT BUBBLES

Rieslings from Germany's Mosel Valley are renowned for their remarkable balance of steely acidity, gently sweet fruit, delicate texture, and low alcohol, all of which are perfectly displayed in this example from one of the country's most popular producers, Ernie Loosen.

Loosen Bros Dr. L. Riesling, Mosel, Germany
8.5% ABV $$ W

91

Golden Wedding Anniversary

NEITHER YOU NOR YOUR PARTNER have much time for gold: With the exception of your wedding bands and a couple of fillings, you've never owned anything made from it. You know it's an old-fashioned word, but you've always thought the display of gold to be not for you. You're aware, however, that it's customary to celebrate this remarkable anniversary by buying something made out of the confounded stuff for your partner. That's why you're out today. But you would dearly like that gift not to be one of those gaudy trinkets in the jewelry store or one of those appalling vases, even if it is an antique. Then inspiration strikes from an unlikely place. Catching your eye in the wine-store window as you make your way home, is something—yes, you're sure you can get away with it—golden: a bottle of dessert wine, made from grapes with an extended ripening that has concentrated its color. It's expensive. But you must have it. Not only will it match each of the desserts and cheeses you have lined up for the celebratory dinner. Just looking at it takes you back to your first sips of wine, on honeymoon, with your beautiful partner, half a century ago.

*"The Grape that can
with logic absolute
The two-and-seventy
jarring sects confute:
The sovereign alchemist
that in a trice
Life's leaden metal into
gold transmute."*

OMAR KHAYYÁM

ROYAL TOKAJI MÉZES MÁLY TOKAJI ASZÚ 6 PUTTONYOS

FROM Tokaj, Hungary
STYLE Sweet White
GRAPE VARIETY Blend
PRICE $$$$
ABV 9%

THOUGH THE COUNTRY'S BURGEONING post-Communist wine scene produces a number of fine dry wines, Hungary's greatest vinous gift to the world remains the spectacular sweet wines of the Tokaj region, some 150 miles (240 km) north of the capital Budapest. Tokaji wines have a long association with European nobility (who had good taste in wine, whatever else you might say about them), and they get their extraordinary sweetness and richness from the aptly named noble rot, *Botrytis cinerea*, a fungus that forms around the grapes, concentrating its flavors and sugars. The wines are graded by sweetness levels, with 6 *puttonyos* being toward the sweeter end of the scale, which starts at 3 *puttonyos*. From one of the region's most highly rated vineyards, Mézes Mály, this is wine as you might have imagined it from reading 19th-century novels as a schoolchild: an elixir of barley sugar and marmalade, with a ballerina's poise, balance, and clarity of expression.

Drink it with: *A fruit-based tart, or anything with toffee or caramel (though avoid chocolate if you can, since its bitterness disrupts the flavors of most wines). Tokaji also contrasts well with blue cheeses and, if it doesn't disrupt your conscience, foie gras.*

BUDGET CHOICE

Like their dry wine partners in Bergerac, the sweet wines of Monbazillac lack the cachet of Sauternes in Bordeaux. A shame, perhaps even an injustice, for them. But a boon for drinkers who can find unctuous but brilliant (in both senses) sweet wines such as this for relatively affordable prices.

Domaine de l'Ancienne Cure Monbazillac, France
12.5% ABV $$$ SW

BREAKING THE BUDGET

Historic, much in demand, and (the word genuinely applies here) exquisite, Château d'Yquem is one of the world's most expensive wines for a reason. Variously described as like drinking light or gold, you may simply, if more prosaically, note its complexity, length, and grace.

Château d'Yquem Sauternes, Bordeaux, France
14% ABV $$$$$ SW

A GOLDEN DINNER WHITE

Burgundy's Chardonnays come in many different guises, but the dry white wines produced around the village of Meursault tend to be richer in style, broader in their feel in the mouth. Made by top winemaker Denis Morey from grapes supplied by local growers, this example has a seam of brightness along with the trademark richness.

Morey-Blanc Meursault, Burgundy, France
13% ABV $$$ W

IN SEARCH OF EL DORADO

Inspired by the wines of Beaujolais in France (hence the punning name) but made in California, this is a red wine that emphasizes the bright berry fruit and sheer drinkability of the Gamay grape variety, providing the perfect precursor for the richer fare to follow.

Edmunds St. John Bone-Jolly Gamay Noir El Dorado County, California, USA
12.5% ABV $$ R

92

80th Birthday

WHEN YOU WERE YOUNGER, you tended to view the elderly in one of two ways: Either they were wise, kindly, and spry, or they were grumpy, pompous, and resistant to anything new. As you've grown older, you've learned that people rarely fit into such binary categories. But now that you've reached an age that is—and there's no way of finessing it anymore—definitively old, you do wonder how younger people see you. You hope they've noticed how you've always tried to disprove the lazy assumption that we naturally grow more conservative the older we get. This has nothing to do with politics. It's to do with staying open to the world and its possibilities, of staying on guard against the insidious hardening of the mind into prejudice. Tonight, you've asked your grandchildren to prepare the music, you've picked out a fashionable restaurant that the newspaper described as "daring," and you'll only order wines the sommelier says are "different" or "edgy" in some way. These may be wines from off-the-beaten-track locations such as Lebanon, or from unusual grape varieties such as Bastardo. They may just have something different in their winemaking approach or flavor, perhaps favoring minerals or savory characters over fruit. In choosing them you'll be doing what you've always done: searching for the shock of the new to keep the heart young.

"The advantage of being 80 years old is that one has many people to love."

JEAN RENOIR

DOMAINE MATASSA BLANC

FROM Roussillon, France
STYLE Rich Dry White
GRAPE VARIETY Blend
PRICE $$$
ABV 13%

THE APPEAL OF MOST WINES lies in their fruit character, and all those florid tasting-note descriptions (not least in this book) have trained us to reach for fruit analogies as we taste. But there are other things in wine besides its ability to conjure up an orchard or a fruit salad. This white blend of Grenache Gris and Maccabeu from the wilds of the Roussillon in Catalan France, for example, embodies what might be called the mineral side of wine, with a texture and flavors that seem to have been wrung from the slate and schist soils where the grapes are grown (using biodynamic principles). You may also detect a herbal note—a nod to the aromatic scrubland that surrounds the vineyards perhaps? And finally, there is fruit, too: citrus and white peach, as well as nuts and flint. In short, it's a remarkable, genuinely complex wine, from a well-traveled winemaker of New Zealand origins, determined to do things his way.

Drink it with: *The natural acidity, richness, and salty minerals make this one to serve with tangy, well-matured hard cheese.*

EDGY PORTUGAL

You don't get much of the amusingly named Bastardo grape variety (also known as Trousseau) made on its own, and it's generally thought of as one of the lesser grapes of Portugal's Douro Valley. But this mother-and-daughter outfit has always set out to do things differently, and this is a delightfully fluent, lighter-styled red.

Conceito Bastardo, Vinho Regional Duriense, Portugal
13% ABV $$ R

FUNKY LEBANON

Lebanon's most celebrated red is a law unto itself. This wine flirts with being faulty on occasion but has a savory, gamey, animal edge that you'll either love or hate. There is also an array of more exotic perfumed notes and rather more conventional layers of dark fruit—a true original.

Château Musar, Bekaa Valley, Lebanon
13.5% ABV $$ R

NATURAL FIZZ

This is a high-quality Prosecco with a difference, made like Champagne with the second fermentation in the bottle (most examples of this Italian wine get their fizz in pressurized tanks), but like a bottle-conditioned ale, the yeast is left in the bottle. Notes of honey, fresh apple, and citrus peel, a fine mousse, and driving, refreshing acidity make for a graceful but full-flavored fizz.

Casa Coste Piane di Loris Follador Prosecco di Valdobbiadene, Italy
11.5% ABV $$$ SpW

EMBRACING THE WINTER OF LIFE

Inspired by techniques used in the Germanic world, Canada has become adept at making sweet wines from grapes that have been harvested in winter, when they are frozen on the vine. It produces an elixir of a dessert wine, with live-wire acidity and sweet crystallized orchard fruit. Just a drop is all you'll need, and it's available in very small bottles (20 ml) to keep the outlay low.

Pillitteri Estates Vidal Icewine, Ontario, Canada
11% ABV $$$$ SW

93

The Friend Who Hates Wine

MOST FRIENDSHIPS FORM OVER SHARED TASTES. But just as we tend to feel attracted to people who like the same things we do, feeling a little less alone in the world as a result, so there are few things more dispiriting in life than when someone you like—or love—just doesn't get something you like or love. That moment you emerge from the movie theater full of talk about this life-changing experience of exquisite beauty, and your companion . . . Well, they may be too polite to say what a pretentious farrago they thought it was, but you can see in their eyes that they just want to change the subject. Or the book you pressed on your partner that was rejected after a handful of pages and now sits by the bed, mocking your assumptions about what you thought you knew about them. Friendships have been lost over less. Wine also has this power both to bring together and to alienate. All those lifestyle ads saying wine is for sharing are not entirely without truth: Swapping thoughts about a wine can be a bonding experience; if we agree on what we taste, we feel a little less alone. Still, if someone you love has declared they're not interested in that experience, you're hardly going to fall out with them over it. Even the delicate, oversensitive oenophile flower behind these words wouldn't go that far. Better to try a little gentle persuasion, choosing wines that share some of the attributes of the drinks they do like—little vinous Trojan horses to smuggle in all the other tastes you want your friend to share.

"Friendship is born at that moment when one person says to another: 'What! You too? I thought I was the only one.'"

C. S. LEWIS

DARIO PRINČIČ JAKOT

FROM Friuli-Venezia Giulia, Italy
STYLE Dry White
GRAPE VARIETY Friulano
PRICE $$$
ABV 12%

MOST WHITE WINES are made with very little contact between the juice and skins of the grapes. This so-called "orange" wine, however, is made with three weeks of skin contact, and that leads to a wine with a very different color (copper), flavors, and textures, pitched somewhere between a rosé and a white, without quite being like either. Your beer-drinking buddy won't care about any of that technical stuff: A wine, after all, is a wine, no matter how you dress it up. What may cause them to sit up and take notice, however, is the way this wine has more than a little in common with aromatic, citrusy wheat beers, sharing the herbal tang, whisper of astringency, and twist of bitterness and exotic spice, as well as the color.

Drink it with: *A platter of hard cheese and salami, or perhaps try some more conventional beer snacks, such as peanuts or potato chips.*

FOR THE GIN DRINKER

Gin is all about the perfume—the different blends of aromatic herbs, spices, and citrus peel that each distiller uses to give their creations a unique character. There is an aromatic kinship between those "botanicals" and this exotically scented dry white that may well appeal to a martini- or Negroni-loving friend.

Kebrilla Grillo, IGP Sicilia, Italy
13% ABV $$ W

FOR THE BROWN-SPIRITS DRINKER

A bit of a cheat this, since, as with all fortified wines, it actually contains some spirit. But something in its aromatic range—caramel, figs, dried fruit, sweet cedar, and oak—must surely set off a bell of recognition in the mind of any Cognac or bourbon fan.

Seppeltsfield Para Grand 10 Year Old Tawny, Barossa Valley, Australia
19% ABV $$$ F

FOR THE COFFEE DRINKER

Using the Pinotage grape variety, which tends to have an espresso-like smokiness, a handful of South African winemakers have created a new genre of wine that deliberately accentuates the note of mocha or coffee imparted by new oak barrels. It's not to everyone's taste, but it might be a way to win a reluctant coffee lover over to wine.

Diemersfontein Coffee Pinotage, Wellington, South Africa
13.5% ABV $$ R

FOR THE SOFT-DRINK DRINKER

Made from the Gamay grape variety in Beaujolais, though in such an unusual fashion that the local authorities won't permit the producer to put that on the label, this is the closest wine gets to high-quality sparkling fruit juice— a gently fizzy, gently sweet blend of raspberry, cherry, and apple that is, as the name suggests, extremely thirst-quenching.

Jean Paul Thevenet On Pete La Soif!, France
7.5% ABV $ SpR

94

Christmas Dinner

IN THE UNITED STATES, THE CHRISTMAS meal is less strictly defined than Thanksgiving, where most families stick to the same menu each year. At Christmas there is more regional variation—whether it's tamales in the Southwest, lutefisk in the upper Midwest, or oysters in the South—and it's less likely your family will be as hung up on its traditions as they are elsewhere in the world. Many of us, however, will take as our inspiration the classic roast dinner that we find in Dickens's *A Christmas Carol*, a meal based around a roasted bird (goose, turkey, or duck) with all the trimmings, followed by the classic Christmas pudding. The wines for this style of Christmas meal may be equally classic and traditional, the kind of thing the Victorians themselves may have drunk: Champagne to start, claret or Burgundy for the bird, and Port to take us through to the evening. We might also seek out a suitably classic match for the pudding in the sweet golden dessert wines of Sauternes in Bordeaux, although the best matches for this sweetly dense and dark concoction are those that have some of the same dried-fruit character: Australia's greatest "sticky" wine, Rutherglen Muscat, or the treacly sweet Sherries made from and labeled as Pedro Ximénez.

"I heard the bells on
Christmas Day
Their old, familiar
carols play,
And wild and sweet
The words repeat
Of peace on earth,
good-will to men!"

HENRY WASDSWORTH
LONGFELLOW

JOSEPH DROUHIN CHOREY-LÈS-BEAUNE

FROM Burgundy, France
STYLE Elegant Red
GRAPE VARIETY Pinot Noir
PRICE $$$
ABV 13%

AS WE HAVE SEEN ELSEWHERE, Burgundy is not known for value, but it needn't cost the earth, particularly if you find a reputable producer in a lesser-known village. Joseph Drouhin is one of the best examples of what's known in France as a négociant, meaning it sources grapes or even finished wine from other producers, then bottles and labels it for sale. Here the company is working in Chorey-lès-Beaune—a village in the northeastern part of the Côtes de Beaune area of Burgundy, without the reputation of more famous names such as Pommard or Volnay—to make a fluently red-fruited and subtly earthy Pinot Noir.

Drink it with: *Something in the character and flavor of this wine is reminiscent of cranberries, and though it is dry, when served with goose or turkey it has a similar effect to cranberry sauce, providing a counterpoint to the richness of the meat.*

A TRUSTY WHITE BURGUNDY

Burgundy's most southerly appellation, St.-Véran, is a star of the Mâcon area, which is generally the best place to uncover the region's facility with Chardonnay without scorching your credit card. Olivier Merlin's example is tangy and rich enough to cope with strong flavors, as well as being crystal clear and clean on the finish.

Olivier Merlin St.-Véran, Burgundy, France
13% ABV $$ W

A RELIABLE CLASSIC CLARET

If you have a bigger budget, Château Léoville Barton's eponymous top wine is one of Bordeaux's most consistent ageworthy reds. But their second wine, made using fruit from the same vineyards, for younger drinking (though it will keep for five years or so) and smaller wallets, has a purring cassis-and-graphite power typical of the St.-Julien commune.

La Réserve de Léoville Barton, St.-Julien, Bordeaux, France
13.5% ABV $$$ R

THE ONE FOR CHRISTMAS PUDDING

If there's a better wine than Rutherglen Muscat for the dangerously sweet, dark dried-fruit and brandy of a classic Christmas pudding, I've yet to discover it. Matching the pudding's flavors mouthful for luscious mouthful, this sweet Australian fortified wine is almost a pudding in itself.

Campbells Rutherglen Muscat, Victoria, Australia
17.5% ABV $$ F

THE AFTER-DINNER PORT

In the UK, supermarkets do a very tidy trade in gift packs of blue Stilton cheese and Port. Plump, sumptuous, and Christmas spicy, Ramos Pinto's Late Bottled Vintage also works very well with the dark chocolates just before you doze off on the sofa.

Ramos Pinto Late Bottled Vintage Port, Douro, Portugal
20% ABV $$ F

95

When You're the Guest

ON THOSE OCCASIONS WHEN YOU'RE THE GUEST, it can be worth taking a minute before you arrive to remind yourself why you're bringing a bottle. That wine you've chosen so carefully is a gift, which means that once you've handed it over, it's no longer yours and you no longer have any say in when and with whom it will be consumed. No matter how much you might long to try it, no matter how much better you know it will be than the stuff your host is serving, and no matter how much you feel that they simply won't appreciate it, you cannot ask or even hint, at any point, that they might want to go and open it right now. Those are the rules! You've waved that bottle good-bye. After all, you wouldn't expect to take the flowers you brought along back home with you, would you? Of course, if you're on your way someplace where you know the wine is going to be dispiriting, you could always bring two bottles along, one as the gift and one to suddenly remember halfway through the meal saying, "I really think you should try this." And if that second bottle just happens to be more appealing than the first one? Well, as a wise man once said, what they don't know can't hurt them.

"When it comes to giving, some people stop at nothing."

ATTRIBUTED TO
JIMMY CARTER

SHAW & SMITH M3 VINEYARD CHARDONNAY

FROM Adelaide Hills, Australia
STYLE Rich, Dry White
GRAPE VARIETY Chardonnay
PRICE $$$
ABV 13.5%

FOR THE GENEROUS OF SPIRIT, this very smart white wine is the perfect bottle to take to a dinner party—smart in all senses. The bottle looks classy, which is always more of a consideration when you're buying wine as a gift, but it's not crazy expensive. It's also a wine that will be delightful now but, if your host chooses to stash it away, will keep for several years. And if they are kind enough to open it while you're around, it's a wine to prompt conversation, one of a number of restrained, elegant, textured Chardonnays that have been bucking the oaky Aussie fruit-bomb stereotype and changing perceptions of what the grape can do in Australia in recent years. Oh, and most importantly of all, it just happens to be delicious, a wonderful combination of the rich, the creamy, and the nutty, underscored with cool, precise acidity.

Drink it with: *This versatile wine (another good reason for bringing it along when you're the guest) goes equally well with fish, white meat, and rich creamy sauces.*

SMART ON A BUDGET

Condrieu, the great white wine of France's Northern Rhône Valley, tends to be very expensive, but this extremely expressive alternative, made using the same grape variety, Viognier, has much of the same juicy, ripe apricot-and-honeysuckle character that never fails to appeal at a fraction of the price in a classically smart package.

Domaine Les Grands Bois Viognier, Côtes du Rhône, France
14% ABV $ W

THE RED GUEST

As with the Shaw & Smith, this red wine looks the gifting part and allows your host the option of keeping it for a few years or sharing it over dinner immediately. At either stage, it's a wine with broad appeal—a suavely polished Tempranillo with abundant fruit, lifted acidity, and spicy oak.

Bodegas Emilio Moro, Ribera del Duero, Spain
14% ABV $$ R

THE SWEET GIFT

Botrytis (or *Botrytis cinerea* to give it its full name) is a form of fungus that grows over grapes in some sweet-wine production, concentrating the sugars and flavors inside; it is often known as noble rot. This classic Australian Botrytis sticky's intense flavors of marmalade and barley sugar are a delectable treat for your host, with or without you.

De Bortoli Noble One Botrytis Semillon, New South Wales, Australia
10% ABV $$ SW

A FIZZ TO SHARE

That you've gone to the trouble of bringing the bottle chilled would surely prompt your host into serving this Champagne as soon as you arrive. And you wouldn't want to miss out on its distinctive charms or the chance to share a bit of trivia about how it uses an unusually high proportion of the least heralded of Champagne's trio of grape varieties, Pinot Meunier.

Aubry & Fils Premier Cru Brut NV, Champagne, France
12% ABV $$$ SpW

96

New Year's Eve

THOSE CLEVER PEOPLE in Champagne, northeast France, have cornered the market for vinous celebrations and expressions of joy—from the spray of victorious sporting stars to the glasses charged for the wedding toast. And so it is that, for many of us, the end-of-year party has become synonymous with Champagne. The trouble is, not all of us can spare the kind of cash that even the cheapest Champagnes require, particularly if we're hosting a party and need plenty of bottles to go around. (And if truth be told, aggressively tart, cheap Champagne is, anyway, one of the world's most mean-spirited drinks.) Fortunately, Champagne no longer has the monopoly on quality sparkling wine, and if your choice of lubricant for an assault on "Auld Lang Syne" really must have bubbles, you can choose from a range of options from all over the world.

> *"Hope*
> *Smiles from the threshold of*
> *the year to come,*
> *Whispering 'it will be happier.'"*
>
> ALFRED, LORD TENNYSON

With the New Year being, with a few exceptions, one of those rare occasions when people across the globe celebrate the same thing (you can picture a kind of time-lapse wave effect of popping corks as midnight arrives in each time zone), this is an opportunity to embrace the internationalist spirit with a bottle from as many wine-producing continents as you can.

JACKY BLOT TRIPLE ZÉRO

FROM Montlouis, Loire Valley, France
STYLE Sparkling White
GRAPE VARIETY Chenin Blanc
PRICE $$$$
ABV 12%

SPARKLING WINES are made all over France, labeled as *crémant*, *blanquette*, and *pétillant*. Few have the ambition and savoir faire of the top Champagne producers, but this sparkling Chenin Blanc from one of the Loire's best producers of still wines, Jacky Blot, most certainly does. Its name refers to the fact that it is emphatically dry: No sugar has been added either at harvest time to the juice, or must, before it ferments, or before bottling (a process known as *dosage*). What it is, however, is remarkably pure, clean, and invigorating, like the crispest, ripest, tastiest green apple imaginable.

Drink it with: *Try it accompanying deep-fried battered fish—English-style fish 'n' chips or Japanese tempura.*

THE AFRICAN CHOICE

South African sparkling wines made using the traditional Champagne technique, in which the bubbles come from a second fermentation in the bottle, are known as *cap classique*. Made from Chardonnay and Pinot Noir and named after an emigré Hungarian count turned Cape-based maker of sparkling wine, this is an excellent, great-value example, full of toasty richness and clean, crisp fruit.

Pongrácz Brut Méthode Cap Classique, South Africa
12.5% ABV $$ SpW

THE NORTH AMERICAN CHOICE

The California outpost of famed Spanish sparkling-wine producer Freixenet in Carneros has become one of the most reliable names in North American fizz. This good-value example is refreshingly zesty and crisp, with citrus and apples.

Gloria Ferrer Sonoma Brut, California, USA
12.5% ABV $$$ SpW

THE SOUTH AMERICAN CHOICE

Those of us outside of South America are more used to seeing Chile and Argentina as that continent's vinous representatives, but Brazil trumps both for sparkling. From the country's largest producer, this is uncomplicated frothy fun, with lots of strawberry and red currant fruit.

Miolo Cuvée Tradition Brut Rosé, Rio Grande do Sul, Brazil
12% ABV $ SpRo

THE AUSTRALASIAN CHOICE

The grapes used in sparkling wine prefer a cooler climate, which helps preserve the acidity that gives the finished wine its freshness. So, it's no surprise that one of Australia's cooler regions, Tasmania, has made such a success of the style. This example, a blend of Chardonnay and Pinot Noir, is a crisp, brisk, and tangy mix of fresh fruit and patisserie flavors.

Jansz Premium Cuvée Sparkling Wine, Tasmania, Australia
12.5% ABV $$ SpW

90th Birthday

You've been thinking, as you cast your eyes around the people at the party tonight, about Shakespeare's seven ages of man. There are players representing each age tonight—from your "mewling and puking" great-grandchildren, to your children comfortable now "in fair round belly," and your friends, shifting "into the lean and slippered pantaloon" (or the elasticated velour tracksuit) of the sixth age. Inevitably, as you go through Jacques's "All the world's a stage" monologue from *As You Like It* (your voice, in your mind's eye at least, still sonorous, and not yet turned "again toward childish treble, pipes, and whistles"), you begin to ask where you, at this grandest of ages, fit in and how closely your own life has squared with the Bard's scheme. Well, you think with a wolfish smile, you've certainly played the lover and, in your own way, a soldier, but how near are you now to the seventh age, to "second childishness," at 90 years old? It's true the great-grandchildren are the only people who seem to laugh at your jokes anymore. And it's true that you are "sans teeth," at least your own. But you are not "sans taste"—quite the reverse. After all, would the younger you have had the knowledge, patience, and experience to appreciate this historic wine that you have before you now? Of course not, and neither would any of their equivalents here tonight. That's why you've smuggled it away backstage, to sip all by yourself in secret; it's too good to waste on those without sufficient wisdom. And if that seems like second childishness, so be it. However many ages there may be, you only live once.

"All the world's a stage,
And all the men and
women merely players;
They have their exits
and their entrances,
And one man in his
time plays many parts,
His acts being seven ages."

from As You Like It
by *William Shakespeare*

HENSCHKE HILL OF GRACE

FROM Eden Valley, Australia
STYLE Powerful Red
GRAPE VARIETY
Shiraz
PRICE $$$$$
ABV 14%

IF YOU THINK Australia's is a young wine industry, then this wine is proof to the contrary. Made by the Henschke family, it comes from the titular vineyard in South Australia's Eden Valley, where the oldest parcel of vines, known as "The Grandfathers," is thought to have been planted in the 1860s. The wine itself now commands national-treasure status and prices, a reputation it has earned through the high quality it has displayed over more than half a century of vintages. It's a red wine that, on the few occasions I've tried it, combines power and depth of dark fruit with an elegance of texture that is quite unlike anything else from this corner of South Australia, and it ages as gracefully as its name suggests.

Drink it with: *As elegant as this wine is in its aromatics and silk texture, it is not without tannin and acidity, making red meat such as tender roast haunch of venison its most suitable partner.*

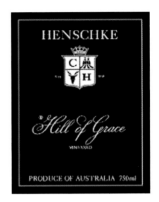

A PIECE OF HISTORY

Schloss Johannisberg is one of the world's oldest wine producers, having started its life way back in the 12th century, and the oldest Riesling specialist, having switched entirely to the variety in the early 18th century. Currently in the throes of a renaissance, the estate has produced this typically delightful, racy, elegant off-dry white, flowing with peach, lime, and orange.

Schloss Johannisberg Riesling Feinherb QbA, Rheingau, Germany
12% ABV $$ W

GRAND OLD VIN

Vin Jaune, a non-fortified dry white wine that ages like Sherry in barrels under a layer of yeast, reaches its zenith of nutty, Granny Smith apple complexity at Domaine Jean Macle in the Château Chalon appellation of the Jura in eastern France. It's a wine remarkable for its longevity, and it only begins to hit its stride a decade after the vintage.

Jean Macle Château Chalon, Jura, France
14% ABV $$$$ W

A SECOND CHILDHOOD

To relish to the full your second childhood, be sure to include this Beaujolais-meets-Burgundy blend of Gamay and Pinot Noir from a historic producer. It hums with an energy and zip-a-dee-doo-dah joy that works best when it's still in the first flush of youth and its red-fruit flavors are at their most beguiling.

Louis Jadot Les Roches Rouges Mâcon Rouges, France
12.5% ABV $ R

A SHAKESPEAREAN SHERRY

William Shakespeare was famously fond of Sherry, his character Falstaff in *Henry IV Part II* extolling its manifold benefits. This venerable 30-year-old Sherry, complete with its Shakespearean name, would surely have appealed to Falstaff, too, with its sweet/savory mix of salted-nut caramel and a freshly opened bag of mixed dried fruit.

Williams & Humbert As You Like It Amontillado Sherry, Jerez, Spain
20% ABV $$$ F

98

Diamond Wedding Anniversary

How special the table looks. It's the light from all those candles. It catches the cutlery, the glasses, and the eyes of all these people, all these precious people here tonight. "A sparkling occasion," you think, laughing at how silly and old-fashioned that sounds—you're not Jackie Onassis; this isn't a society ball. And then your mind snags on the word "sparkle" for a moment. You like the sound of it, and you let it roll around your inner ear a little. "Did our marriage always sparkle?" you ask yourself. Well, perhaps you've just been lucky that you found the right person, someone who even in the most difficult times—yes, you think, let's use that word again—made your life sparkle. How happy you are, sipping this sparkling drink with them tonight, a drink that is somehow as giddy and glamorous as you now feel. It comes from one of the best houses in the region. It's a wine that justifies its price with its electrifying focus, precision, and length of flavor. Champagne. Yes, you like the sound of that word, too: Champagne and a diamond as big as the Ritz.

"Better a diamond with a flaw than a pebble without."

Confucius

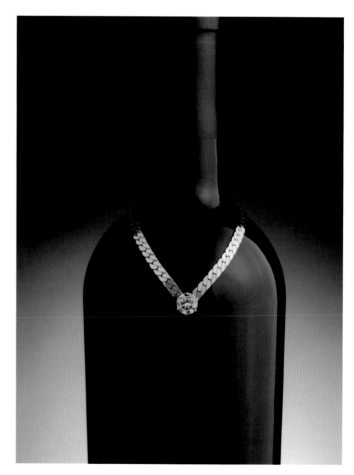

CHAMPAGNE SALON CUVÉE "S" LE MESNIL

FROM Champagne, France
STYLE Sparkling White
GRAPE VARIETY
Chardonnay
PRICE $$$$
ABV 12.5%

EXPENSIVE, RARE, AND MUCH IN DEMAND, Champagne Salon is also (and that's not always the case with cult names) one of the world's great wines. Produced only from Chardonnay grapes from a special vineyard in the top grand cru village of Le Mesnil, Salon is made only in the best years—generally three times a decade. Its luminous precision and harp-like resonance should be experienced by every wine lover at least once in their lives. And what better time than tonight?
Drink it with: *Much more than an apéritif, it can be served with fish, poultry, or mushrooms with a creamy sauce.*

THE BRILLIANT BARGAIN

A wine made from grapes grown in the top-rated grand cru village of Bouzy but with a lesser-known name on the label, this is one of the best-value Champagnes around: rich with stone and red fruits, brioche, and the striking clarity of all good Champagne.

Champagne Barnaut Grand Cru Réserve, Bouzy, France
12% ABV $$$ SpW

THE RISING STAR

Champagne has been transformed in recent decades by the rise of small producers, making wines from their own grapes rather than selling them to the bigger houses. Egly-Ouriet is one of the best of these *récoltant-manipulants*, and this wine shows off the intensely flavored but free-flowing style to great effect.

Champagne Egly-Ouriet Brut Tradition Grand Cru, France
12.5% ABV $$$ SpW

THE DIAMOND DINNER WHITE

From a biodynamic producer in the heart of the Mosel Valley, this dry Riesling has an effortless, racy charm, some tangy lime and peach fruit, and an almost saline mineral quality that stimulates the palate, the mind, and conversation.

Clemens Busch Estate Riesling, Mosel, Germany
11% ABV $$ W

THE DIAMOND DINNER RED

From a part of the world associated with gutsy, robust reds, here is a lighter red from Grenache and Syrah that is all about fluency and drinkability. Like the Clemens Busch Riesling, it feels unforced and natural—and the picture on the label could not be more appropriate.

Mas Coutelou Classe, Languedoc, France
13.% ABV $$ R

New Year's Day

99

IF NEW YEAR'S EVE is the biggest party of the year for many of us, New Year's Day is, inevitably, the biggest hangover. And so, you start the New Year with an urgent quest for an antidote. Strong black coffee and fried food, a mindless soak in the bath, an unchallenging movie, a bracing walk in the great outdoors—all will be attempted, with varying degrees of success. Sound medical advice, backed up by the distress signals being sent by your own body, suggests that today is not the day for wine. Indeed, many people see January 1 as the beginning of a month of abstinence from all forms of alcohol. However, the rest of us—either because we are the kind of people who have learned not to overindulge on New Year's Eve or because we want to believe in the restorative powers of the hair of the dog— can find what we need in the rich red wines of the southern Rhône Valley in southeast France. Warming, hearty blends of several grape varieties (generally including Grenache, Syrah, and Mourvèdre), these wines often have an herbal streak—rosemary, thyme, what the French call *garrigue*—that calls to mind the sun-baked hills of Provence, acting as summer's envoy in the bleak midwinter and lending the wines a (no doubt illusory) medicinal air.

"I pray thee let me and my fellow have A hair of the dog that bit us last night— And bitten were we both to the brain aright."

JOHN HEYWOOD

CHÂTEAU ST.-COSME GIGONDAS

FROM Rhône, France
STYLE Powerful Red
GRAPE VARIETY
Blend
PRICE $$$
ABV 14%

NEARBY CHÂTEAUNEUF-DU-PAPE may be more celebrated, but the appellation of Gigondas is no less historic, capable of producing wines that are every bit as good and, generally, at much better prices. Certainly, the wines of Château St-Cosme exude tradition and class. Proprietor and winemaker Louis Barroul has wine in the blood: He's the 14th generation to work the family estate. The wines he makes nod to tradition, with savory pepper and wild herb adding a cooling note to the berry fruit.

Drink it with: *A slow-roasted lamb—stuffed with garlic and olives and spiked with rosemary—echoes its flavors and is easy to cook.*

CORNER-STORE CURE

Wines labeled Côtes du Rhône can use grapes from across the Rhône Valley, and they are among the best bargains in the wine world. This fine red staple, one of the region's best-selling wines from the esteemed house of Guigal, is as juicy and lively as it is robust and spicy.

**E. Guigal
Côtes du Rhône,
France**
13% ABV $ R

UPMARKET MEDICINE

One of the great wines of the southern Rhône, this is made from very old vines and only in the best vintages. It's superbly rich, dense, chocolaty, and spicy— a worthy tribute to Beaucastel's former driving force, Jacques, and a fabulous way to start the New Year.

**Château de Beaucastel
Hommage à Jacques
Perrin, Châteauneuf-
du-Pape, France**
14% ABV $$$$ R

THE SOFT LANDING

The remarkably consistent Penfolds makes excellent wines at all prices, right up to Australia's most famous—and expensive— red wine, Grange. This plush Rhône-inspired blend has the producer's trademark harmonious feel and wonderfully vibrant black fruit.

**Penfolds Bin 138
Grenache/Shiraz/
Mourvèdre,
Barossa Valley, Australia**
14% ABV $$ R

THE BLOODY-MARY INGREDIENT

There's a salty-savory streak to this Sherry from coastal Sanlúcar that adds depth like a stock in a stew when added to the tomato juice and vodka of a Bloody Mary, the classic hangover-recovery cocktail. Alternatively, you could just cut to the chase and serve it as a chilled pick-me-up on its own.

**La Gitana Manzanilla
Sherry, Sanlúcar de
Barrameda, Spain**
15% ABV $ F

THE HANGOVER CURE

Though many of us try to convince ourselves otherwise, alcohol will, at best, offer a temporary suspension of a hangover's symptoms. But then, current medical thinking suggests the search for a cure of any kind is a fool's errand. Prevention, of course, is the most effective way of avoiding the whole sorry business; alternating a glass of water for every glass of alcohol is the next best thing. But if that advice comes too late for you, the most sensible action, says the Surgeon General, is just to stay in bed.

100th Birthday

ONE HUNDRED YEARS; OR—AND DOESN'T IT SOUND even more incredible?—a century. You've been around long enough now to know that this kind of landmark means nothing in the grand scheme of things (not that you're sure, even now, that there is anything so helpful as a scheme, even a humble one, in life). People keep telling you what an achievement it is to reach this age, as if you'd set your heart on it and worked single-mindedly at bringing it about, like running a marathon or making some scientific breakthrough. You think about telling them that it doesn't really work that way—that you feel lucky and blessed, not skilled, canny, or strong-willed. But you don't. Neither do you mention that your age doesn't make you some kind of exotic or magical species: You're the same as everyone else; you've just taken up a bit more temporal space. "Don't sweat the small stuff"—isn't that what they say in those peculiar books your grandchildren read. What are they called . . . Is it self-help books? Well, they're right in this case. You have more important things to do, a party to plan, and you need to find a wine that has been through as much as you have. One hundred years old and still with a twinkle in its eye: vintage Madeira.

"And in the end, it's not the years in your life that count. It's the life in your years."

ATTRIBUTED TO
ABRAHAM LINCOLN

BLANDY'S VERDELHO VINTAGE MADEIRA

FROM Madeira, Portugal
STYLE Fortified
GRAPE VARIETY Verdelho
PRICE $$$$$
ABV 21%

THE FORTIFIED WINES OF MADEIRA age like no other wine. While you may not be able to source one that matches your precise age, with the help of a reputable broker you should be able to find vintages of this wine from several decades back and maybe more. Judging by my recent tastings of the 1822 and 1952 vintages of the remarkable Blandy's Verdelho, the experience will not merely be of historic interest; these were densely flavored but still delicate wines of astonishing verve; floral, like jasmine tea, with hazelnuts, oak furniture, dried citrus peel.

Drink it with: *Nothing more than your nearest and dearest.*

A RICHER STYLE

Producing a richer style than Terrantez or Verdelho, the Bual variety takes on characters of treacle, caramel, figs, dates … I could go on; Madeira does tend to encourage the would-be poet. My personal experience of the island's oldest shipper goes back only as far as the 1950s, but I've heard amazing tales of the 1908.

Cossart Gordon Bual Vintage Madeira, Portugal
14% ABV $$$$$ W

A VENERABLE, EXOTIC RARITY

Terrantez is the rarest of the grapes used on Madeira, but for many it is the most favored, thanks to its mix of elegance and asperity, richness and blistering acidity. Barbeito's 1795 (yes, really) is, by all accounts, thrilling. The single tiny drop of the 1950 I tried lingered for hours.

Barbeito Vintage Terrantez Madeira, Portugal
18.5% ABV $$$$ R

MADEIRA ON A SMALLER BUDGET

If your budget is limited, or if you simply can't be bothered with the hassle of sourcing rare wines, Henriques & Henriques' range of age-dated Madeiras is consistently excellent and much easier to find. The Malvasia is sweetly sumptuous, with caramel and faintly smoky mocha notes.

Henriques & Henriques 15 Year Old Malvasia Madeira, Portugal
20% ABV $$$ F

THE WARM-UP WINE

Before the richness of Madeira, try a dry white wine from an innovative producer on the mainland to focus and energize the palate. With more body and weight than is usual for Vinho Verde, this still has the area's quicksilver character: It fairly quivers with citrus (lemon, lime, orange) and white peach.

Anselmo Mendes Vinhos Muros de Melgaço Alvarinho, Vinho Verde, Portugal
13% ABV $$$ W

HEAT: THE SECRET TO A LONG LIFE?

The remarkable longevity of the best Madeira wines is attributed to an unusual and ingenious winemaking technique that goes back to the 18th century. Producers in Madeira noticed that their wines were improved by long boat voyages in the tropics. They decided to mimic the process in their lodges back in Madeira, placing barrels of wine in sun-heated lofts for years. This *canteiro* system is still used for the best wines. Other wines are aged in rooms heated by hot-water pipes, known as *estufas*.

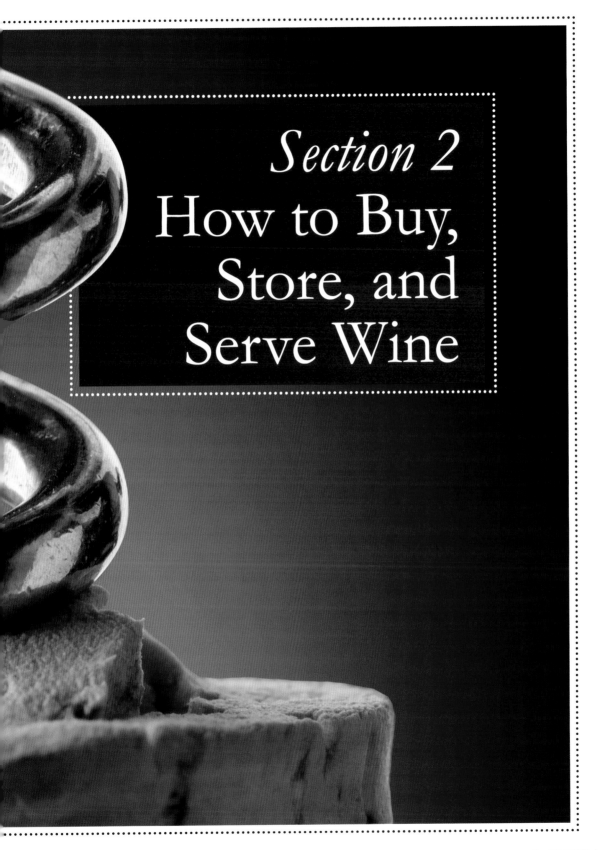

Section 2
How to Buy, Store, and Serve Wine

How to Buy Wine in a Store

In much of the world, supermarkets now dominate the sale of wine. In Europe, around 80 percent of bottles pass through the checkouts of the big grocery groups, and even in the USA, where some states don't allow you to pick up a bottle with your groceries, more than half are sold in this way. The reason is simple enough: convenience. Why go through the hassle of seeking out another, specialist store when you're buying everything else for the week in one place, especially when those other stores are likely to be more expensive?

In fact, there are plenty of reasons why you might want to give the supermarket a miss when you're buying wine, and at the top of the list is service. In your average cavernous out-of-town barn of a supercenter, wine is generally stacked up into an intimidating wall of bottles, but the only means of navigating what seems like a vast choice are the unfailingly hyperbolic, chirpy, and uninformative blurbs on shelf-tags: Very few supermarkets have real, breathing people trained to help you make a wine choice.

In most specialist stores, by contrast, the staff will tend to be, if anything, too enthusiastic. As with the snooty sommelier (see p. 220), the days when specialist wine merchants were peopled only with stuck-up wine bores operating on the assumption that "if you have to ask the price, you can't afford it" are, in all but a few instances, consigned to the past. Most wine stores today are staffed by enthusiasts who have a borderline-evangelical mission to get more people drinking more interesting wine. Many of them will either own the store or have taken an active role in buying the wines. And they won't (for the most part) talk down to you—they understand that kindly and helpful personal service is one of a pair of potent weapons they have in their battle with supermarkets and other discount chains.

Their other weapon is the quality and interest of their range. That's not to say that every specialist has better wines than every supermarket; there are bad specialists and good supermarkets. But to generalize wildly, a specialist has greater flexibility to list more interesting bottles. It's a question of scale. Supermarkets and discount stores like to buy wines in large quantities from large suppliers. It makes it easier to manage their supply chain; it means they can offer the same wines in as many of their stores as possible; and buying in bulk helps secure better prices (for them, that is; the savings won't always be passed on to you). But while there are producers around who are capable of producing good wines in large quantities, an overwhelming majority of the world's most delicious and interesting wines are made by smaller producers or by large producers in small quantities. Only on very rare occasions do these make it to the supermarkets, but they are the specialist's stock in trade.

Shopping for wine in supermarkets or discount warehouses can be intimidating, with many wines literally out of reach

Small production doesn't necessarily mean high prices, however, and this brings us to the central myth that drives many of us to the supermarkets—that they are cheaper than anywhere else. A myth? Well, it's true that supermarkets will offer the cheapest wines, but that doesn't mean they offer the best value, and it doesn't mean that specialists are, de facto, more expensive. Again, it comes down to the way supermarkets usually operate, which is to create the illusion of low price by carefully selecting a handful of well-known brands, common to a number of stores, and to sell them at the lowest possible margin, with great fanfare, while making up what they've lost by bumping up the price on the less familiar products. Taken as a whole, then, you'll often get more wine for your money in specialist stores, which, in these days of Internet price-comparison sites such as snooth.com or wine-searcher.com, tend to be much more careful about their prices than they may have been in the past.

But if you're still in need of convincing that a local specialist is likely to offer the wine with the highest pleasure-to-cost ratio, why not at least give it a trial. Ask around, either in person or on Internet message boards or social media, for recommendations of the best specialist wine retailers in your area. When you've settled on your choice, put the store through its paces with a simple test. First, give them a budget—the same amount you would have spent in a supermarket. Next, tell them about a few bottles you've enjoyed before, to give them a sense of your taste. Finally, tell them about the food you might be drinking your wine(s) with. If the merchant is worth its salt, the chances are you'll be back for more and swearing off supermarket wine for good.

And if you do find yourself back in front of the wall of wine, remember there are a few tricks to getting the best out of the experience. The first is to avoid the more extravagant deals on unfamiliar brands where the off-promotion price of the wine has almost always been inflated, and the wine's true value is likely to be the discounted one, if that. The second tip is not to shy away from own-label brands, which may not look as smart or have the cachet of their branded equivalents but often represent the best value in the store and are sometimes made by highly reputable producers (though you'll need to scan the tiny print on the back label to find out who they are). And finally, if you're buying a familiar brand, it's worth running a check on the prices at other stores online before you set out; deals tend to rotate through the different supermarket groups, and you could end up paying considerably more than you need to.

One of the advantages of shopping at a specialist wine store is that knowledgeable staff can help you choose

How to Buy Wine in a Restaurant

WHEN PEOPLE TALK ABOUT their fear of buying wine, what they usually seem to have in mind is the stereotypical restaurant situation familiar from a million comedy sketch shows and movies. You know the scene: a snooty male sommelier in a penguin suit arrives at your table with a book that compares with *Finnegans Wake* or *Infinite Jest* in its length, breadth, and exotic syntax. Five minutes later, he returns, eyebrows and nose set northward, to pass judgment on your mangled pronunciation and unimaginative, not to mention cheap, selection with a crisp, "Interesting choice. I see that madam won't be requiring the decanter then," in a tone that suggests a vast, unknowable chasm between his refined world of elegant taste and your irredeemably vulgar swamp of ignorance. No wonder most of us, anticipating a shameful loss of face, take refuge in that old classic, the Second Cheapest Wine on the List, thinking, Okay, we can't win here, but at least we're not the cheapest people in the room.

If situations like this were ever the norm, however, they are highly unusual today. Most sommeliers in most restaurants with a halfway decent wine list really aren't there to make you look stupid or inadequate. For one thing, it's plainly not in their, or their employer's, interest to upset their customers in any way. For another, it's a rare person who goes into a service job to express their sociopathic tendencies. Just as most doctors don't leave the examination room sniggering to their colleagues about your embarrassing ailment, so most sommeliers aren't swapping stories about your lack of knowledge of vintages and obscure appellations at the service pass. In fact, your average sommelier is only in the job at all because he or she likes wine and wants to share that passion. They are there to help you, in other words, and will take pleasure in finding the right wine for you.

If you have ever struggled with a wine list, then, there really is no shame at all in tapping into a sommelier's knowledge. How much of the decision-making you want to cede is entirely up to you. You could give them a budget, tell them what you want to eat, and ask them to pick out the best wine for the dish. Or you could ask them to come up with a few alternatives in a certain style that you know you've enjoyed before. It's a trick that works even for the savviest of wine drinkers—after all, nobody knows a restaurant's wines better than the person who serves and may even have bought them.

Of course, many restaurants don't have the budget or the desire to employ a sommelier. In those instances, you're flying blind, as it were, and though a restaurant with no sommelier is unlikely to have a brick-like wine list, you may still feel lost at the choice. Your best advice would be to follow some of the basic rules we saw for buying in a supermarket (see p. 216) Alternatively, you could use your smartphone to act as a kind of virtual sommelier. It's amazing how much information you can turn up on almost any wine or wine style in the world with a couple of Web searches.

Knowing how to get the best out of the sommelier or the wine list should help you enjoy your experience to the full

There's no need to get too complicated, however. Ordering restaurant wine is really no different from ordering food. Just as not every dish is a success, neither is every wine: Some you win, some you lose. But however you make your choice, remember that you can always send it back if you don't like it. Even in the most outlandishly snooty restaurants, the customer is always right.

Top Tips for Happy Wine Buying

1. The producer is king.

A region, appellation, or grape variety may give you a guide to a wine's style, but the producer is generally a more reliable indicator of its quality. If you find a wine you like, remember the name on the label. More often than not, you'll like their other stuff, too.

2. Vintage isn't everything.

Wine merchants and the press tend to make sweeping statements about vintages, and that can give the impression that every wine made in a given vintage is of the same level of quality. But the best producers will make good wines in even the harshest of vintages, while the worst will make duds no matter the conditions. In bad vintages, your favorite producer's wine may not be quite as sharp or lively as you remember it, but often with the best producers, the difference between vintages is more one of character than absolute quality—and good wines in "off" vintages often provide the best value.

3. The house wine may well be better than the Second Cheapest Wine on the List.

Many restaurants view their house wine as their showpiece wine—their ambassador—and of all the bottles on the list, it will often be the one that the wine buyer puts the most effort into getting right. It may not be an afterthought exactly, but the SCWL gets significantly less attention and is therefore frequently poorer in quality but higher in price.

4. Love thy neighbor.

The reputation of the region where a wine comes from has a big part to play in its price. That reputation may be justified when it comes to that region's top producers, but lower down the ladder, others may simply be coasting on the region's reputation, and you will usually be better off looking to the better producers making similar styles in neighboring appellations. Examples may include a Loire Sauvignon Blanc from the Coteaux du Giennois rather than Sancerre, or a Syrah from Crozes-Hermitage rather than Hermitage.

5. Get a map and explore.

One of the things that make wine special—arguably the single most beguiling thing about it—is how it reflects the specific soils, climate, and winemaking traditions of the place where it is made. Whenever you buy a wine, it's worth looking on a map to see where it came from. You'll soon identify flavors with places as you travel the world, bottle by bottle.

The great hill of Hermitage (right) produces superb wines, but those from Crozes-Hermitage may be better value

How to Store Wine

FOR THE MOST PART, the question of where to keep your bottles of wine once you've bought them doesn't arise. The vast majority of wines are consumed within a day or two of purchase, and most of them aren't built to last for much longer than a year or two after bottling anyway. As you'll have seen throughout this book, however, some wines do improve after a few years in the bottle (or at least evolve in a way that some people find pleasing; not everyone likes the taste of old wine). And if you are planning to keep your bottles for an extended period, there are a few things to consider so that you ensure it remains in the best of health.

The two great enemies of wine are extremes of temperature and bright light, so look for a dark place with a consistent, cool temperature (roughly 50–60°F [10–15°C]), and good humidity. Since very few of us live in a house blessed with the kind of traditional cellar that meets these precise conditions, however, we have to improvise.

Although few of us have special storage rooms (below) or traditional cellars, it is still possible to keep wine at home

Provided it is away from radiators or other heat sources, a space at the bottom of a cupboard or under the bed would do if you have just a couple of bottles—but not a high shelf. If your collection is growing to a little more than that, you might want to consider an old refrigerator with the temperature turned up as close to 55°F as possible, or even, if you're really serious, a professional wine fridge, which will have a capacity of between 33 and 80 bottles and is designed to mimic the conditions of a traditional wine cellar, including optimum humidity.

Wherever you lay your bottles, if they're sealed with a cork, remember to lay them down on their side. This is to prevent the cork from drying out and splitting, which is tantamount to leaving the bottle with no seal at all; it will spoil very rapidly.

Finally, if you've spent a lot of money on a case of wine to store for a long period and you're not confident you have the right conditions for it, for a small fee many wine merchants offer a cellar service, guaranteeing that your wine will be kept in perfect conditions (and providing a replacement or compensation if the bottles are broken).

How to Serve Wine

Temperature Just as nobody drinks their tea or coffee at precisely the same temperature, so no two people will have the exact same optimum temperature for a glass of wine. In general, however, there is a tendency to go to extremes, with white wines served too cool and red wines too warm.

As a rough guide, sparkling wines, light crisp whites, rosés, and lighter fortified styles such as Fino Sherry are wines that are geared toward refreshment, and they work best at cooler temperatures—chilled right down in the fridge for a few hours if possible, or if time is short, in a bucket filled with ice cubes and water for as long as you can.

For whites and rosés with a little more richness and flesh, including sweet wines, too much chilling has a kind of muting effect on the aromas, flavors, and textures, so they're generally at their best if you take them out the fridge a few minutes before you're going to drink them (though it's not the end of the world if they're served too cool, since they're going to warm up in your glass anyway).

Lighter reds (see the list of Top Ten lower-alcohol reds for examples, p. 238), the more robust rosés, and richer styles of fortified wines such as Amontillado Sherry are, like richer whites, best served a little cool and can be stored in the fridge for around half an hour to emphasize their refreshing qualities, particularly on summer days.

Finally, the more powerful reds and fortified styles have the highest serving temperature, but not too high. If you were going to be really fastidious about it, the thermometer would read around 60°F (16°C)—that is, room temperature in a house before the invention of central heating. Once wines start warming up too much above 70°F (21°C), they start feeling soupy and, to mix metaphors, lose their definition and focus.

Decanting and breathing There are three reasons why you might want to use a decanter. The first is that it looks smart on the table. The second is when a wine, generally an older, unfiltered red wine, has accumulated harmless sediment and you want to avoid pouring it directly into a glass. The third is to give the wine a little oxygen, to soften its tannins and awaken its aromas and flavors. The decanter will have a long spout, and pouring the wine in from as high a point as possible will hasten the process still further, as will a gentle swish of the decanter once the bottle has been emptied. The wines that respond best—or at least, most noticeably—to decanting are powerful reds (including fortified reds) with high tannin levels, though richer white and sparkling wines can also respond well to the process. Some people try to replicate this process by simply taking the cork out an hour or two before serving to allow it to "breathe." This will have very limited effect, however, since the surface area in contact with the wine is so small.

Aerating a wine to open up its aromas and flavors and soften its texture is just one of the reasons for decanting

Glasses and pouring This is where wine lovers take their instinctive nerdiness to still greater extremes, on a par with the hi-fi equipment fetishist. A vast range of wine glasses is available, with some companies, led by the Austrian glass-maker Riedel, offering specific glasses for specific styles. I've never been convinced that the infinitesimal differences in the experience of drinking, say, a Bordeaux wine in a glass specifically tailored for the style and drinking it from one designed for a Burgundy justify the expense of buying a full set (though I should say that many respected wine experts swear by them).

In a more general way, however, it's widely accepted that some wine styles work better in a certain glass shape or size than others. Champagne, for example, is at its best in glasses with a long fluted shape and a narrow top to help retain the bubbles. Crisp white wines, where freshness is all important, generally prefer a smaller glass than richer whites and lighter reds, while powerful red wines—where you're looking to get as much interaction with the air as possible—suit a still larger glass. Finally, fortified or dessert wines generally work best in smaller glasses (though not the tiny thimbles or schooners of yore), since the smaller measures we have of these stronger wines will get lost in a large wine glass.

It's also clear that the better the quality of the wine glass, the greater your experience of wine. Just try comparing the same wine out of a mug and a basic wine glass if you don't believe me. The wine in the glass just seems to have much more aroma. That

While you don't need myriad glasses, some suit some styles of wine better than others:
1. Pinot Noir
2. Cabernet Sauvignon
3. Port/Sherry
4. Riesling
5. Chardonnay
6. Syrah
7. Gamay

1   2   3

doesn't mean you have to spend a fortune; by "better," I mean thin rather than thick glass, an oval shape, and a decent size—all of which give the wine a better chance of showing off its full array of aromas.

Whatever the quality of your glasses, to get the most out of them in terms of aroma and flavor (as opposed to volume), try pouring up to a third full, which again gives the wine space to breathe and spread out its aromas. The only exception is sparkling wines, where the escaping bubbles bring out the bouquet, and (for me at least) the glass is better poured (at an angle, as you would a beer) nearer to the top. (And while we're on the subject, another tip with Champagne is to open the bottle at a 45-degree angle, with the top of the bottle pointing away from you and any other people, holding the cork firmly in one hand, and twisting the bottle at the base.)

Gadgets and gizmos There's a flourishing mini-industry devoted to accoutrements for the credulous wine lover—most of them unnecessary and some of them bordering on snake-oil levels of charlatanism. Many are variations on a theme of corkscrew, and very few have improved on the elegance, simplicity, and efficiency of the basic Waiter's Friend that I use. If you struggle with those and you're feeling flush, however, the Le Creuset Screwpull is a smoothly functioning bit of engineering—until, in my experience, it comes up against a synthetic cork, though that seems to be the case with all corkscrews.

Section 3
Top-Ten Tables

If you are departing from an occasional approach and want
instead to start from the wine, here are some of my
favorites across a broad range of prices and styles

10 AFFORDABLE CLASSIC REDS

E. GUIGAL / **Côtes du Rhône** / *Rhône, France*

FONTODI / **Chianti Classico** / *Tuscany, Italy*

DOMAINE HUDELOT-NOËLLAT / **Bourgogne Rouge** / *Burgundy, France*

COUSIÑO MACUL / **Antiguas Reservas** / *Maipo Valley, Chile*

CHRISTIAN MOUEIX / **St.-Emilion** / *Bordeaux, France*

ROBERT MONDAVI / **Cabernet Sauvignon** / *Napa Valley, California, USA*

CVNE / **Crianza** / *Rioja, Spain*

BODEGAS SALENTEIN PORTILLO / **Malbec** / *Mendoza, Argentina*

GRANT BURGE / **Benchmark Shiraz** / *South Australia*

LA PERLA DEL PRIORAT / **Noster Nobili**s / *Priorat, Spain*

10 AFFORDABLE CLASSIC WHITES

DÖNNHOFF / **Riesling Kabinett** / *Nahe, Germany*

SONOMA-CUTRER / **Sonoma Coast Chardonnay** / *California, USA*

DOMAINE CHAVY-CHOUET / **Bourgogne Blanc Les Femelottes** / *Burgundy, France*

HUGEL / **Gentil Classic** / *Alsace, France*

VILLA MARIA / **Private Bin Sauvignon Blanc** / *Marlborough, New Zealand*

DOMAINE MOREAU-NAUDET / **Petit Chablis** / *Chablis, France*

FEUDI DI SAN GREGORIO / **Lacryma Christi Bianco** / *Campania, Italy*

DOMÄNE WACHAU / **Terrassen Grüner Veltliner Federspiel** / *Wachau, Austria*

CHÂTEAU DE SUDUIRAUT / **Lions de Suduiraut** / *Sauternes, Bordeaux, France*

LOOSEN BROS / **Dr. L. Riesling** / *Mosel, Germany*

10 BLOW-THE-BUDGET REDS

RIDGE / **Monte Bello** / *Santa Cruz Mountains, California, USA*

DOMAINE JEAN GRIVOT / **Richebourg Grand Cru** / *Burgundy, France*

VIEUX CHÂTEAU CERTAN / *Pomerol, Bordeaux, France*

MASCARELLO GIUSEPPE E FIGLO / **Barolo Riserva Monprivato Cà d' Morissio** / *Italy*

DOMAINE JAMET / **Côte-Rôtie** / *Rhône, France*

GRAMERCY CELLARS / **Walla Walla Valley Syrah** / *Washington State, USA*

HENSCHKE / **Hill of Grace** / *Eden Valley, Australia*

BIONDI-SANTI / **Brunello di Montalcino** / *Tuscany, Italy*

ACHAVAL FERRER / **Malbec Finca Mirador** / *Mendoza, Argentina*

MARQUÉS DE MURRIETA / **Castillo Ygay Gran Reserva Especial** / *Rioja, Spain*

10 BLOW-THE-BUDGET WHITES

CHÂTEAU D'YQUEM / *Sauternes, Bordeaux, France*

COULÉE DE SERRANT / **Clos de la Coulée de Serrant** / *Savennières, Loire, France*

CHÂTEAU GRILLET / *Rhône, France*

SADIE FAMILY WINES / **Palladius** / *Swartland, South Africa*

TRIMBACH / **Cuvée Frédéric Emile Riesling** / *Alsace, France*

PIEROPAN / **Le Colombare Recioto di Soave Classico** / *Veneto, Italy*

ROYAL TOKAJI / **Mézes Mály Tokaji Aszú 6 Puttonyos** / *Tokaj, Hungary*

JEAN MACLE / **Château Chalon** / *Jura, France*

DOMAINE LEFLAIVE / **Chevalier-Montrachet Grand Cru** / *Burgundy, France*

JOH JOS PRÜM / **Wehlener Sonnenuhr Riesling Spätlese** / *Mosel, Germany*

10 REALLY GOOD-VALUE REDS

WEINERT / **Carrascal Tinto** / *Mendoza, Argentina*

BODEGAS JUAN GIL / **El Tesoro Monastrell/Shiraz** / *Jumilla, Spain*

CONO SUR / **Bicicleta Pinot Noir** / *Central Valley, Chile*

CASILLERO DEL DIABLO / **Cabernet Sauvignon** / *Central Valley, Chile*

HEDGES / **CMS Red** / *Columbia Valley, Washington State, USA*

BODEGAS BORSAO / **Garnacha** / *Campo de Borja, Spain*

VIÑA FALERNIA / **Syrah** / *Elquí Valley, Chile*

DOMAINE LES YEUSES / **Les Epices Syrah** / *Languedoc, France*

TORRES / **Sangre de Toro** / *Penedès, Spain*

PAOLO LEO / **Primitivo di Manduria** / *Puglia, Italy*

10 REALLY GOOD-VALUE WHITES

PRODUCTEURS PLAIMONT / **Les Bastions Blanc** / *Saint-Mont, France*

VIÑA TABALÍ / **Late Harvest Muscat** / *Limarí, Chile*

TORRES / **Viña Sol** / *Penedès, Spain*

DOURTHE / **La Grande Cuvée Sauvignon Blanc** / *Bordeaux, France*

LAURENT MIQUEL / **Nord-Sud Viognier** / *IGP Pays d'Oc, France*

DOMAINE LES YEUSES / **Vermentino** / *IGP Pays d'Oc, France*

KEN FORRESTER / **Chenin Blanc** / *Stellenbosch, South Africa*

DOMAINE TARIQUET / **Classic** / *Côtes de Gascogne, France*

CHÂTEAU DU CLÉRAY / **Muscadet Sèvre et Maine Sur Lie** / *Loire, France*

PERRIN & FILS / **La Vieille Ferme Blanc** / *Côtes du Luberon, France*

10 VERSATILE FOOD WINES

ANDRÉ DEZAT / **Pinot Noir Rosé** / *Sancerre, Loire, France*

TRIMBACH / **Pinot Gris Reserve** / *Alsace, France*

D'ARENBERG / **The Hermit Crab Marsanne/Viognier** / *McLaren Vale, Australia*

CEDERBERG CELLARS / **Bukettraube** / *Cederberg, South Africa*

LA MONACESCA / **Mirum** / *Verdicchio di Matelica Riserva, Italy*

SANCHEZ ROMATE / **Fino Sherry** / *Jerez, Spain*

BODEGAS OCHOA / **Garnacha Rosado** / *Navarra, Spain*

PLANETA / **Cerasuolo di Vittoria** / *Sicily, Italy*

DOMAINE COUDERT / **Clos de la Roilette** / *Fleurie, Beaujolais, France*

BILLECART-SALMON / **Brut Rosé NV** / *Champagne, France*

10 WINES TO ENJOY WITH OR WITHOUT FOOD

CERUTTI / **Moscato d'Asti Suri Sandrinet** / *Cassinasco, Piedmont, Italy*

ST HALLET / **Gamekeeper's Reserve** / *Barossa Valley, Australia*

CHÂTEAU DE SOURS / **Rosé** / *Bordeaux, France*

MT BEAUTIFUL / **Cheviot Hills Riesling** / *Canterbury, New Zealand*

DOG POINT / **Sauvignon Blanc** / *Marlborough, New Zealand*

SUSANA BALBO / **Crios Torrontés** / *Cafayate, Salta, Argentina*

MAS COUTELOU / **Classe** / *Languedoc, France*

WILLUNGA 100 / **Grenache** / *McLaren Vale, Australia*

CASTRO CELTA / **Albariño** / *Rías Baixas, Galicia, Spain*

ALVEAR / **Pedro Ximénez de Añada** / *Montilla-Moriles, Spain*

10 EXCITING AND UNUSUAL REDS

PHEASANT'S TEARS / **Saperavi** / *Kakheti, Georgia*

MANUEL JOSÉ / **Colares** / *Portugal*

S. C. PANNELL / **Tempranillo/Touriga Nacional** / *McLaren Vale, Australia*

J. HOFSTÄTTER / **Lagrein** / *Südtirol-Alto Adige, Italy*

DOMAINE DU CROS LO SANG DEL PAIS / **Marcillac** / *Southwest France*

DE MARTINO / **Viejas Tinajas** / *Itata Valley, Chile*

GUÍMARO / **Tinto** / *Ribeira Sacra, Galicia, Spain*

CONCEITO / **Bastardo** / *Vinho Regional Duriense, Portugal*

CHÂTEAU MUSAR / *Bekaa Valley, Lebanon*

THYMIOPOULOS / **Earth and Sky** / *Naoussa, Macedonia, Greece*

10 EXCITING AND UNUSUAL WHITES

KOZLOVIĆ / **Malvazija** / *Istria, Croatia*

DOMAINE GEROVASSILIOU / **Malagousia** / *Epanomi, Macedonia, Greece*

HATZIDAKIS / **Assyrtiko** / *Santorini, Greece*

TXOMIN ETXANIZ / **Chacolí** / *Spain*

STÉPHANE TISSOT / **Arbois Savagnin** / *Jura, France*

KABAJ / **Rebula** / *Goriška Brda, Slovenia*

CAVE DU VIN BLANC DE MORGEX ET DE LA SALLE RAYON / *Valle d'Aosta, Italy*

CONUNDRUM / **White Wine** / *California, USA*

CEDERBERG CELLARS / **Bukettraube** / *Cederberg, South Africa*

DARIO PRINCIC / **Jakot** / *Friuli-Venezia Giulia, Italy*

10 RISING-STAR REDS

SANDHI / **Evening Land Tempest Pinot Noir** / *Santa Barbara, California*

MEYER-NÄKEL / **Blauschiefer Spätburgunder** / *Ahr, Germany*

PYRAMID VALLEY / **Howell Family Vineyard Cabernet Franc** / *Hawkes Bay, New Zealand*

BODEGA CHACRA / **Barda Pinot Noir** / *Rio Negro, Patagonia, Argentina*

GRACI / **Passopisciaro Etna Rosso** / *Sicily, Italy*

MORIC / **Blaufränkisch** / *Burgenland, Austria*

BODEGAS Y VIÑEDOS PONCE / **Clos Lojen** / *Manchuela, Spain*

ERIC TEXIER / **Brézème Côtes du Rhône** / *Rhône, France*

MATETIC / **Corralillo Syrah** / *San Antonio, Chile*

MENDEL / **Malbec** / *Mendoza, Argentina*

10 RISING-STAR WHITES

MULLINEUX / **Estate White** / *Swartland, South Africa*

GREYWACKE / **Wild Sauvignon** / *Marlborough, New Zealand*

WINE & SOUL / **Guru Branco** / *Douro, Portugal*

VIÑA LEYDA / **Reserva Sauvignon Blanc** / *Leyda, Chile*

DOMAINE LES GRANDS BOIS / **Viognier** / *Côtes du Rhône, France*

DIRLER-CADÉ / **Saering Grand Cru Muscat** / *Alsace, France*

FILIPA PATO / **Nossa Branco** / *Bairrada, Portugal*

HERENCIA ALTÉS / **Garnatxa Blanca** / *Terra Alta, Spain*

DOMAINE MATASSA / **Vin de Pays des Côtes Catalanes** / *Roussillon, France*

CAPE POINT VINEYARDS / **Stonehaven Sauvignon Blanc** / *Cape Point, South Africa*

10 LOWER-ALCOHOL REDS

ROBERT SÉROL / **Vieilles Vignes** / *Côte Roannaise, France*

LOUIS JADOT / **Les Roches Rouges** / *Mâcon Rouges, France*

BROWN BROTHERS / **Tarrango** / *Victoria, Australia*

DOMAINE FILLIATREAU / **Saumur-Champigny** / *Loire, France*

EDMUNDS ST. JOHN / **Bone-Jolly Gamay Noir** / *El Dorado County, California, USA*

AFROS / **Vinhão Tinto** / *Vinho Verde, Portugal*

CHÂTEAU THIVIN / **Brouilly** / *Beaujolais, France*

CAVE DE SAUMUR / **Réserve des Vignerons Saumur Rouge** / *Saumur, Loire, France*

CLOS DU TUE-BOEUF / **Cheverny Rouge** / *Loire, France*

HENRY FESSY / **Beaujolais-Villages** / *Beaujolais, France*

10 LOWER-ALCOHOL WHITES

PAULINSHOF / **Urstuck Riesling Trocken** / *Mosel, Germany*

CLEMENS BUSCH / **Estate Riesling** / *Mosel, Germany*

MEULENHOF / **Erdener Treppchen Riesling Auslese Alte Reben** / *Mosel, Germany*

TYRRELL'S / **Vat 1 Hunter Valley Semillon** / *New South Wales, Australia*

DÖNNHOFF / **Riesling Kabinett** / *Nahe, Germany*

ELIO PERRONE / **Moscato d'Asti** / *Piedmont, Italy*

QUINTA DE AZEVEDO / **Vinho Verde** / *Portugal*

SCHLOSS SCHÖNBORN / **Hattenheimer Pfaffenberg Riesling Spätlese**, *Rheingau, Germany*

DOMAINE DE L'IDYLLE / **Cuvée Orangerie** / *Savoie, France*

TE WHARE RA / **D Riesling** / *Marlborough, New Zealand*

10 SPECIAL-OCCASION CHAMPAGNES

CHAMPAGNE TAITTINGER / **Comtes de Champagne Blanc de Blancs** / *Champagne, France*

CHAMPAGNE HENRIOT / **Cuvée des Enchanteleurs** / *Champagne, France*

CHAMPAGNE GOSSET / **Grande Réserve Brut** / *Champagne, France*

CHAMPAGNE GIMONNET / **Premier Cru Brut** / *Champagne, France*

DOM RUINART / **Blanc de Blancs Vintage** / *Champagne, France*

CHAMPAGNE EGLY-OURIET / **Tradition Grand Cru Brut** / *Champagne, France*

CHAMPAGNE SALON / **Cuvée "S" Le Mesnil** / *Champagne, France*

CHAMPAGNE KRUG / **Grande Cuvée** / *Champagne, France*

CHAMPAGNE DOM PÉRIGNON / *Champagne, France*

CHAMPAGNE LOUIS ROEDERER / **Cristal** / *Champagne, France*

10 GOOD-VALUE SPARKLING WINES

ANTECH / **Brut Nature NV Blanquette de Limoux** / *Limoux, Languedoc, France*

RAVENTÓS I BLANC / **De Nit** / *Cava, Spain*

BODEGAS SUMARROCA / **Cava Brut Reserva** / *Catalonia, Spain*

LA JARA / **Prosecco Spumante Extra Dry** / *Veneto, Italy*

BISOL / **Jeio Prosecco di Valdobbiadene** / *Veneto, Italy*

JANSZ / **Premium Cuvée Sparkling Wine** / *Tasmania, Australia*

CLOUDY BAY / **Pelorus** / *Marlborough, New Zealand*

SCHLOSS GOBELSBURG / **Sekt Brut Reserve** / *Kamptal, Austria*

DOMAINE PFISTER / **Crémant d'Alsace** / *Alsace, France*

CHAMPAGNE DELAMOTTE / **Brut NV** / *Champagne, France*

10 FORTIFIED TREATS

FONSECA / **Vintage Port** / *Douro, Portugal*

TAYLOR'S / **Vintage Port** / *Douro, Portugal*

QUINTA DO NOVAL / **Nacional Vintage Port** / *Douro, Portugal*

EQUIPO NAVAZOS / **La Bota de Amontillado Sherry** / *Sanlúcar de Barrameda, Spain*

BLANDY'S / **Verdelho Vintage Madeira** / *Madeira, Portugal*

BODEGAS TRADICIÓN / **30 Year Old VORS Palo Cortado Sherry** / *Jerez, Spain*

LUSTAU / **Almacenista Obregon Amontillado del Puerto Sherry** / *Jerez, Spain*

MARCO DE BARTOLI / **Marsala Superiore 10 Anni** / *Sicily, Italy*

SANDEMAN / **40 Year Old Tawny Port** / *Douro, Portugal*

SEPPELTSFIELD / **Para Grand 10 Year Old Tawny** / *Barossa Valley, Australia*

10 AFFORDABLE FORTIFIED WINES

LA GITANA / **Manzanilla Sherry** / *Sanlúcar de Barrameda, Spain*

VALDESPINO / **Inocente Fino Sherry** / *Jerez, Spain*

GONZÁLEZ BYASS / **Tío Pepe Fino Sherry** / *Jerez, Spain*

DOMAINE SARDA-MALET / **Le Serrat Rivesaltes Ambré** / *Roussillon, France*

WARRE'S / **Bottle Matured Late Bottled Vintage Port** / *Douro, Portugal*

RAMOS PINTO / **Late Bottled Vintage Port** / *Douro, Portugal*

NIEPOORT / **Ruby Port** / *Douro, Portugal*

QUADY'S / **Batch 88 Starboard** / *California, USA*

VINHOS BARBEITO / **10 Year Old Sercial** / *Madeira, Portugal*

BACALHÔA / **Moscatel de Setúbal** / *Portugal*

Index of Occasions

Index of Wines

M

N

Author's Acknowledgments

Author's thanks to:

Sara Morley for being the original driving force behind the book.

Neil Beckett for being the best editor around.

Johanna Wilson for her patience and support.

The Tombesi-Waltons for their eagle eyes.

Bob Morley for his all-round design brilliance.

Kazumi Suzuki for her tireless work in sourcing images and colored Kit-Kats.

Claudia, Raffy, and Mathilde, for putting up with a grumpy old soul.

Ann and Geoff Williams for the Dengie School of Asti Spumante, elderberry wine, and Rioja.

Photographic Credits

Page 32: © Peter Cassidy, from Paul Gayler, *Steak* (Jacqui Small; London, 2006).

Page 106: © Michel Smith; www.les5duVin@wordpress.com.

Page 182: © Jon Wyand.